AQA Media Stu...

AS

Exclusively endorsed by AQA

Nelson Thornes

Julia Burton
Elspeth Stevenson

Published in 2008 by:
Nelson Thornes Ltd
Delta Place
27 Bath Road
CHELTENHAM
GL53 7TH
United Kingdom

08 09 10 11 12 / 10 9 8 7 6 5 4 3 2 1

A catalogue record for this book is available from the British Library

ISBN 978 0 7487 9814 8

Cover photograph by Alamy
Page make-up by Pantek Arts Ltd, Maidstone, Kent

Printed in Great Britain by Scotprint

Acknowledgements
The authors and publisher would like to thank the following for permission to reproduce
photographs and other copyright material:

p. iv Getty; p. 4 BARB; p. 7 Nielsen EDI/UK Film Council analysis, supplied by British
Film Institute; p. 8 Alamy; p. 9 © NI Syndication Limited, The Sun, 9 April 1992 © NI
Syndication Limited, *The Sun*, 11 April 1992; p. 10 Associated News; p. 12 IPC/*Woman's
Weekly* Magazine; p. 20 The Ronald Grant Archive; p. 21 ACP-Natmag Magazines; p. 22
PSB Broadcaster Returns; p. 24 The Kobal Collection (left), © Chris Clough, Company
Productions Limited (top), Capital Pictures (bottom); p. 27 Logo courtesy of Channel 4 and
Endemol UK; p. 28 © BBC Photo Library; p. 30 RAJAR Ltd./Ipsos-MORI/RSMB;
p. 33 Copyright BBC *Girl Talk* magazine, BBC Worldwide (top), *Amnesty Magazine*,
Amnesty International UK, March 2007 (bottom); p. 37 Top 20 websites in the UK by share
of visits, December 2007. Source: Hitwise (hitwise.co.uk) (bottom); p. 42 The Ronald Grant
Archive (left), Alamy (right); p. 43 Fotolia (top right), iStock (remainder); p. 44 The *Daily
Telegraph*/Paul Grover; p. 49 Martin Argyles/Guardian News & Media Ltd. 2005;
p. 50 XLeague TV, broadcast by Portland TV; p. 55 Alamy; p. 56 The Ronald Grant Archive;
p. 59 Alamy; p. 61 Pearl & Dean; p. 63 The *Daily Telegraph* 2007; p. 69 copyright 2008
virgin.com; p. 83 *Radio Times*; p. 86 reproduced with permission of Yahoo! Inc. © 2007 by
Yahoo! Inc. YAHOO! and the YAHOO! logo are trademarks of Yahoo! Inc.; p. 97 4Creative/
photo Jim Fiscus © 2008; p. 99 Guardian News & Media Ltd. 2007; p. 101 copyright O_2;
p. 103 copyright Orange; p. 106 courtesy Livelistingsmag.com; p. 107 © BBC Photo Library;
p. 108 Penguin; p. 132 www.firstnews.co.uk (top), *The Times Educational Supplement*
(bottom), August 24, 2007. Photo: Jess Hurd. Text: Warwick Mansell and Nick Holborne.

Contents

Introduction

Nelson Thornes and AQA

Nelson Thornes has worked in collaboration with AQA to ensure that this book offers you the best support for your AS or A level course and helps you to prepare for your exams. The partnership means that you can be confident that the range of learning, teaching and assessment practice materials has been checked by the senior examining team at AQA before formal approval, and is closely matched to the requirements of your specification.

Blended learning

Printed and electronic resources are blended: this means that links between topics and activities between the book and the electronic resources help you to work in the way that best suits you, and enable extra support to be provided online. For example, you can test yourself online and feedback from the test will direct you back to the relevant parts of the book.

Electronic resources are available in a simple-to-use online platform called Nelson Thornes learning space. If your school or college has a licence to use the service, you will be given a password through which you can access the materials through any internet connection.

Icons in this book indicate where there is material online related to that topic. The following icons are used:

Learning activity

These resources include a variety of interactive and non-interactive activities to support your learning.

Progress tracking

These resources include a variety of tests that you can use to check your knowledge on particular topics (Test yourself) and a range of resources that enable you to analyse and understand examination questions (On your marks…).

Research support

These resources include WebQuests, in which you are assigned a task and provided with a range of web links to use as source material for research.

Study skills

These resources support you develop a skill that is key for your course, for example planning essays.

Analysis tool

These resources help you to analyse key texts and images by providing questions and prompts to focus your response.

When you see an icon, go to Nelson Thornes learning space at www.nelsonthornes.com/aqagce, enter your access details and select your course. The materials are arranged in the same order as the topics in the book, so you can easily find the resources you need.

How to use this book

This book covers the specification for your course and is arranged in a sequence approved by AQA. The book is divided into two Units. Unit 1 is designed to aid you in preparation for the examination. To help you with section A of the examination, media platforms, media forms, and media concepts and ideas are discussed, using real-life examples. Section B of this book focuses on section B of the examination by describing in detail how to apply what you have learned so far when preparing for and writing the cross media study.

Unit 2 is written to provide you with detailed guidance on your coursework, explaining how to use the knowledge gained from Unit 1 to research, plan, create and evaluate your coursework product.

Definitions of any words that appear in bold can be found in the glossary at the back of this book.

Learning objectives

At the beginning of each section you will find a list of learning objectives that contain targets linked to the requirements of the specification.

The features in this book include:

 Key terms

Terms that you will need to be able to define and understand. These terms are coloured blue in the text book and their definition will also appear in the glossary at the back of this book.

Investigating media

Activities which develop skills, knowledge and understanding that will prepare you for assessment in your Media Studies course.

 Media in action

Information on key events, products, companies, and points of interest which enhance your understanding of media.

 Links

Links to other areas in the text book which are relevant to what you are reading.

 Case study

A study of specific company, genre, platform, etc.

 Thinking about media

Short reflective activites that extend your understanding of key ideas.

Technical tip

Useful suggestions and reminders.

 **Examiner's tip**

Hints from AQA examiners to help you with your study and to prepare for your exam.

End of topic summary

A summary of what has been taught in the topic.

 Web links in the book

Because Nelson Thornes is not responsible for third party content online, there may be some changes to this material that are beyond our control. In order for us to ensure that the links referred to in the book are as up-to-date as possible, the websites provided are usually homepages with supporting instructions on how to reach the relevant pages if necessary.

Please let us know at **webadmin@nelsonthornes.com** if you find a link that doesn't work and we will do our best to correct this at reprint, or to list an alternative site.

Supporting resources referred to in the text can be found by going to **www.nelsonthornes.com/agagce/media.htm** and clicking on the link to the supporting resources.

AQA examination questions are reproduced by permission of the Assessment and Qualifications Alliance.

Introduction to media studies

What will I be doing on this course?

Studying the media means looking differently at the culturally shared products of our everyday lives as people living in the 21st-century technological world. This is the world where a film, a television programme, music or news on the internet can be accessed and understood by audiences and consumers across the globe. A world where a quotation from an advertisement or a television sketch show can become a catchphrase used by people of all ages and nationalities.

If you studied Media Studies as one of your GSCE subjects you will already have some knowledge of the media and will have studied television, the press and perhaps the film or music industry. You will have had the experience of planning and making media products yourself. If you are new to the subject you will have first-hand experience as a consumer of the media as part of your everyday life.

One of the main appeals of any Media Studies course is that the content of the course is based on **media texts** that are part of the **contemporary media landscape** and you will be investigating these texts with an analytical perspective. You will be analysing a wide range of media texts from television, radio, newspapers, magazines and the internet and will build up throughout the course a body of knowledge about how media texts are constructed and the **terminology** and theoretical ideas to describe and evaluate them. You will also make a **case study** of how a selected topic is presented across the media and will have the chance to investigate that topic in some depth. You will be looking at the processes by which texts are produced and, importantly, at the ways in which texts are received and responded to by their audiences. The knowledge and understanding you gain from the investigation of existing media texts in the contemporary media landscape will prepare you for your written AS examination and for your coursework. You will be investigating texts across the media, looking at the similarities and differences between, for example, the coverage of Formula 1 racing in the press, on television and on the internet and keeping up to date with developments in the technologies used by media producers and media audiences.

One of the most exciting parts of the media course is the active part you will be playing in planning and creating media texts as individuals and as groups. You will learn the skills of using the media technologies and have the chance to produce texts for different audiences. These skills combined with what you have learned through your investigations of media texts and topics will enable you to evaluate your coursework critically.

A conceptual framework

We all have personal views about the media and can readily give an off-the-cuff opinion of a media text based on like or dislike and our personal experience of similar texts. People in the media will comment on and criticise media content on a daily basis. Discussion about media content can be 'common sense' or expressed in a journalistic way. As media students you need a set of concepts to help you understand how texts are constructed by examining their different parts.

A set of **concepts** has been developed to provide a framework to help you understand how media texts work and this book will enable you to understand and apply this 'toolkit' when investigating and creating media. You will also learn and apply some theories that are relevant to the study of the media.

Key terms

Media texts: anything that has been constructed to appear in the media. A text can consist of words and still and moving images, sound and moving images or any combination. A feature film, a television advertisement, a magazine cover, a website are examples of media texts.

Contemporary media landscape: where media texts can be found – the changing contexts within which media texts are produced and consumed, for example multi-channel television, web radio, on-line newspapers and downloadable filmed and audio material.

Terminology: specialised vocabulary used in any particular sphere of life. For example, doctors use medical terminology and lawyers use legal terminology. As students of the media you will need to use media terminology.

Case study: A factual example or a set of related examples about media platforms, media institutions or media products. Used to make or illustrate a point.

Concepts: ideas that can be applied to a media text in order to understand it, i.e. Representations in the media; Languages of the media, including Narrative and genre; Media audiences; Media institutions.

Using such a conceptual toolkit encourages you take an analytical and objective approach to every text you encounter. The same toolkit can also be used for constructing your own texts. You can use it as a checklist to make sure that you haven't left out a vital component or included too much of another.

Link

Topic 3 is all about Media concepts and ideas.

AQA Examiner's tip

Start your own notebook or e-notebook, to which you can add throughout the course. Make notes, using terminology and concepts on the media texts you consume. Building on the skills learned in the classroom by applying them to what you experience outside the classroom deepens your understanding of how the media works and will give you a wider range to draw on in the examination and in your coursework.

■ How will my work be assessed and examined?

Fifty per cent of the AS marks are assessed by the Unit 1 examination, which will normally be taken at the end of the AS course in the summer term. The examination lasts for two hours and will be marked by external examiners. This paper will assess your knowledge and understanding of media concepts and contexts and your ability to analyse media products and processes and show how meanings and responses are created.

Fifty per cent of the AS marks are assessed by the Unit 2 coursework component. The coursework and the written evaluation will asses your ability to plan and construct media products and to do research and your ability to analyse media products and processes and show how meanings and responses are created. Your coursework will be assessed by the teachers at your school or college who will then send off some of the work to the examination board for checking.

■ The units at a glance

Unit 1: Investigating media

AS Unit 1 is assessed by a written paper, divided into two sections, A and B.

Section A contains four compulsory questions based on a text that you will be provided with in the examination. The text could be moving image, audio

or print in form. You will have 15 minutes to study the text and will spend approximately 15 minutes writing each answer in Section A. Each question will be based around the media concepts: Media forms, Media representations, Media institutions, Media audiences.

In Section B you will write one essay question in 45 minutes. There will be a choice of question but for whichever one you choose you will use the material from your cross-media case study to support your answer. Cross media topics include: Broadcast or film fiction, Documentary and hybrid forms, Lifestyle, Music, News and Sport.

Your teacher will guide you in your choice of case study.

Link

Topic 4 is all about the cross-media study.

Unit 2: Creating media (coursework)

For this unit, you will produce two pieces of linked practical coursework. You will be able to choose what to make from a choice of three briefs provided by the examination board. Each brief will offer three choices covering print, moving image or audio or web-based technologies and you will choose two technologies from one brief. You will work individually when researching and evaluating your chosen topic but might work as one of a group when actually making a moving image based product. This will depend on the equipment and time available but your group must not be bigger than four people. You will be assessed on your own contribution to the product and, as technological competence carries the majority of the marks, you need to make sure that you have the opportunity to show these skills.

Link

See Topics 7, 8 and 9 for advice about pre-production choices.

■ Pathways through the course

The linear structure of this book takes you through Unit 1 and then Unit 2. However, it is likely that you will be working on Unit 2, the coursework topics, before you have covered all the Unit 1 topics.

You will need to have studied Topics 1, 2 and 3 before you are ready to start the coursework planning and research. Topic 4, The Cross-Media Study will help you start your research for Unit 2.

Enjoy your AS Media Studies course.

1 Investigating media platforms

💡 Key terms

Media products: products or texts are TV and radio programmes, films, advertisements, websites, newspapers and magazines etc., produced for audiences.

Media platforms: the technology through which we receive media products.

Institutions: the organisation or company, public or privately owned that produces and/or distributes media.

AQA Examiner's tip

For your case study you will need to know some facts about each platform: the **institutions** that use the platforms and the ways in which the platforms are financed and controlled.

▨ Media platforms

The contemporary media landscape is one in which you, the individual consumer, have a great deal of choice as to what you watch, listen to, read or even participate in, and when and where you want to do this.

Thinking about media

- ▨ What media products were you in contact with yesterday? How did the media reach you?
- ▨ How much time did you spend with magazines, newspapers, television, radio, cinema and internet or something else?
- ▨ What was the purpose of using each media form; entertainment, information, communication or something else?
- ▨ How did you consume the media form; read, view, listen or something else?

There are a number of technologies that carry media content and from which we can choose the particular product that we want to consume at that moment or, if it suits us, save it for later. An item of content can be called a product or a text: a newspaper, a film trailer, an advertisement, a documentary, a piece of recorded music, anything that can be received by an audience through media technologies is a **media product**. We can choose how and when to get hold of information and entertainment wherever we might be thanks to technologies that are relatively cheap and easily available to us. Reckon up the hardware you have available in your house: television sets, radios, DVD players, games consoles, MP3 devices and computers. Which of these are shared with others and which of these are personal to you? For example, we often consume music as individuals while carrying out other tasks and can receive pre-selected news and advertisements on our mobile telephones.

This is a very different landscape from that of 50 or so years ago when, alongside newspapers and magazines, there were only two television channels broadcasting for a limited period each day, mostly in the evening; three BBC radio channels, namely the Home Service, the Light Programme and the Third Programme; and when the pop music appealing to teenagers was only accessible by listening to Radio Luxembourg late at night. All you could do was watch or listen, as there was no interactivity, whereas now you can participate in and even contribute to media content in a number of ways, including, for example, taking part in a radio phone-in, sending in a photo from a mobile phone to a news programme or voting on a television show. Now, in the 21st century we can consume media offered by a variety of producers over a range of **media platforms**. A media platform can be compared to a stage, showcasing what is available within a particular technology and for the AQA media studies specification the platforms on which we find media content are classified as broadcasting, e-media and print.

■ Thinking about media

See how many of these questions you can answer using your general knowledge and experience as a media consumer. Think about the range of media platforms:

1 Name the BBC radio stations available to listeners. What sort of content does each carry? How, when and where can listeners access these stations?

2 How many non-BBC radio stations can you receive? On which media platforms are these available? What sort of content is carried?

3 Name television channels aimed at the under 10s. What sort of content does each carry? On which media platforms are these available?

4 How many television channels are dedicated to popular music? What type of musical content does each carry? Where else in the media can you listen to popular music?

5 Many broadcasters show films. How many dedicated film channels can you receive? Where would you see promotional material and trailers for upcoming films?

6 On which media platforms might you find local news and events listings?

7 On which media platforms could you buy or sell band memorabilia?

Broadcasting

This section covers television, radio and films. Films are, of course, initially exhibited in cinemas, but also viewed at home, or indeed on the move, on screens of varying sizes – from the large screen in the living room to computer or even small mobile phone screens.

A definition of broadcasting is the institutionalised practice of sending television and radio content to large numbers of receivers. A large and ever growing selection of channels is carried on satellite, cable and digital terrestrial television services. At the time of writing, there are six major broadcasters in the UK: BBC, ITV, Channel 4, Five, BSkyB and Virgin Media. Households pay to receive television and radio content through the TV licence fee and through subscription packages with additional opportunities to pay for view and buy top up stations. To an extent we can choose what we take into our homes and how we take it.

There are constant changes in the world of media institutions, some of which will involve new companies but much of which will be mergers and expansions of existing media providers. You can keep track of these changes by researching the business news in quality newspapers and on the internet. Broadcasting is big business and most broadcasting institutions also have a presence in the other media platforms, for example, the BBC publishes magazines and has a large web presence.

Television and radio

The content of television programmes and films is the moving image while radio is audio, although when radio is received through a screen there is accompanying visual content. Some television and radio programmes, or parts of these, are broadcast live to audiences, whereas films and the majority of television and radio output are pre-recorded.

In the UK, until the mid 1950s, the British Broadcasting Corporation (BBC) – a **public service broadcaster** founded on the concept of service to the public within a democracy – was the institution that had the

■ Link

The next section of this book, Investigating media forms, will deal in more detail with the range of media products available on the broadcast platforms.

■ Key terms

Public service broadcasting (PSB): a broadcasting system whose first duty is to a public within a democracy, serving to inform, educate and entertain rather than to make commercial profit.

monopoly and was the only producer and distributor of all audio and visual content. When commercial television broadcasting began in the mid 1950s the rules laid down for independent television were taken from the standards already established for the BBC with its mission to inform, educate and entertain. Today, it is the responsibility of Ofcom (see below) to regulate the Public Service Remit (see below) but many of the new digital channels are outside of this remit. There is continuing debate about whether, in the contemporary media landscape, imposed responsibilities limit the ability of broadcasters to keep audiences and advertisers and remain commercially viable.

Public Service Publisher: in 2007 Ofcom began planning a new organisation, Public Service Publisher. They say that information and entertainment is not enough in 'the networked learning age'. The mission of the PSP is to provide:

- media content
- democratic value
- cultural and creative value
- educational value
- social and community value
- global value.

This embraces the convergence of media organisations. While broadcasters and print companies continue to invest in the internet, internet companies are converging also and to do this it will embrace the idea of sharing of the production and distribution of media content.

Media in action

Ofcom: the Office of Communications formed in 2003, which regulates television, radio, telecommunications and wireless communication services. It deals with complaints, regulates competition, monitors standards and deals with licences.

Public Service Remit: the legally binding obligation that the five main television channels have to provide a wide range of programmes that inform, educate and entertain their audiences.

The Charter and Agreement sets six Public Purposes for the BBC:

1 sustaining citizenship and civil society

2 promoting education and learning

3 stimulating creativity and cultural excellence

4 representing the UK, its nations, regions and communities

5 bringing the UK to the world and the world to the UK

6 in promoting its other purposes, helping to deliver to the public the benefit of emerging communications, technologies and services and, in addition, taking a leading role in the switchover to digital television.

Requirements for Channel Five, when it launched in 1997, included the obligation to provide minimum amounts of programming from various genres, including news, programming originally commissioned by the channel and of European origin, and maximum limits on the number of repeats. There are a large number of institutions producing

Link

We will look at the ways audiences are classified and measured in Topic 3.

and distributing television and radio content, and there is a diversity of financial support, including advertising revenue, sponsorship, subsidy, subscription and licence fees that pay for the programme making. The role of advertising revenue will be investigated later in this book but for now you should understand that advertisers need audiences and commercial broadcasters have to sell audiences to advertisers. The BBC has to have a reasonable **audience share** in order to justify funding through the licence fee. The study of audiences, who they are, and how they respond and interact with the media is a major topic. All media producers need audiences and audiences are measured and classified by broadcasters and marketeers.

HOURS OF VIEWING AND SHARE OF AUDIENCE Including Timeshift - 5 weeks ending 2nd Dec

	Average Weekly Viewing per person		Share of Total Viewing	
	November(Hrs:Mins)	October (Hrs:Mins)	November(%)	October(%)
ALL/ANY TV	26:57	25:12	100.0	100.0
BBC 1 (incl. Brkfast News)	6:04	5:33	22.5	22.0
BBC 2	2:20	2:04	8.7	8.2
TOTAL BBC1/BBC2	8:24	7:37	31.2	30.3
ITV (incl. GMTV)	5:23	5:15	20.0	20.8
CHANNEL 4/S4C	2:04	1:50	7.7	7.3
five	1:19	1:15	4.9	5.0
TOTAL/ANY COMM. TERR. TV	8:47	8:20	32.6	33.1
Other Viewing	9:40	9:08	35.8	36.2

Fig. 1.1 *BARB chart of audience share of television from web www.barb.co.uk/viewing summary*

Television and radio **schedules**, some of them broadcasting 24/7, need to be filled with content that attracts audiences. Broadcasters compete with each other to gain and maintain their audiences and keep their position in the busy marketplace. Major broadcasters have a portfolio of channels available to audiences. For example, Channel 4 (a public service broadcaster started in 1984 with one channel) has developed a range of off-shoots including Film4, E4, More4, learning4, 4Radio and, on the internet, 4oD.

The major broadcasters make programmes in-house and also use independent production companies. Some minor broadcasting channels do not produce original media content but buy content from production companies or other broadcasters. Endemol UK is responsible for 5,000 hours of television programming annually.

Major broadcasters produce media content over a number of channels, each with a particular **brand image** showing its difference from other channels and each intended to appeal to specific audiences. Individual channels will have their own **ident**, a symbol or **logo** that appears on screen. On radio the ident may be signified by a jingle or slogan.

Case study

Here are two examples of broadcasters, one a major British **network**, ITV, originally broadcasting on analogue television; the other a smaller operator Disney Channel UK, which at the time of writing is available as part of a subscription package linked to the larger networks of Sky and Virgin. ITV has a portfolio of channels and Disney Channel UK has two sister channels, Disney Cinemagic and Playhouse Disney, and two time shift plus 1 services.

ITV

On its website, the institution describes itself as follows: 'ITV is the biggest commercial television network in the UK, broadcasting the most talked about television and making a major contribution to the UK's culture, economy and communities.'

At the time of writing, ITV Network is made up of 15 regional licences, providing television to viewers across the UK. Eleven of the licences in England and Wales are owned by ITV plc, formed in 2004 following the merger of Carlton and Granada. SMG owns the two Scottish licences, Scottish Television and Grampian; UTV and Channel Television own the licences for Northern Ireland and the Channel Islands respectively. ITV1 is subject to a series of public service obligations and regulation concerning relationships with producers and between the various companies within the ITV Network. As well as Network programming, each of the ITV licences provides regional programming to cater for the interests of people living in each area of the UK. The obligations placed on ITV by the communications regulator Ofcom are contained in licences to broadcast.

ITV Network is responsible for the commissioning, scheduling and marketing of network programmes on ITV1. Programmes from ITV are provided by ITV's in-house production unit and by the independent sector. Network programming covers a full range of **genres**, including drama, entertainment, news, current affairs, factual, sport and children's programming. It is also responsible for advertising sales on ITV1 across the UK.

ITV plc also owns the digital channel portfolio – ITV2, ITV3, ITV4 and CITV. ITV plc also provides a range of new media and interactive services via the internet, mobile phones and broadband.

Disney Channel UK

Disney Channel's website is lively, colourful and noisy, designed to appeal to children, the potential Disney audience. The Disney logo, common to all Disney brands, is a version of Mickey Mouse's ears, an **iconic** symbol of all things Disney. The programming content consists of live action shows, animated series and original movies made especially for kids. The website links to another channel, Disney Cinemagic and a third channel, Playhouse Disney, which caters for younger children and is 'the place where preschoolers can laugh and learn and play'.

Disney Channel UK was initially aimed at both children and families and has been available since 1997. Like its American counterpart it does not broadcast commercial advertisements, relying instead on subscription fees. Despite the lack of commercials most non-movie programming is broken up by commercial breaks during which trailers for Disney programming and specially commissioned short programmes are usually shown. All content on these channels is produced by the Walt Disney Company.

The BBC, like Disney channels, also advertises its own products in breaks between the programmes.

Link

For more information on Endemol UK, look at their website (you will find the address in the e-resources, or do a search).

Thinking about media

- How many logos could you draw from memory?
- Look at the logos for a number of broadcasting channels – what do they suggest about the channel?

Key terms

Genre: a term of classification that groups together media texts of a particular type.

Iconic: a sign which in some way resembles its object, looks like it or sounds like it.

Link

See the e-resources for website addresses for ITV and Disney Channel, or do a search on the web.

AQA Examiner's tip

When studying broadcasting, do not forget radio. BBC and commercial radio stations are available on broadcast and e-media platforms.

Investigating media

1. As a group, choose a major broadcaster with several television channels. Investigate some of the channels, noting the channel ident and how it is displayed. Compare your findings and present them to the class, explaining the reasons for any similarities or differences you have discovered.

2. As you watch television, make a note of how much content was produced in-house by the broadcaster and how much by independent production companies.

3. How many television channels are available in the UK and on what broadcasting platforms can they be received?

Films

Early days of cinema

The history of the cinema, the development and power of the Hollywood Studio system, the glories and struggles of the British Film Industry, the Bollywood, Japanese, Chinese and other world cinema movements, and the role of independent and alternative cinema are not central to this course. Media Studies focuses on the products (film texts) themselves, the producers of the products and the audiences. However, you do need to have an overview of how enjoying movies has developed since the invention of cinema.

It can be said that the British started to enjoy moving pictures, the movies, in 1896 when the Lumière Brothers gave a brief demonstration of their cinematograph in Regent Street, London. The images of a horse and cart on the move captivated audiences and they wanted more. In the very early days short films were a fairground attraction drawing gasps from audiences but it was not long before custom-built cinemas were built and the industry developed. Advertisers quickly saw the advantages of this new attraction and cinema advertising itself started in the 1890s.

The film industry was traditionally made up of producers whose business was making films, distributors who sold films and exhibitors who showed films to audiences. It was very big business indeed, with film-going a major popular leisure activity during the first half of the 20th century. By the 1930s many people were in the habit of visiting a cinema twice a week and at each visit seeing two feature films together with a newsreel and cartoons. Most towns had a number of cinemas and children had special shows on Saturday mornings offering short adventure films and animations.

Keeping the film industry viable

Following the coming of cheaper television sets in the 1950s and colour in the 1960s cinema audiences dropped off. They reached an all-time low in 1984 when there were just 1,200 screens in the UK and only 54 million admissions a year. Commercial cinema was revived with the adoption of an American business model; the idea that cinemas with 10 or more screens would attract audiences. The multiplexes, owned by large groups such as UCI and Warner Village, having large screens and powerful sound systems, can be said to have rescued commercial cinema. Although some multiplexes, and megaplexes, offer a range of films, including arts and independent cinema, most of them give priority to Hollywood blockbusters, popular genre films or films written for teen audiences. The production, distribution, marketing and exhibition of films is often in the hands of the very large companies, making films to appeal to specific audiences; multiplex operators and film producers have been accused of ignoring certain groups of cinemagoers. The results of a survey among cinemagoers in 1997 found that while around 90 per cent of those aged 16–35 believed that going to the cinema provided a good night's entertainment, only 56 per cent of the 45–64 age group agreed with this view. For the over-65s the figure dropped to just 36 per cent.

The British film industry revived itself in the 1980s and 1990s through the ways in which television has become an important backer of filmmaking. Being able to exhibit a film in more than one place – cinema, television and on DVD – increases the opportunity for recovering money used in the film making process. Since the advent of the National Lottery some of the money has been used to help finance film production and there have been tax breaks introduced to support filmmaking. The UK Film Council was set up by the government to encourage cultural and commercial film activity.

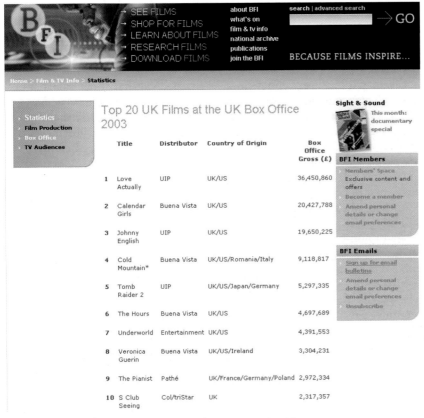

Fig. 1.2 *Top 10 box office films for a year (from* BFI Yearbook*)*

Films across the media platforms

We enjoy watching films in the cinema, on broadcast television, on DVD and on portable electronic devices, and films are marketed across a range of media.

> 'Movie production [can] be seen as the creation of entertainment software that can be viewed through several different windows and transported to several tightly diversified media corporations. Less than 20 per cent of total film revenues come from the domestic box office.'

> *Richard Maltby 'Nobody Knows Everything', which is included in* Contemporary Hollywood *(page 24), edited by Murray Smith and Steve Neale (Routledge, 1998)*

Films form an important part of broadcasters' schedules, screening peak-time movies that attract and hold audiences. Some films are made for TV, and all are made with television audiences in mind. We buy DVDs, the movie and extras, and watch them, or parts of them, over and over again. We download trailers from the internet, and exchange views about films over a variety of media platforms. We play computer games produced at the same time as the movies from which they come.

Print

Print media is the institutional practice of producing content: copy and images using ink on paper. Cheap printing became possible after the invention by Johannes Gutenberg of the printing press, which led to rapid developments in sciences, art and religion by enabling the distribution of texts to large numbers of people. This system, basically rolling ink over the raised surface of movable letters and pressing it on to paper, was

■ Thinking about media

The title of a newspaper gives some suggestion of its role in passing on news and information, for example, the *Guardian*, the *Independent*, the *Express* and *Echo*. Some of the newer newspapers, or those that have been renamed by new proprietors, have less grandiose titles: *Sun*, *Star* and *Metro*. But the idea of being able to observe events from a lofty, godlike viewpoint or transporting messages quickly and connecting with a large number of citizens is still there. Think about the connotations of the name of your local newspaper.

■ Key term

Masthead: the top of the front page, which gives the title and publication date of the newspaper.

superseded in the 20th century by the technique of offset lithography. It is the oldest platform for media content and consumers now, as they did in the 17th century, pay the cover price, hold it in their hands and read it.

Newspapers

A newspaper has long been defined as a periodical that is published at least once a week. Since the 17th century in the UK there has been a demand for news but until 1855 printing was strictly controlled and there were taxes restricting the production and distribution of printed news. During the 19th century improved communication developed alongside the public's need for information. The *Daily Universal Register* started in London in 1785, later becoming *The Times*. In Scotland, *The Herald*, published in Glasgow, has been in continuous production since 1783. A number of newspapers were founded by groups with specific interests and viewpoints, for example *The Manchester Guardian* in 1821, by a group of non-conformist businessmen and later a number of socialist and labour newspapers. The first cheap newspaper was the *Daily Telegraph and Courier*, in 1855. Newspapers then, as now, do more than record events; they also provide opinions on the events. However, the titles of newspapers and their **mastheads** give the impression that they report accurately, responsibly and quickly.

There are a range of daily newspapers, national and local, and a number of Sunday newspapers. Some newspapers are free, often pushed into one's hand or delivered through the letterbox. At the time of writing there are around 680 newspapers in the UK, of which 290 are free and 390 are paid for.

One of the most famous newspaper publishing companies is News International, publishing *The Times*, *Sunday Times*, *Sun*, *News of the World* and *thelondonpaper*. The company is the UK subsidiary of News Corporation, which has a portfolio of media platforms including 20th Century Fox, Myspace and BSKyB, a media empire founded by Rupert Murdoch, an Australian-born US citizen. He is one of the 'press barons' who have expanded their interests to encompass newer media. It is commonly thought that Murdoch himself hires and fires editors of his national newspapers, and it has been debated that his newspaper influenced the outcome of the 1992 UK General Election when the *Sun* campaigned against the Labour Party leader.

Fig. 1.3 *A range of daily newspapers published in the UK*

Fig. 1.4 *Two illustrations from the* Sun *1992.*
1 *Front page of the* Sun *9th April 1992. Note the Tory blue background and biased headline.*
2 *A couple of days later, 11th April, 1992, the headline 'It's the Sun Wot Won It.'*

It is a debatable point as to whether newspapers can swing elections but newspapers can and do influence readers. We must consider issues such as the selection and presentation of news and the way in which people, places and events are represented, which are very important in the study of the media. However, we live in a political climate that can best be described as liberal pluralism. By liberal we mean that individual choice and freedom is seen as a crucial human right; while pluralism means that more than one political view and opinion is allowed. This view sees the mass media as having a beneficial role that is generally positive: the media, along with other social institutions is expected to be the subject of healthy criticism and debate. Journalists are free to investigate stories, express views and not reveal the sources of their information and this scrutiny is thought to create a situation in which corruption cannot thrive. The mass media help to ensure that people have a good understanding of the issues when they vote. The British press is free to express opinions and there is no censorship of the press. Journalists are expected to abide by a Code of Practice and the PCC (Press Complaints Commission) is charged with enforcing this code which begins, 'All members of the press have a duty to maintain the highest professional standards. This Code sets the benchmark for those ethical standards, protecting both the rights of the individual and the public's right to know. It is the cornerstone of the system of self-regulation to which the industry has made a binding commitment.'

As newspaper sales have declined in recent years, newspaper publishers have attempted to attract and maintain readers using a variety of tactics, including price cuts, competitions and free gifts, but essentially a newspaper and all newspapers rely to a greater or lesser extent on advertising revenue. Newspaper publishers have invested in on-line editions and expanding their own media outlets. In the knowledge that the press is free to express opinions, and the opinions might be those of the newspaper owner, you need to know who owns the media you consume and consider the implications.

Media in action

Code of Practice: the code by which journalists abide. It begins 'All members of the press have a duty to maintain the highest professional standards. This Code sets the benchmark for those ethical standards, protecting both the rights of the individual and the public's right to know. It is the cornerstone of the system of self-regulation to which the industry has made a binding commitment.'

PCC (Press Complaints Commission): charged with enforcing the Code of Practice. It is a self-regulatory body that deals with complaints from members of the public about the editorial content of newspapers and magazines.

Link

For DMGT's website, see the e-resources, or do a web search.

Daily Mail

The *Daily Mail* newspaper was first published in 1896 and is now one of the newspapers owned now by DMGT, Daily Mail and General Trust plc, one of the largest and most successful media companies in the UK. DMGT's website states that the company 'invested in editorial excellence to become one of the most successful information providers in the country'. One of their businesses, Associated Newspapers, publishes the *Daily Mail*, *Mail on Sunday*, *Evening Standard*, *Metro*, *London Lite* and *Loot*. Another arm, Northcliffe Media produces, prints and distributes regional newspapers with titles ranging alphabetically from *Aberdeen Citizen* to *Yeovil Times*. Northcliffe has 36 publishing centres and produces 18 daily titles selling 800,000 a day, 29 paid-for weeklies selling almost half a million per week and 62 free titles distributed to more than 2.4 million a week. Northcliffe produces an on-line version of each paper; the 'this is… co.uk' network. They also produce a series of specialist magazines, some free and some paid-for 'to further reach the disparate markets and audiences within our circulation area'.

■ Investigating media

Look at the following illustrations and note the differences in the advertising rates in the free publication, *Primary Times*, and the paid-for publication, *Hooked on Fishing*. Account for the differences.

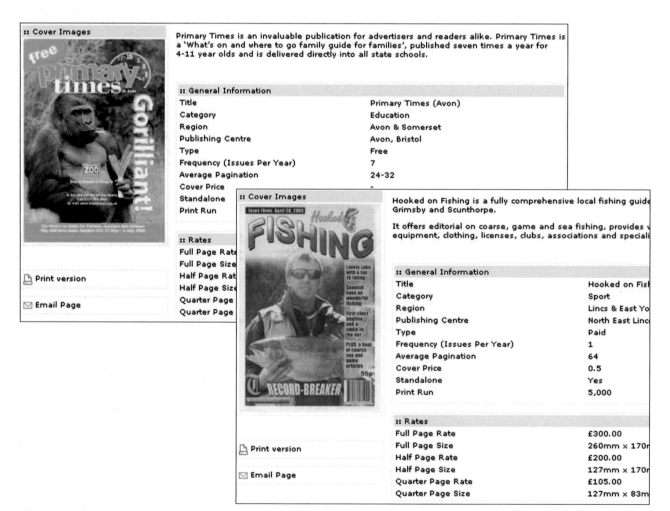

:: Cover Images

Primary Times is an invaluable publication for advertisers and readers alike. Primary Times is a 'What's on and where to go family guide for families', published seven times a year for 4-11 year olds and is delivered directly into all state schools.

:: General Information

Title	Primary Times (Avon)
Category	Education
Region	Avon & Somerset
Publishing Centre	Avon, Bristol
Type	Free
Frequency (Issues Per Year)	7
Average Pagination	24-32
Cover Price	
Standalone	
Print Run	

:: Rates

Full Page Rate	
Full Page Size	
Half Page Rate	
Half Page Size	
Quarter Page	
Quarter Page	

Print version

Email Page

:: Cover Images

Hooked on Fishing is a fully comprehensive local fishing guide Grimsby and Scunthorpe.

It offers editorial on coarse, game and sea fishing, provides equipment, clothing, licenses, clubs, associations and speciali

:: General Information

Title	Hooked on Fish
Category	Sport
Region	Lincs & East Yo
Publishing Centre	North East Linc
Type	Paid
Frequency (Issues Per Year)	1
Average Pagination	64
Cover Price	0.5
Standalone	Yes
Print Run	5,000

:: Rates

Full Page Rate	£300.00
Full Page Size	260mm x 170r
Half Page Rate	£200.00
Half Page Size	127mm x 170r
Quarter Page Rate	£105.00
Quarter Page Size	127mm x 83m

Print version

Email Page

Fig. 1.5 *Cover images and accompanying copy for* Primary Times *and* Fishing *(from www.thisisnorthcliff.co.uk/specialistpublications)*

Investigating media

Find out as much as you can about a local newspaper, free or paid-for, for example:

1 Where is it produced, printed and distributed?

2 What is the approximate content balance between editorial and advertising?

3 What is the approximate content balance between local news and national content?

4 How many journalists are employed by the paper and how many people are employed to sell advertising space?

5 What are the advertising rates? Is any advertising content free?

6 Who is the editor? Who is the owner?

7 How does the on-line version compare with the print version?

Thinking about media

■ Is anyone who reads the *Daily Mail* in the morning and the *Evening Standard* or *London Lite* later in the day – all part of Associated Newspapers – likely to be getting a range of opinions about people, events and politics?

■ What effect does what you read in the newspaper have on your own ideas and opinions?

💡 *Magazines*

'A magazine is a paperback periodical publication, usually an illustrated one, containing articles, stories etc. by various writers.'

Chambers 21st Century Dictionary

Magazine publishing is a crowded market with many titles and a range of categories to reach a variety of audiences. Most magazines are financed from the cover price and advertising while some are free to the consumer. Some people are regular readers of a specific magazine, buying it from the newsagent or subscribing to it. Traditionally, magazines have given information and advice to their readers and included readers' letters and often competitions.

Thinking about media

■ How many different types of magazine do you buy or read?

■ Do you read magazines bought by other members of the household?

■ Are there any particular magazines aimed at you?

■ Investigate the information on magazine cirulation figures on the ABC Consumer Magazine Roundup website. To find the address, look in your e-resources or do a search.

Case study

IPC

IPC media have 150 years of publishing history. Some of the earliest magazines were leisure magazines for upper- and middle-class men who had the time and the money to pursue hobbies. The earliest titles were: *Country Life, Horse and Hound, Shooting Times, Yachting World, Amateur Gardening, Cycling Weekly, Amateur Photography* and *The Railway Magazine*. In 1899, to attract readers there was a competition offering £1 a week for life to any reader who could guess the amount of gold and silver in the Bank of England on a given date.

Woman's magazines currently published by IPC media are *Chat, Pick Me Up, Woman, Woman's Own, Woman's Weekly, Look* and *Now*, the oldest one being *Woman's Weekly*, which was first launched in November 1911 under the editorial banner 'our motto – practical and useful'. Currently *Woman's Weekly* describes its brand profile to advertisers as offering 'Help, advice and inspiration for mature women'.

Thinking about media

You can probably think of other genres of magazines that are aimed at specific audiences that can be classified in terms of age, gender, interests or lifestyle.

The two magazine publishers with the largest number of general interest titles in UK are Emap and IPC Media but you will notice that specialist categories such as gaming/computer magazines may have specialist publishers.

■ Thinking about media

- How do the images shown on the web page match up to the audience profile?
- What products and services do you think will be advertised in the magazine?

Woman's Weekly®

Help, advice and inspiration for mature women

No.1 in the Mature Sector

Circulation:	387,098
Female Readership:	808,000

Unique position in the weeklies market, between classic and mature sectors

Female:	90%
Average Age:	59
ABC1:	46%
Main Shoppers:	90%
Working Profile:	40%
Home Owners:	68%

Readers are happy and settled, with a real lust for life

66% are happy with their lives	
68% think its worth paying extra for quality goods	
68% I get a great deal of pleasure from my garden	
83% want to be fit and active in life	

Open to new Experiences

89% feel it is important to continue learning new things throughout life	
62% want to have fun and enjoy life's pleasures	

Image Conscious

72% want to look attractive and well groomed	
68% look after their appearance	

Loyal Readers

Read 3 out of 4 issues	67%
Actively purchase the magazine	61%
Average time spent reading the issue	55 mins

Sources: ABC JD 06 / NRS JD 06 / TGI 06/ QRS

Fig. 1.6 *The readership profile for* Woman's Weekly

Every magazine uses market research to gather a profile of its readership to include age, class, attitudes and aspirations. For *Woman's Weekly* the profile can be summarised as: 'The 59-year-old mature woman reader is said to be happy and settled with a real lust for life, open to new experiences and image conscious' (see Fig. 1.6).

🇮 E-media

The World Wide Web, the internet and other platforms on which media products can be produced and received is the third area that we need to investigate. It is the newest form of media communication and has grown rapidly in terms of technology and use by ordinary people. For example, mobile phones that can be used to text, send pictures, receive news and advertising and satellite navigation were the stuff of science fiction stories until relatively recently.

The internet has grown into a method of exchanging ideas and information. Since the 1990s, technological developments and the inclusion of computer skills in the education system have led to computers and hand-held devices becoming consumer tools. Initially it was the telephone companies that set up as internet service providers (ISPs) but anyone with enough money and expertise can provide a service, often a combination of services, including domain name registration and web-hosting. Most 'old media' companies have set up their own websites

■ Investigating media

Group research activity

The ABC (Audit Bureau of Circulations) publishes circulation figures of consumer magazines, broken down into different genres. On their website (see the e-resources for the address or do a search on the web), scroll through the list of genres. Each person should choose a category and click through to the titles in that category. What do the titles tell us about the lifestyles and interests of UK readers?

and some have bought up internet companies. Advertisers have been quick to use the opportunities offered by e-media. Consumers use digital technology to shop, e-mail, research, listen to the radio and for gaming but the most interesting debate about the platform is about the changing way we use it. Much of the internet content is free to the user and subscriptions to an ISP provider are inexpensive. Recent developments have provided the widespread adoption of collaborative software that enthusiasts of the second generation **Web 2.0** see as the architecture of participation and democracy, with web-based communities such as social networking sites and **wikis** facilitating collaboration and sharing of user generated content. We can post our comments on websites, upload home-made videos, photos and music and comment on others' contributions.

There are those like Andrew Keen (*The Cult of the Amateur: how today's internet is killing our culture and assaulting our economy*) who have criticised the value and virtue of a situation where 'people endlessly **Google** themselves and expertise counts for nothing' and 'a knowledge of history and literature becomes smothered by an avalanche of blogs from self-obsessed teenagers'. Many others have reservations about this revolution that has resulted in users creating and editing content, cutting out the editorial function and responsibilities that still exist on the broadcasting and print platforms.

No one owns or controls the internet and there are few checks in place to screen what's out there. Legal actions have been taken against the use of the internet for criminal purposes and the music industry has challenged sites offering free downloading and filesharing. There are unresolved issues around copyright, virtual vandalism, on-line abuse and bullying but at the time of writing there is no legislation. Tim O'Reilly, who coined the phrase 'Web 2.0' and Jimmy Wales, the founder of Wikipedia, have suggested a code of conduct for users.

Case study

Wikimedia

The Wikimedia Foundation owns the Wikipedia Free On-line Encylopedia and its sister sites and encourages its community of users to edit the content. The owners rely on contributions from users – contributions of content and of funding. Wikimedia Foundation Inc. is a not-for-profit organisation devoted to sharing free information with every person in the world. There are tens of thousands of regular editors and also 'mechanisms that help community members watch for bad edits, over one thousand administrators with special powers to enforce good behavior [sic], and a judicial committee which considers the few situations remaining unresolved, and decides on withdrawal or restriction of editing privileges or other punishments when needed, after all other consensus remedies have been tried.'

Its fundraising page appeals to us to imagine a world in which every single person can share freely in the sum of human knowledge and to help them support that aim. 'Our projects collect this content from people around the world, process it, and make it readily available on-line in over 200 languages. These efforts are supported through the generosity of people like you, who believe that knowledge means power and that knowledge should be free.'

Key terms

Web 2.0: a term coined in 2004 to describe the second generation of web based communities such as social networking sites, wikis and folksonomies. These changes are in the ways the platform of the World Wide Web or internet is used and not an update in technical specifications.

Wikis: a wiki is a software that enables documents to be written collaboratively using a web browser.

Google: a leading search engine which has become so well-used that the verb 'to google' has become synonymous with searching on the internet.

Investigating media

Wikipedia, like similar sites, is a useful resource for research but remember it is only vetted by users themselves and may contain inaccuracies or a biased viewpoint. Go to the Wikipedia site and follow the links to read the text of the GNU Free Documentation Licence. What would you have to do to contribute an article to Wikipedia?

AQA Examiner's tip

You will need to keep as up to date as possible with what is going on in broadcasting, print and e-media and emerging media platforms including the developments in technologies and changes in legislation. When you are doing your case study (see Topic 4) you will need to investigate how the topic is presented and received across the three media platforms, know some details about the institutions involved and understand the reasons for the interconnections.

Thinking about media

Audiences are encouraged to consume a range of media products from one source. Think about *The Simpsons* television show: this was shown on Sky before it became available on terrestrial channels. The original programme has since produced a range of spin-offs, including *The Simpsons* the movie, *The Simpsons* comics, *The Simpsons* images in merchandising and *The Simpsons* computer games.

Key terms

Convergence: the coming together of the media technologies.

UGC (user generated content): contributions to media texts from audiences.

Synergy: the process through which a series of media products derived from the same text is promoted in and through each other.

End of topic summary:

- In the contemporary media landscape, we can communicate with others; receive and provide information and entertainment wherever we might be through technology readily available to most people.

- There has been a **convergence** of computer technology, telephone communication and television and before long there may be one piece of hardware to do everything.

- Now we can consume broadcast content through the internet and access the internet through the television; we can read the newspaper or place an advertisement in it on the internet.

- We can play a part in the production of content on media platforms; media producers employ people to deal with user generated content **(UGC)** in their products. For example, visual first-on-the-scene news images are sent to traditional media institutions by members of the public.

- We have the technology to access ideas from all over the world, publish our words and images, even record and market our own band.

- Media owners operate across the media platforms using the opportunities for **synergy**, the process by which it uses various products to sell one another, for example a film, a soundtrack and a computer game.

Investigating media forms

Link

The media languages used in the construction of forms will be explored in detail in the next section of this book, Media Concepts and Ideas.

Key terms

Media forms: the distinguishing characteristics of types of media products.

Codes and conventions: a code is a network of signs, written, visual, artistic or behavioural, which signify meanings that are culturally accepted and shared. A convention is a conduct or practice or method that is commonly accepted and has a tradition. Media texts are constructed using a number of codes and conventions including technical codes that have agreed meanings.

Expectations and pleasures: audiences understand genre through their familiarity with the codes and conventions used in the text. They take pleasure in the anticipation of familiarity; they expect and take pleasure in repetition and recognition of the generic elements of content, style and form.

Media forms

Having looked at the media platforms, the broader contexts in which and on which products are made available to audiences, we need to identify the **media forms** themselves. During the AS course you will investigate a wide range of media products and create texts from more than one platform. In the examination you will have to respond to an unseen media product and comment on how the features are typical or otherwise to others of its type.

To identify a media form we consider the features of the text in the light of our previous experience and knowledge of media products. We all recognise a website, a magazine cover, a film trailer or a radio news bulletin by the characteristics it shares with other media products and by the **codes and conventions** used that signify it belongs to a particular genre. These codes can be technical codes, such as the colours or the type of background music, or concerned with such factors as the structure of the narrative or the presence of a star or stock character. These factors help us classify media forms into genres that can be consistent across the media. Superficially, the way the news is presented in newspapers, on the internet and on television is similar and news as a form, with recognisable generic features, is understood by audiences.

Thinking about media

- What would you expect to see and hear in a trailer for a disaster movie?
- Who would you expect to star in a new ITV drama about vets?
- What would you expect to see in a TV newsroom set?
- Where in the newspaper would you find the music reviews?

Audiences and genre

Genre is a useful concept that can be critically applied to any media text. By classifying the features, comparing texts, noting similarities and differences in content and form, and considering the **expectations and pleasures** that genre offers audiences, we become aware of trends in popular taste; we also understand why producers respond to these by making more texts of the same sort in order to maintain an audience. Investing in producing genre texts can be a risky business: a mere copy of an existing product is not enough for success; there needs to be a difference, a development, something to excite audiences. The producers of the Spiderman franchise or the Big Brother shows have to carry on coming up with something fresh to keep their audiences happy.

Audiences enjoy the mixture of repetition and variation; they take pleasure in familiarity as well as anticipating a new twist, an added ingredient. Genre studies have shown that audiences can have specific expectations from a text that they wish to be fulfilled; that they enjoy recognising familiar features and that recognition of genre attracts audiences. We're comfortable with what we know and what we can predict. We gain satisfaction by engaging with a text, we consume

Discourse: the language associated with a particular situation; a set of statements or body of language on a particular topic or theme unified by common understanding. For example, in a situation comedy, the discourse might suggest that the mother rather than the father is the centrally important figure.

Narrative: the processes by which stories, fictional and non-fictional, are constructed by producers and understood by audiences.

Media in action

Discourse has been classified into four basic forms:

1 Communication

2 Exposition (providing information)

3 Argument (giving an opinion)

4 Description and narration.

(in Brooks, Cleanth and Robert Penn Warren (1972) *Modern Rhetoric* (Shorter 3rd edn), New York: Harcourt Brace Jovanovich)

Thinking about media

Consider McQuail's research into why people say they use media to come to some opinions about:

- Why people watch soap operas. Consider a range of soap operas.

- What pleasures are available to audiences. Consider a range of audiences.

texts for specific purposes and can recognise the function of a text, the **discourse** by which it addresses us and the ways in which we can respond to it. We recognise the function of the discourse through our knowledge of the patterns of genre built up by our experiences as media consumers.

The concept of **narrative**, the ways in which stories are structured by producers and understood by audiences, is fundamental to the study of media forms. We encounter stories in television programmes, films, advertisements, news on television and radio and via the internet. Our own lives follow a narrative pattern and we learn about the world primarily through following stories about people and events. The media caters for our love of narrative: television, radio, internet and the newspapers will cover the story of a missing child to its conclusion, perhaps using all four discourses. All media texts have a narrative, all tell a story of some kind and the basic structure of beginning, middle and end is used, reused and varied in all types of media products. Narrative often involves conflict of some kind, for example the essence of television soap opera is conflict between characters, and audiences understand how such conflicts start, continue and how they might be resolved.

Soap operas, sometimes called continuing narratives, gain higher television audiences than any broadcast genre. *EastEnders* consistently has more than eight million viewers, more than any other continuing television programme.

The narratives involve dramatic conflicts, large casts of 'everyday' characters, often whole families. Action takes place in a limited location, the domestic sphere of the living room and kitchen and public spaces such as shops, streets, pubs and cafes.

The uses of television

(from Denis McQuail in McQuail 1987: 73)

Information

- finding out about relevant events and conditions in immediate surroundings, society and the world
- seeking advice on practical matters or opinion and decision choices
- satisfying curiosity and general interest
- learning; self-education
- gaining a sense of security through knowledge

Personal identity

- finding reinforcement for personal values
- finding models of behaviour
- identifying with valued other (in the media)
- gaining insight into one's self

Integration and social interaction

- gaining insight into circumstances of others; social empathy
- identifying with others and gaining a sense of belonging
- finding a basis for conversation and social interaction
- having a substitute for real-life companionship
- helping to carry out social roles
- enabling one to connect with family, friends and society

Entertainment

■ escaping, or being diverted, from problems
■ relaxing
■ getting intrinsic cultural or aesthetic enjoyment
■ filling time
■ emotional release
■ sexual arousal

This theory, which was advanced by Blumler and Katz (1974) and developed by others including McQuail, is called **Uses and Gratifications.** It can be applied to television audiences or to consumers on any other media platform. In the next chapter we will look at other ideas about audience.

Genre as a critical tool

Certain genres connect with certain audiences; producers want to maintain this connection and genres don't remain static. Genres develop and change with changes in technology, changes in popular culture and changes in the nature of audiences. Genres that are a mixture of existing ones are called **hybrid genres.** For example, the film *Shaun of the Dead* can be described as a romzomcom as it contains elements of the romantic comedy and zombie horror film genres.

We can examine the codes and conventions within a text and a series of texts to identify generic conventions. A way of doing this is to look at the aspects that could be said to be typical of this type of text.

Four typicals that are useful to consider are:

■ typical narratives
■ typical **iconography**
■ typical characters
■ typical settings.

A very simple, stereotypical example would be a *narrative* about solving a series of murders; *iconography* of guns, blood and cool jazz music; *characters* including detectives, victims and villains set in an urban *setting* with dark streets and alleyways. These features are recognisable as some of the **repertoire of elements** associated with the crime drama.

Another way of classifying texts is to look at the style and the format of the text. A detective story can be told in a one-off two-hour television drama, a film, an interactive game, a drama serial with a **cliff-hanger** ending to each half-hour episode. The style of filming can be fast-paced like the US *CSI, Crime Scene Investigation* series or the slower and gentler pace of an Inspector Morse television drama.

Producers classify products into genres to market them to audiences. Keep an eye out for generic classes used by media producers when buying or renting a DVD for instance, and think about the four typicals and elements of style and format the texts share.

Many modern texts are **post-modern** inasmuch as our large media world needs so much content to fill it that the practice of recycling is common and acceptable. Ideas, styles and icons are appropriated, sometimes from another medium, and reworked or sampled. Taking ideas and styles and incorporating them into a new text is playful and contemporary audiences enjoy this. We like to get the joke and understand the reference.

■ **Media in action**

The Uses and Gratifications theory suggests that media audiences make active use of what the media has to offer arising from a complex set of needs that the media in one form or another gratify. This theory, first put forward in the 1970s, contrasted with earlier theoretical models that saw the audience as passive consumers of media.

■ Key terms

Hybrid genres: texts that are formed with elements from more than one genre, perhaps producing sub-genres.

Iconography: particular signs we associate with particular genres.

Repertoire of elements: the number of codes and conventions, technical, symbolic, narrative and setting, from which a selection can be made.

Cliff-hanger: a dramatic device at the end of an episode in a series that leaves the audience eager to discover what happens next.

Post-modern: the idea that in our society old certainties no longer apply, that with the globalisation of the media and the interactive virtual reality of the internet, the cultural meanings and forms of the media are subject to constant change.

Recognising its origin and the way the image may have been subverted gives us the pleasure of being knowledgeable about popular culture, being one of the 'in-crowd'. Advertisers, needing to get their message across in a short space of time, rely on audiences recognising **intertextuality** with their prior knowledge of the form of genre conventions. For example, in the 2007 VW Golf nightdriving.com television advertisement, the film of a car being driven through a dark and urban landscape is accompanied by voice-over soundtrack of the late Richard Burton reading from the poetry drama, *Under Milk Wood*. The highly regarded and famous recording of Dylan Thomas's play, which starts by describing the night scene in a sleepy Welsh village, is recognised with pleasure by literary, educated audiences. There are elements of brand transference: the classical, classy and stylish qualities of the actor and the verse are associated with the same features in the advertised product.

By looking at the text itself, and beyond it to the relationship between the target audience and the placing of a media product in the schedule or **layout** on the media platform, you will be able to account for differences within a generic form.

■ Broadcast and film forms

The significant features of all visual broadcast and film products are, of course, moving images and sound. Music videos also share this basic form. Radio and other audio-only products are formed entirely from sound codes: the spoken word, music and sound effects. We will look at some of the generic forms and the codes and conventions used in film, television and audio texts, and consider how particular forms are organised and scheduled by producers and consumed by audiences.

Film and genre

Movies can be classified in terms of narrative, director, star or films associated with a specific artistic movement. Some studies of film genre have looked at the output of a particular production company, for example the Hammer horror films made in the UK in the 1950s and 1960s; others have made studies of the work of directors such as Alfred Hitchcock, Tarantino or the Coen Brothers, or of the work of actors such as Bruce Willis or Robert de Niro.

Other approaches to genre in film are from the point of view of the film industry producing and distributing the movies, for example the Hollywood blockbuster or the Bollywood musical; from the point of view of the ideas and values they contain and the aesthetic and stylistic traditions common to them; or from the point of view of the audiences, how they understand and respond to certain genres.

If we consider what is typical of certain types of film we begin to understand how genre works.

Case study

Horror

The horror genre is often associated with low budgets but major studios and well-respected directors have made films in the genre. The horror genre is almost as old as cinema itself and contains a number of sub-genres and repeated themes: slasher themes, vampire themes, zombie themes, demonic possession, alien mind control etc. Horror is a feeling of dread and anticipation that occurs before something frightening is seen or otherwise experienced, a feeling of fear, revulsion and helplessness. It is particularly suited to the darkness of the cinema and the Internet Movie Database lists well over 1,000 vampire films. Well-known stories and legends have inspired vampire filmmakers and there have been countless versions based on the Victorian novel by Bram Stoker. He coined the name of Dracula, and based his story on a real character, a 15th-century Romanian count, and Irish myths about blood-sucking monsters.

One of the earliest silent movies, *Nosferatu, a Symphony in Horror*, was made in Germany in 1922. The director, Friedrich Murnau, was unable to obtain rights to the story but although he changed the names and some of the details of the story the film narrative was so close to Bram Stoker's book *Dracula* that Stoker's widow sued and some prints were destroyed. Some vampire movies portray the blood-sucking vampire as a terrifying animated corpse and others show him as a romantic, sexy aristocratic figure. Audiences familiar with the story enjoy the dread and anticipation of what will happen when the count shows an interest in someone's wife or fiancée. The narrative of Dracula films follows a straightforward, predictable pattern; the monster, the victims, the hero are fairly predictable; the iconography includes garlic, crucifixes and coffins; the setting might vary in location in time and place but much of the action will take place in the darkness necessary for the vampire's dastardly deeds.

Audiences enjoy change, perhaps of location in time or place, but are left unsatisfied if the film fails to frighten. Horror fans approached Francis Ford Coppola's 1992 *Bram Stoker's Dracula* anticipating pleasures shaped by prior viewing experiences.

'They were aware of the diverse attractions, the hybrid elements were flagged through advertising, publicity and other merchandising products but there was no consensus about the generic status of the film. It was described by some as a 'sad and romantic', or a 'gothic-horror-love-story', a 'thriller' or 'a normal Dracula movie with a bit more sex' but disappointed fans of the genre because it failed to frighten them.'

(taken from Austin in *Hollywood, Hype and Audiences*)

So, a horror film that doesn't scare doesn't work for audiences.

In the contemporary media landscape, films often come as part of a series. Sometimes a whole series is planned along with merchandising, such as a video game, a DVD, a soundtrack. Producers can buy and sell a **media franchise,** which is the rights to the intellectual property involving the characters, setting and trademarks of an original work of media such as a film, a work of literature, a television programme or a video game. The franchise allows different actors and different directors to be used such as in Star Trek, James Bond and the Batman movies. Other series like the Pirates of the Caribbean trilogy and Lord of the Rings are conceived to be released over a more limited period of time using the same cast and crew and are released at times to maximise box office, video games and DVD sales.

■ Key term

Media franchise: the capacity to extend the life of characters, settings or trademarks by producing further products.

■ Thinking about media

Notice that the cinema releases at the beginning of the school holidays appeal to family audiences.

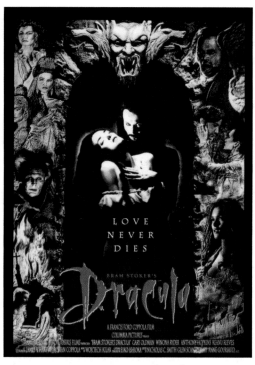

Fig. 2.1 Bram Stoker's Dracula *(1992) and* Nosferatu *(1922)*

Investigating media

Choose a film genre and consider at least three films that could be included within it. Present your findings in chart form. Copy the chart below.

Typical features of a film genre

Film genre Title	Film 1 Title	Film 2 Title	Film 3 Title
Narrative: what sort of story, what happens, what 'set pieces' might there be (for example a car chase in a crime film, a gun-fight in a Western)			
Iconography: what significant objects, what sort of lighting, sound codes			
Characters: what types of men, women, other creatures			
Setting: where the narrative is located in place and time			
Themes: underlying message (for example families are more important than consumer goods, that romance is more valued than arranged marriage)			
Technology: for example use of CGI, stunts			
Audience response: for example, engaged in the mystery, excited			

Media in action

The watershed: the BBC Editorial Guidelines on harm and offence say that programmes broadcast between 5.30 and 21.00 must be suitable for family audiences including children. If there is to be an exception, clear content information is given, for example images that children might find distressing in natural history programmes or in the 6 o'clock news.

Television forms: production and reception

The content of linear television schedules can be broken down into the types of programmes, factual and fictional, and the idents, trailers and commercial advertising. It can be further broken down roughly into programming aimed at specific audiences such as children, families, young people and the adult programming, which is screened after the 21.00 (9pm) watershed.

The major television broadcasters want to appeal to large numbers of people and their schedules reflect this but at the same time they have varying obligations to provide programmes of specialist interest. In the multi-channel digital age we are seeing a number of specialist channels that focus on specific genres such as the History Channel, the Sci Fi Channel, FilmFour.

Television and daily life

Television schedules are in tune with the patterns of life in our culture. Many people watch the news while eating their evening meal or settle

Investigating media

Search on-line for a TV listings guide, such as TV Easy. Compare the schedules of the five major terrestrial channels.

1 When does news appear and how does this chime in with the pattern of everyday life?

2 When do the broadcasters compete by scheduling two programmes of appeal to the same audience at the same time?

3 Why do you think that continuing dramas (soaps) are not scheduled head to head?

Thinking about media

Read through the information about the scheduled programmes for Friday evening from 6pm to 11pm on the five main television channels:

■ Is there a clear difference between pre and post-watershed programming?

■ Try to classify the content of each channel's Friday evening programming into genres. *(Do this by thinking broadly in terms of fictional drama, comedy, news, talk shows, competitions and quizzes, documentary and factual programmes. Some of the many hybrid television forms can't be classified without studying the programme in detail as you did when you investigated film genre.)*

■ What differences can you see in the pleasures offered to the Friday night television audiences by each channel?

Fig. 2.2 *Friday 26 October pages in TV Week 20–26 October 2007*

down to watch a film or drama programme at a particular time each evening. Saturday and Sunday evening programmes offer different content to weekday evening programmes.

Early morning weekday schedules include young children's programmes from 6am to 10am on BBC Two, Channel 4 and Five, while BBC One's *Breakfast* and ITV1's *GMTV* compete for viewers with three hours of news magazine programmes. The rest of their morning schedule reflects stay-at-home audiences with consumer programmes, debates and human interest programmes led by familiar presenters.

Broadcasters compete to appeal to certain audiences. With television broadcasting this is most apparent at peak-time evening viewing when all broadcasters try to maximise their audience share and keep viewing figures high by scheduling the most popular genres. The BBC and other broadcasters actively promote their products by trailing programmes, including those screened on other channels in their portfolio. Other tactics include hammocking, namely positioning a programme in between two more popular ones; and inheriting, in other words placing a new programme, perhaps the first of a series, after one that shares the same genre hoping to hold the large audience of the first programme. It is becoming common practice to show consecutively programmes from the same series on channels such as More4. There may be, for example, two continuing dramas, two home decorating programmes and then three US drama series between 18.00 and midnight.

Of course, in the contemporary media landscape, we are not reliant on television schedulers for our evening's viewing, but the patterns of watching particular types of programming at particular times is still current. BBC One and ITV1 both compete for Saturday night family audience share, presenting entertainment shows involving competitions with a chance for audiences to influence the outcome by casting a vote. For example, viewers can sing along karaoke style through interactive technology to *Joseph*; the interest awakened in 'old' musicals will, it is hoped, lead to successful box office and soundtrack sales for the new West End productions and a boost in sales for the original products: an example of synergy and maximising of profit.

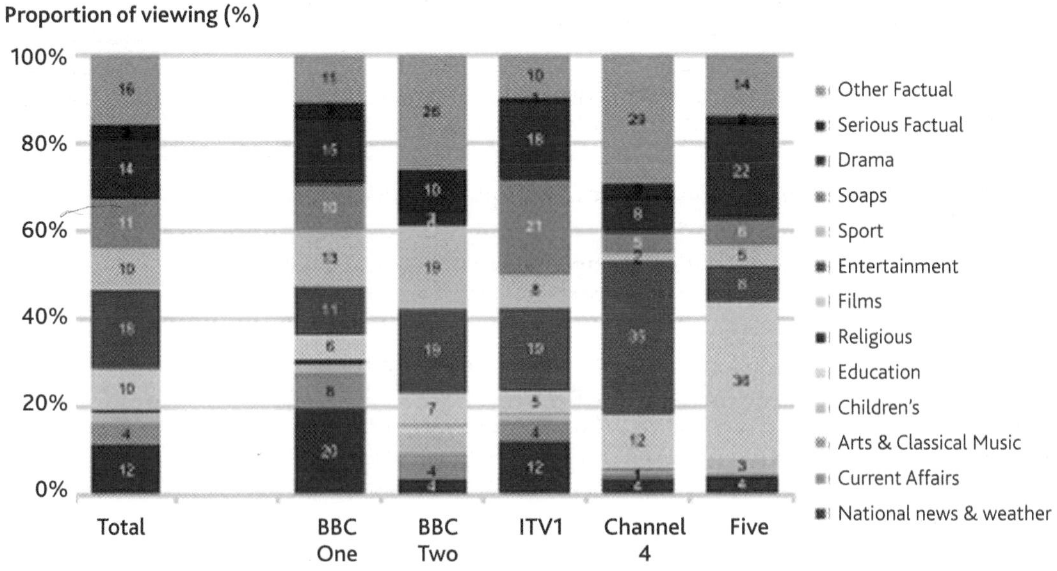

Proportion of viewing (%)

Source: BARB 2006, network, terrestrial channels only, all individuals, all time (0600–0300)

Fig. 2.3 *What do the channels show?*

The proportions of output vary between channels and each channel is seen by viewers as having different strengths. Part of an Ofcom survey in 2006 revealed that BBC One is seen as strong on delivering news and big national events, BBC Two as stimulating knowledge and learning and ITV1 is appreciated for its quality drama. Channel 4 is rated highly by 16–24 year olds for high quality and challenging programmes.

Television genre

There are two ways of understanding television genre: one is the broad programming categories of drama, entertainment (including comedy, music and game shows), sports, news, factual programmes, education, religion, arts and children's programmes; and the other is to look at the repetition within products of formulas. The broader categories, fiction and factual programming, could be said to relate to what audiences gain from the products, entertainment or knowledge, but as we know many knowledge based television products offer entertainment and tell interesting and entertaining stories using similar narrative techniques to fiction programmes.

Genre can be identified by looking at products that include similar characteristics, character types, themes, backgrounds and situations. A limited studio location, such as a house or an office, a family or a small social group, a new situation in each episode when a minor problem is set up and solved, a soundtrack with laughter, a 'natural' style of lighting and use of the camera equals a traditional form of situation comedy. These formulas are adapted over time. As characters grow up, for example, storylines and relationships may change.

Broadcast fiction

Broadcast fiction is scripted, directed and acted and popular drama programming includes the following formats:

- Continuing stories (sometimes known as soap operas) with a large number of characters, sometimes with multiple storylines (such as *EastEnders*) with several 30-minute episodes a week.
- Drama series with familiar characters, with some continuation of stories but one major dramatic event contained within each weekly show. Drama series such as *Heartbeat* and *House* fall into this category.
- Drama series can range from mini-series that might take two or three one-hour shows to draw to a conclusion or a series of eight or more episodes.
- One-off dramas, which can sometimes be scripted dramatisations based on real people or events.
- Comedy drama includes 30-minute situation comedies and shows consisting of shorter sketches with characters that become familiar with repetition.

We enjoy the familiarity of characters we come to know, groups we are familiar with, locations we understand; such features are the mainstay of television drama continuing stories. We also want variation, and producers and writers provide a new twist, a change in narrative, setting or characters to maintain our interest. As genres develop, variations are added to the basic formula.

■ **Media in action**

The Ofcom report said 2006 was 'a transitional' year for UK television. With advertising revenues continuing to fall and subscription revenues from pay TV continuing to rise, the gap between the public service broadcasters with the remit to broadcast a number of genres of programming, and pay TV, which are not subject to these restrictions, had widened. Ofcom recognised that regulation of public service broadcasting will have to change to reflect the new digital world.

■ Investigating media

Look at the title sequences and the first ten minutes of two hospital drama programmes – continuing dramas such as *Holby City* and *Casualty*.

Note the shared features in terms of the language of the moving image (visuals and sound), characters and the way the narrative develops.

■ **Media in action**

Broadcasters provide their own publicity, fan material and merchandising opportunities on the internet. The BBC Press Office provides Press Packs on its programmes. There is a synopsis and full cast and production details on *Life on Mars* and information about spin-off products: in this case there are two DVDs for *Life on Mars* from Contender Home Entertainment; *Life on Mars: The Official Companion Book*, by Guy Adams and Lee Thompson, published by Simon & Schuster UK and the original soundtrack to *Life on Mars* released by Sony BMG.

■ **Case study**

Three examples of changes to a formula: setting, character, approach to audience.

Life on Mars, a popular BBC One police drama, started with a short series of one-hour programmes in 2006 in which a detective is transported back to 1970s Manchester after a car accident. The time travel itself, the change of setting, gave audiences the pleasure of the pastiche of the 1970s settings, the colours, the clothes, the cars; they loved to be knowingly appalled like the hero, DI Tyler, at the police style and attitudes that would be unacceptable today. The show was a hit resulting in a second series of eight episodes. *Life on Mars* won the Best Drama Series at the International Emmy Awards in November 2006; it was a police drama with a difference. The idea will be carried on but with a significant change; the leading actor does not want to participate in future shows.

Ugly Betty is an American television drama product that runs to over 20 programmes in each series. First aired on British television in 2007 with the workplace setting that of a New York fashion magazine, the twist in the genre was in the placing of an unsophisticated, naive, honest and hardworking character in a situation that would seem to be unattainable for her. The blurb on the Channel 4 website sums up the theme of the narrative: 'In the superficial world of high fashion, image is everything. Styles come and go, and the only constants are the super-thin beauties who wear them. How can an ordinary girl – a slightly plump plain Jane from Queens – possibly fit in? In the world of high fashion, Betty is

Fig. 2.4 *Stills from* Life on Mars *BBC1,* Ugly Betty *Channel 4 and* Skins *E4*

an oversized peg in the petite round hole.' If this had been made a few years ago, viewers might have expected a Cinderella make-over transformation story but the theme fits in with the contradictory ideas current across the media: an awareness of the dangers of audiences identifying with the conventionally ultra-slim, blonde women in television drama. Viewers are happy to see the ordinary girl winning in situations where the glamorous people fail.

Skins, a British drama series, made for E4, aimed at the 16–24 age range, reflected the cutting edge nature of its storylines with a different way of promoting itself before transmission. Conventionally, television programmes are previewed and reviewed in newspapers, magazines and on the internet. Broadcasters finance marketing campaigns to build awareness, interest and desire to watch the first episode of a series, hoping that further publicity and word of mouth will attract further viewers. Instead of the usual advertising campaign two weeks before the show, the E4 show *Skins* put material on MySpace two months before transmission. A series of short films, showing each character talking to camera about their lives and likes followed the flash-animation storylines and broadcast dates, allowing potential fans to get to know their characters before the show had started. There were opportunities to act in the show, to create a costume, to redesign the logo, vote on a storyline and the entire first episode was on its MySpace site a week before its television release. Audiences feel involved not just with the characters and themes in the story but also in the construction of the programme. There is a feeling of ownership and belonging, which builds audience loyalty to the community of the producers of *Skins*.

Factual television

Factual television is about real people and real events, with much of the content scripted and shaped to tell a story within a specific period of time. Some factual programmes are classified as documentaries and there are many hybrid forms. A documentary can be defined as a film, television programme or book that presents a social, political, historical or scientific subject in a factual or informative manner. It is concerned with actuality – what actually happens – but as it is shaped and organised into a media product it can never be reality itself. The 'truth' has been mediated by the very processes used to make the product acceptable to an audience.

Documentaries fulfil a variety of functions and provide valuable sources of information, education and illumination about historical, geographical, scientific, artistic and social subject matter. They can present a case, highlight an injustice and give a voice to issues that may not otherwise be aired. Documentaries can have a campaigning role and be designed to provoke thought and action from their audience. Docu-soaps became very popular with audiences and producers in the 1990s. The public enjoyed getting to know 'ordinary' people, going behind the scenes at, for example, a hotel or an airport. These are a hybrid format of the expository and observational modes. The content of the programmes was focused on how the people selected by the producers on the basis of their personalities dealt with dramatic situations. Other hybrid forms: reality TV shows that follow real people in situations that have been set up sometimes to provoke particular reactions from the participants; make-over shows that change people, animals, children, houses and gardens are also 'documentary' inasmuch as they show real people and are not

Media in action

Most of American television's recent hits have been structured as 'television novels' (Steve Bochco described *Murder One*, his 1995 legal series that followed a single case across a 20-week season as a television novel), breaking the traditional pattern where a plotline was resolved within a single episode or occasionally in a two-parter. Long-running US series have a large presence in UK television schedules. They stretch to so many episodes as American cable television relies on funding from viewers and audience: long-running series hold both groups over a long time period.

Thinking about media

- What examples can you think of where there have been generic changes to a well-known formula in a broadcast fiction genre?
- What sort of changes are they and why?

Link

Broadcast fiction is a Cross-Media topic. In Topic 4 broadcast fiction, and the processes of its production and reception across the media platforms, will be discussed further.

scripted. However, without exception, much of what actually happened has been mediated, selected and edited to tell a particular story in a particular way in a particular time frame.

The documentary text may be a one-off programme or part of a series. There are some recognisable techniques used by the makers of factual programmes that are chosen to convey a sense of realism.

💡 *Conventions of the documentary*

Conventions of news and traditional documentary forms

- Actuality footage
- Archive footage
- Visible recording
- Talking head
- Interview
- Use of experts
- Vox pop (voices of ordinary people)
- Witness testimony
- Reconstruction
- Voiceover narration
- Graphical information

Newer conventions of the hybrid documentary

- Contrived situation
- Set-ups
- Characters chosen for personality or contrast
- Competition or game
- Characters talk direct to camera

The ways in which audiences respond to a nature documentary, for example, are different from the response to a reality show such as *Wife Swap*. For example, the documentaries in the BBC's Life series, written

---

💡 **Investigating media**

Using a copy of this table, view two television documentaries and note the use of these documentary conventions:

Conventions of factual television programmes

Conventions 1. Traditional forms 2. Hybrid forms	First programme Title – channel – time	Second programme Title – channel – time
Actuality footage Archive footage Interview Talking head Use of experts Vox pop Witness testimony Reconstruction Voiceover narration Graphical information		
Contrived situation Set-ups Characters chosen for personality or contrast Characters talk directly to camera		

and presented by Sir David Attenborough, have been seen by millions of people throughout the world and have influenced the movement for the conservation of the natural world. Some documentaries like *Planet Earth* and other high concept products have a large production budget. They involve months or years of research and filming and post-production work that requires funding by co-producers. Production companies are increasingly exploiting the filmed material by making DVDs for home viewing or educational purposes, or selling library footage to advertisers, museum exhibitors or other documentary producers.

Many contemporary television documentaries are relatively cheap to make, using ordinary people and limited locations. A documentary series such as *Airline*, about the easyJet budget airline, is based at four airports, Bristol, Luton, Liverpool and Newcastle, filming characters and events that can later be moulded into television shows. Each programme has a pattern: the locations will be familiar to viewers and new characters will be introduced; three or more stories will be told from beginning to end in 30 minutes. These stories are intercut with each other, the problems are set up, the action develops and the problems are resolved. The blurb for *Airline*, episode 7 of 10 in series 10 highlights 1 of the 4 strands of the programme. 'Plenty of things can go wrong when flying, but most people do manage to actually book their tickets. Not so the Spears who need to get to Glasgow for Alison's mum's birthday. Alison thought she'd booked, but there's no sign of their tickets on the system, leaving husband Paul with a hefty bill.' This programme did make a drama out of a crisis.

Such programmes give audiences the opportunity to see how other people react in situations and some put us in the position of a voyeur, looking at other people's lives through the window of our television screen.

Both the nature documentaries and the reality television shows are popular in television schedules; both share characteristics such as a voiceover; both are heavily edited to shape a narrative into the time allocation of the programme and both show 'real life'. The documentary factual genres have developed dramatically with the new technology available to documentary makers and with the ways in which audiences contribute to the documentary. We can make documentaries ourselves and share them with others on the internet, we can send a documentary account of an experience into a broadcaster and some of us can participate in reality TV. One of the newer developments in reality TV involves competitions running over a time period with participants facing a challenge of some kind. In some shows members of the public vote on who is to be eliminated and in others the contestants are assessed by a panel of studio judges.

Thinking about media

- Why do people watch these documentaries?
- What pleasures are available to viewers?
- Look at the television schedules for the five major channels and consider the documentaries on offer throughout a week's viewing. What pleasures do they offer viewers?
- Are they primarily for information, entertainment or a mixture of both?
- Note any differences in the types of documentaries screened on different channels. Why might this be so?

■ Media in action

The Life series started with *Life on Earth* in 1979. The ninth series *Life in Cold Blood* is due in 2008. All are written and presented by Sir David Attenborough on BBC.

Fig. 2.5 *We're watching you*

■ Media in action

In *The Apprentice* series on BBC, aspiring executives compete for a job with Sir Alan Sugar; in *How Do you Solve a Problem Like Maria?* and *Any Dream Will Do*, hopefuls compete for a part in a forthcoming West End show. ITV have gained large audiences with *Strictly Come Dancing*, featuring celebrities partnered by professional dancers and *The X Factor* in which contestants sing for the chance of a recording contract.

■ Link

You may choose documentary and hybrid forms for your case study. The topic will be discussed in more detail in chapter 4.

Investigating media

You are producing two short documentaries, about your neighbourhood, both for different audiences.

1 Plan the content of each programme, suggesting scene, characters and conventions you might use. Don't forget to plan the soundtrack. What music or voiceover would you include and why?

2 What view of your neighbourhood do you want to get across to your audiences?

Key terms

News agenda: the planned content of the news programme, the running order and the time allocation.

News values: the relative importance of certain stories over others depends on a number of factors both institutional and technological. News and entertainment values will be discussed fully in Topic 4, The cross-media case study.

Vox pop: the voice of the people – short interviews gathering the opinions of members of the public, usually in the street.

Link

News is a Cross-media study topic and in Topic 4 there is more about news selection and news values across the media platforms.

Investigating media

List the stories in a day's early evening news broadcasts on BBC One, ITV1, Channel 4, Channel 5 and BBC Four and the order in which they occur. Share your findings. Can any conclusions be drawn about institutions and audiences?

Case study

News

If we think about news as a genre, certain content comes to mind immediately: many of the conventions in the documentary table above are included in full length news programmes such as the early evening news programmes broadcast by BBC One, ITV1, Channel 4, Channel 5 and BBC Four.

The talking heads are presenters in the studio, always talking seriously, direct to camera while reporters talk to the camera outside the studio and provide the voiceover to the short packages of filmed footage of events. The studio presenter will usually start the story and viewers will be returned to the news desk for the start of the next one. The order of the news stories indicates the relative importance of the stories, according to the agenda of the institution and what producers consider to be relevant and interesting to their audience. Different producers present news differently to different audiences because the **news agenda** may be different. For example, in radio news, Radio 1's *Newsbeat* has different **news values** from Radio 4's *The World at One*.

Shorter news bulletins are delivered in headlines and sound-bites often accompanied by rolling captions on-screen. Many news programmes start with a title sequence, accompanied by dramatic music, a mixture of images and voiceover speaking the headlines in a serious manner.

Other conventions are extracts from interviews, graphics to clarify information, and the use of **vox pop**. These may form elements of the presentation of one news story and packaged within a familiar and accessible narrative structure.

Rolling news stations like Sky News and BBC News 24 and current affairs programmes will include discussion among experts about the events and issues or a more thorough report of a particular event and its significance but some of the conventions remain the same.

Journalists report news but with modern technology there are opportunities for user generated content (UGC, see Topic 1) and the process and practice of newsgathering changes.

Fig. 2.6 *News Studio with presenters*

Radio: production and reception

Radio can be received on all media platforms: the digital television services, through the wavebands FM/AM and DAB multi-plexes on the e-platforms including telephony. Some FM and AM stations are available on the internet and on this platform a multiplicity of radio stations worldwide are available.

Much radio is broadcast live and we listen to radio for the latest travel information, local news updates and sports commentaries and scores. Many of us wake up to a clock radio tuned to our favourite station and the radio is often on as a background to activities, in the home and in the workplace. Breakfast time and drive time are when radio captures its largest audiences; it has the advantage over other media as you can listen to it while doing something else.

We listen to the radio for information and for entertainment, at home and on the move. The radio presenter directly addresses the listener and it is an intimate medium of communication; listeners feel that they are being addressed personally. Even when the presenter is talking and joking with his or her friends in the studio during the popular type of music radio known as zoo format, the listener feels included in the company. The presenter is an important part of the daytime radio schedules and is arguably more of a draw for listeners than the music itself. The presenter DJs are the best paid people on radio.

Many popular radio stations give listeners the opportunity to participate by telephone by expressing an opinion or competing in a quiz or by text providing information about current traffic conditions.

With digital technology we can download radio programmes as podcasts to MP3 players or listen again to programmes on the internet. Popular download genres are comedy programmes on BBC Radio 4 and the chat from the Radio 1 and 2 disc jockey shows. For **copyright** reasons, the music elements cannot be downloaded.

> ### Key term
>
> **Copyright:** the legal ownership of the text. The owner gets a fee for giving permission for a media product or part of a product to be reproduced or shown.

As with all media products, radio stations compete for audiences and statistics on reach and share are published by RAJAR (Radio Joint Audience Research) and available on the internet. The average length of time that listeners spend with a station is calculated based on the number of people aged 15+ who tune to a radio station (are reached by that station) for specified periods of time.

By looking at these statistics it can be seen that although the reach of all commercial stations is not far behind that of all BBC stations, younger listeners are tuning into commercial stations and that older listeners of 45+ listen to more hours of BBC radio than any other group. RAJAR also releases data about listening to radio via digital television, DAB radio, mobile phone and the internet: understandably given the uptake of the technology, figures have been rising significantly.

Radio forms

Basic radio production is inexpensive: all that is needed for basic programming is a presenter and some other content: phone-ins with the presenter doing the desk, chat shows, recorded music. Higher production radio contains inserts of features, commercials, **vox pops** and news packages and radio drama.

Radio is a blind medium and there is a strict layering of sound events to avoid confusing the listener. In talk radio the voice is foregrounded and the balance between the voice and background music is vital. In the domain of radio, the key organisers of form and content are the vocals, sound effects, the ambience, music, noise from non-sentient objects and silences.

Every genre found on television can be found on radio and technical processes such as recording, mixing and editing are conventions common to both.

Radio stations can be classified broadly into those with speech based content and those with music based content. Many music stations play particular music genres, for example Classic FM or The Jazz.com and other stations, Radio 2 and Radio 3 for example, will schedule different music content to suit listeners' habits. Some radio stations have an ident, a jingle perhaps, that identifies the station and acts as a transition point between programmes and between sections of programmes.

Spoken word channels, like BBC Radio 4, cover a range of genre including news and current affairs and plays written for radio. The world's longest running serial is a radio programme, the continuing drama serial *The Archers*, which has been broadcast daily with a weekend catch-up omnibus edition for nearly 60 years.

Fig. 2.7 *RAJAR quarterly summary of radio listening part 4 United Kingdom (Key demographics)*

PART 4 - UNITED KINGDOM (Key Demographics)

	Survey Period	Pop'n '000s	Weekly Reach '000	Weekly Reach %	Average Hours per head	Average Hours per listener	Total Hours '000	Share in TSA %
ALL COMMERCIAL 15+	Q	50334	32005	64	9.1	14.4	459322	43.5
Children 4-14	Q	7872	5550	71	6.1	8.6	47965	67.7
15-24	Q	8104	6112	75	10.2	13.6	83036	59.3
25-44	Q	17109	12111	71	10.4	14.6	177249	51.5
45-64	Q	15302	9688	63	9.4	14.9	143928	40.5
65+	Q	9819	4093	42	5.6	13.5	55110	25.5
Main Shoppers	Q	38266	23804	62	9.0	14.4	343082	42.2
Main Shoppers with children	Q	11593	8407	73	10.5	14.4	121275	52.9
ABC1	Q	26982	17104	63	7.5	11.8	202618	37.6
C2DE	Q	23352	14901	64	11.0	17.2	256704	49.7
ALL BBC 15+	Q	50334	33245	66	11.4	17.3	573516	54.3
Children 4-14	Q	7872	3787	48	2.7	5.7	21491	30.3
15-24	Q	8104	4736	58	6.5	11.2	52922	37.8
25-44	Q	17109	10758	63	9.3	14.8	159422	46.3
45-64	Q	15302	10592	69	13.3	19.2	203657	57.3
65+	Q	9819	7160	73	16.0	22.0	157514	72.9
Main Shoppers	Q	38266	25388	66	11.8	17.8	453173	55.7
Main Shoppers with children	Q	11593	6945	60	8.9	14.8	102821	44.8
ABC1	Q	26982	19515	72	12.1	16.7	326607	60.6
C2DE	Q	23352	13730	59	10.6	18.0	246909	47.8

DEFINITIONS

(1) Audiences in local analogue areas excluded from 'All BBC Network Radio' and 'All National Commercial' totals.
(2) National groups that are a combination of analogue and digital broadcast.
(3) Audience to 'Opt-out' services included.

AREAS

UNITED KINGDOM (Parts 1 and 4)   (including Channel Islands and Isle of Man)
EDITORIAL AREAS (Part 2)   BBC stations' defined service areas
TOTAL SURVEY AREAS (Part 3)   Commercial stations' defined marketing areas

In Part 1 'BBC Local/Regional' and 'All Local Commercial' include listening to local stations outside their own Editorial/Total Survey Areas.
In Parts 2 and 3 'BBC Local Radio' and 'All Local Commercial Radio' are based on the net Editorial/Total Survey Area of the individual services making up the network.

TERMS

WEEKLY REACH	The number in thousands or as a percentage of the UK/area adult population who listen to a station for at least 5 minutes in the course of an average week
AVERAGE HOURS	The total hours of listening to a station during the course of a week, averaged:
	PER HEAD - across the total adult population of the UK/area
	PER LISTENER - across all those listening to the station for at least 5 minutes
TOTAL HOURS	The overall number of hours of adult listening to a station in the UK/area in an average week
SHARE IN TSA	The percentage of total listening time accounted for by a station in the UK/area in an average week

SURVEY PERIODS

CODE	FIELDWORK DATES	SAMPLE SIZE (Adults 15+)
Q	26th March 2007 - 24th June 2007	32,124
H	1st January 2007 - 24th June 2007	64,784
Y	26th June 2006 - 24th June 2007	129,959

Radio Joint Audience Research Limited   www.rajar.co.uk

RAJAR

This radio soap opera, based in the fictional village of Ambridge in the fictional county of Borsetshire and the families who live there, was conceived at a time when the government was urging farmers to grow more food and was seen as an educational tool; today it still deals occasionally with agricultural issues but focuses mainly in its scripts with social issues and domestic drama as do the television soaps.

Radio 4 has been a nursery for comedy shows that later transfer to television on BBC Three, BBC Two and BBC One. *The Hitchhiker's Guide to the Galaxy*, the sci-fi spoof, was a series on Radio 4; *The League of Gentleman*, *Dead Ringers* and *Little Britain* started as half-hour programmes within a short series on the Radio 4 6.30pm slot.

Case study

BBC Radio 2

Radio 2 has the largest weekly reach, a reach similar to all the national commercial stations put together. Its schedules cover a range of radio genres: Arts and Drama; Blues, Soul and Reggae; Classical; Classic Rock/Pop; Comedy and Quizzes; Easy and Soundtrack; Entertainment; Jazz; Music Documentaries; Pop and Rock and Alternative. The weekday 24-hour broadcasting schedule is punctuated, on the hour, by news bulletins with news headlines at half-hourly intervals from 5.30am to 8.30am. Weather news appears half-hourly from 5am to 9am, then at key travel or transition times during the day and evening – 1pm, 5, 6, 7 and 10pm.

The presenter led and named programmes vary in length from one-and-a-half hours to three hours. The presenters who draw the biggest audiences take the breakfast and drivetime slots and the current pattern is to have six regular presenters with a daily weekday show each. There are sometimes surprise celebrity presenters who draw new audiences. The content of the daytime shows is a mixture of music and chat, often involving interaction with the listening audience through phone-ins or text and e-mail. The two-hour lunchtime show presented by journalist, Jeremy Vine, is a topical phone-in show featuring people in the news.

The playlist for the daytime music shows is decided by Radio 2 producers. Each week the committee decides which 30 new releases, singles and albums, will be added to the station playlist and classified into A (receives about 20 plays per week), B (10 plays) and C (5 plays). In the evening, mass radio audiences tend to watch television. From 7pm on the radio there are different slots every evening led by presenters specialising in a particular music genre, such as jazz, country, musicals, big band, etc. Many of these programmes include audience requests for music tracks. The evening schedule also includes music documentaries and occasionally orchestral concerts. BBC Radio 2 caters for live music and broadcasts seasonal festivals such as the Cambridge Folk Festival, Country Awards in Nashville, Blackpool Illuminations and Proms in the Park.

Since the BBC's position was threatened by the challenge of new commercial stations licensed in the 1990s, Radio's 1 and 2 have had makeovers and changed content and style. Radio 1 was positioned as the station showcasing new music appealing to the 16–24 age group with Radio 2 aiming to provide the other types of popular music that appeal to audiences. The hiring of presenters such as Jonathan Ross, Chris Evans and Russell Brand by Radio 2 has brought a wide audience of listeners. At the time of writing,

Investigating media

1 Listen to a spoken word drama programme and note the use of voice, music, silence and sound effects to carry the narrative. Is it more or less difficult to follow the narrative of an audio drama product than a television or film text? Give reasons for your opinions.

2 Listen to the news on Radio 1's *Newsbeat* at 12.45 or 5.45 and Radio 4's *Six O-clock News*. How and why do they sound different?

■ Media in action

The Sony Radio Academy Awards judge achievement across a number of categories of radio: programmes, personalities, production and station. See the e-resources or do a search for the website and follow the links to the winners of the awards; the comments of the judges will give you a good idea of what good radio is about.

Examiner's tip

To become familiar with the codes and conventions of broadcast and film forms you will need to look at least one factual and at least one fictional television programme, one film and one music radio and one speech radio programme. You will need to look at a film and television trailer and examples of other audio/visual promotional material.

though, Radio 2 still provides Pause for Thought, a religious broadcast and programmes of light classical popular music.

- Who listens to Radio 2?
- What does the case study tell you about the lifestyles and interests of Radio 2 listeners?

■ Investigating media

1. Look carefully at the schedules for a week of Radio 2. Account for the differences in the weekday and weekend schedules.

2. Visit the BBC Radio 2 website (see the e-resources for the web address, or do a search) and follow the links to the programmes available for listening again.

3. **Group activity**: listen to part of a breakfast show on a local BBC radio station, a commercial radio station and BBC Radio 4. Chart the content: news, weather, presenter style, presence and type of music, interaction with listeners, user generated content.

4. Produce a script for a two-minute package about a band to be inserted into a radio music documentary about current trends. Include a reporter, interview and music.

■ Print forms: production and reception

Newspapers and magazines

The basic features of print products are the copy (the material prepared by the writers) and pictures (the photographs or other forms of illustration). There are differences in the size and type of paper used and the balance between colour and black and white, typefaces, number and quality of pictures; these factors relate to cover price, advertising revenue, frequency of publication and readership. When investigating print texts we need to look carefully at the content of the product, for example the range of stories and features within a newspaper or magazine and how they are organised within the product and the layout of the pages, how the content is arranged and presented. The choice of words, the use of puns, word play such as alliteration, the use of colour and the size and frequency of pictures are useful indicators of the type of product and how it relates with its audience.

Figure 2.9 (on page 36) from a BBC magazine called *Girl Talk* is one of three pages of quizzes and competitions. The graphology, the visual aspects of the text, is simple and colourful and attractive to its target audience of girls aged 8 to 13. The rest of the content of *Girl Talk* is concerned with its readers' interests, including clothes, cute animals and other media forms like DVDs and television programmes. However, the emphasis in the magazine is on friendships, important to this age group. The cover picture shows a girl smiling as she holds a bunny rabbit and one of the free gifts offered is a paw-print stationery set. Inside the magazine, readers contribute photos of their furry friends. All magazines and newspapers contain contributions from readers, predominantly in the form of letters and e-mails but increasingly as photos.

- Pick out some elements of the content of the page that reflect the interests of the readers.
- Pick out some elements of the copy that you consider to be typical of the discourse of the print media.

A feature common to newspapers and magazines is the presence of an **editorial**, at least one column, in which the editor directly addresses the readers, often highlighting some of the content of the magazine or giving an opinion on one of the leading stories in the newspaper or events of the day.

- Pick out some elements of the language of the pages that reflect the interests of the readers.
- Pick out some elements of the copy and layout that might appeal to readers.

Key term

Editorial: an expression of opinion by the newspaper's editors, reflecting the views of the publisher or owner.

Fig. 2.8 *What's your spring thing?* Girl Talk *28th March–10th April 2007. Compare this format to that of Fig. 2.9 below.*

Fig. 2.9 *Contents page of* Amnesty Magazine *Issue 142 March/April 2007*

A significant feature of newspapers and magazines is the cover or front page. All newspapers and magazines have a front or cover page that serves to announce its identity and invite readers to buy and read the product. There will be headlines in large type summarising the content of the articles and often our attention is drawn to an exclusive story in that particular product.

Study the key terms. They will be useful when analysing the layout of newspaper forms.

Fig. 2.10 *Mock-up of a front page*

■ Key terms

Masthead: the name plate – information printed in every issue stating the date of publication and publisher.

Puff: a promotion of a product or service.

Strapline: a short statement that sums up a story in a newspaper or magazine in a few words and may appear with the main headline for that story.

Headline: words in large type found at the top of the story, summarising it, the head.

Deck: the number of lines in a headline – this is a four-deck headline.

Banner headline: page-wide headline.

Exclusive: story published by only one newspaper, a scoop.

Byline: name of the writer.

Lead: the first paragraph or two of a news story – sometimes in bold or larger typeface.

Caption: headline under a photo.

DAILY TRUMPET

Bringing your news   Friday February 22 2008   www.oxfordshire.co.uk

Half-Term Savers
See Page 39

Win a £500 shopping spree
See page 39

Find your dream home in our property supplement

Children safe – arson suspected

By Emma Smith
newsdest@daily trumpet.co.uk

CHILDREN RESCUED FROM BLAZE

TWO young children were dramatically rescued from a house blaze in Tarrington last night.

Emergency services were called to the fire at a three-storey three bedroomed house in Kingston Road at around 6pm.

Turn to Page 5

Scene: emergency services outside the house last night.

Council to embark on £21.5m spending spree

THE COUNTY COUNCIL are likely to be bracing themselves today, following revelations from a council insider to our reporter yesterday about spending plans for the coming year.

EXCLUSIVE STORY
By Alan Jones
ajones@dailytrumpet

Nelson Thornes has worked in collaboration with AQA to ensure that this book offers you the best support for your AS or A level course and helps you to prepare for your exams. The partnership means that you can be confident that the range of learning, teaching and assessment practice materials has been checked

by the senior examining team at AQA before formal approval, and is closely matched to the requirements of your specification.

One of the main appeals of any Media Studies course is that the content of the course is based on media texts that are part of the contemporary media landscape and you will be investigating these texts with an analytical perspective. You will be analysing a wide range of media texts from television, radio, newspapers, magazines and the internet and will build up throughout the course a body

of knowledge about how media texts are constructed and the terminology and theoretical ideas to describe and evaluate them.

Turn to Page 5

Open evening 5th March 2008 5pm–8pm   Freephone 08000 607080
Full-time/Part time University courses at Tarrington College of Higher Education

Examiner's tip

Many of the conventions of the layout of the content of print products apply also to the e-media platforms and some of the terminology relating to newspapers and magazines can be applied to the material found on websites.

Newspapers come in a variety of types and can be classified in terms of size, ratio of images to words, style and tone, content, language and target audience. Newspaper formats are usually one of three sizes: broadsheets – 600 x 380 mm, generally associated with intellectual newspapers, although the trend towards 'compact' newspapers has changed this; tabloids – 380 x 300 mm often perceived as sensationalist as opposed to broadsheets; Berliner or midi – 470 x 315 mm. News design is the process of arranging material on a newspaper page, according to editorial and graphical guidelines and goals. The terms broadsheet and tabloid are often used to describe the style and content of the newspaper rather than the size. For example the *Daily Mail*, *The Times* and the *Sun* are currently tabloid in size but don't have the same news values or cater for the same readership.

Main editorial goals include the ordering of news stories by importance, while graphical considerations include readability and balanced, unobtrusive incorporation of advertising. Newspapers are printed on inexpensive, off-white paper known as newsprint while magazines use a better quality paper.

Much of the funding comes from advertising and the content that is not paid for by advertising is known as editorial content, written by the editors, journalists and guest writers.

Investigating media

Choose two newspapers, one a red-top tabloid and one quality newspaper for the same day, and compare them.

Look firstly at the front pages of both newspapers and note the following points:

1 ratio of images to words, size of headlines, number of stories

2 style/tone – sensationalist and exaggerated with alliteration and puns or serious and measured

3 language – easy to understand language with short paragraphs or more complex language with longer paragraphs.

Look at the newspaper as a whole and note the following points:

1 How much content is about sport and which sports are featured?

2 How much content is about celebrities from the entertainment or sporting world?

3 How much of the paper consists of advertising material?

4 How much of the paper is about international news?

Case study

Kick

An example of a specialist magazine is *Kick*, published by Attic Media in London and classified as a pre-teen magazine. The advertising is aimed at the parents of pre-teens interested in football. The July 2007 issue consisted of 11 pages devoted to advertising and promoting a new Nintendo game, Mario Strikers, featuring 'footy legend' Ian Wright endorsing the game. Some of the promotional material takes the form of quizzes and word searches involving the reader in the characters and action of the game. The magazine consists of 26 pages of editorial content, 4 of which are puzzles and competitions with 3 pages of readers' letters, photos and drawings. An additional 8 pages are full-size photographs of contemporary famous footballers plus a giant poster, one of a series of '10 Awesome Posters'.

The layout of the cover uses a bold colour palette of reds and orange, a masthead with a football for the dot on the I and an exclamation mark, and most of the pages, all glossy, present the copy on brightly coloured backgrounds. The puff on the cover of the July 2007 issue invites readers to 'WIN! iPod!, Wii! and DVD player! and loads more!', and the strapline shouts that the magazine is 'packed with

Link

More discussion about the selection of news in newspapers and on-line and broadcast news platforms appears in Topic 4, The Cross-Media Study.

More discussion about advertising funding and advertising content in media products appears in Topic 5, Investigating Advertising and Marketing.

Examiner's tip

For Media Studies purposes, the type of news selected and the style and tone of the presentational features, the copy and images are the features that allow us to classify the differences between the different types. There are sharp differences between the quality press and the red-top press, which you should be able to observe and comment on.

prizes and puzzles!' Alliteration is continued with the lead headline 'Sizzlin' Superstars!' and throughout the magazine the exclamation marks and colourful mixed-font headlines continue. The editorial content is entirely about football and the layout of the pages varies from pages that consist of photographs, drawings and colourful short articles or interviews to double-page spreads of 40 Footy Facts.

The tone and style of the magazine is exciting and excitable, appealing to young boys who are enthusiastic about Premier League football stars. All advertisements are full-page display ads; the Nintendo game takes up most space but a further four pages advertise three other games and a TV show on Nickelodeon.

■ E-media: production and reception

All traditional media forms have a presence on the internet platforms; many broadcast products can be consumed on-line and most newspapers and magazines have on-line versions. Advertising has a huge presence on the new digital platforms and appears in various forms. We use the internet to buy and sell, to make friends and communicate socially, to share information, photographs, videos and music. Rapidly developing technology means that some of the forms present at the time of writing will have been superseded and there are likely to be other forms in use. You will need to keep up to date with the latest forms on the internet and emerging media, being sure that you understand the ways in which audiences interact and respond to them.

The most interesting thing about the internet and emerging forms is the extent to which it is bottom-up rather than top-down. You can upload content to your own website or to space on a host website. You can post a comment about current events, television, films or books. You can participate with others in virtual reality gaming worlds, creating an avatar and conducting a range of activities in cyberspace.

A website will be designed with consideration to content, layout and **navigation**. It is important that the visitor can quickly and easily find what they are looking for and navigation is just as important as the actual content. Various navigation methods can be used, depending on the nature of the website, including:

- page links – buttons or text, usually along the top or left
- drop-down menus – enabling visitors to go directly to a topic that they would otherwise have to click through several pages to get to
- **hyperlinks** on text or images throughout the main website content, taking you to other pages
- site maps – like an index – ideal for large websites, and often used to assist with searching.

Content of a website can be static or dynamic, when content is updated automatically or manually. Website graphics are used to enhance the look of websites. Text on websites can only be displayed in a limited number of fonts, so if you want to jazz it up, you need to turn that text into a graphic image. Other website graphics include photos, pictures, buttons, navigation menus, **banner ads**, **animations**.

Interactive websites are those that allow visitors to perform tasks and get a response from the website, rather than just view information. Common examples of this are:

Fig. 2.11 *A page from the Nelson Thornes website*

- registering for a newsletter
- searching for information
- buying products.

Many of us look first to the internet for information as can be seen from the chart.

Shopping including selling, searching and social networking occupy most of the chart. News has a place in the top 20.

Rank	Website - [Show domain]	Related	Market Share
1.	Google UK	▶	7.69%
2.	Windows Live Mail	▶	3.13%
3.	eBay UK	▶	2.66%
4.	Facebook	▶	2.01%
5.	Google	▶	1.72%
6.	MSN UK	▶	1.63%
7.	Bebo	▶	1.49%
8.	YouTube	▶	1.14%
9.	MySpace	▶	1.01%
10.	BBC News	▶	1.00%
11.	BBC Homepage	▶	0.87%
12.	Yahoo! UK & Ireland Mail	▶	0.85%
13.	Yahoo! UK & Ireland	▶	0.81%
14.	Orange	▶	0.78%
15.	Amazon UK	▶	0.77%
16.	Microsoft	▶	0.75%
17.	BBC Sport	▶	0.60%
18.	Google UK Image Search	▶	0.59%
19.	Wikipedia	▶	0.49%
20.	MSN	▶	0.48%

Thinking about media

Look again at the reasons people give for watching television (see page 16).

- Do these uses apply to your use of the internet and emerging media?
- In what other ways do you use these platforms?
- How do you use your mobile telephone other than texting and telephoning?
- Is e-media more useful to you than traditional media?

Fig. 2.12 *Top 20 UK sites, May 2007 from the* Guardian *June 21*

Some e-media forms

Other types of websites are search engines that make their money from advertisers – Google gets more advertising revenue in a year than Channel 4 – and webhosting sites that allow users to upload content to the site.

Gaming is an important form of e-media that has many users who play interactively with other gamers. Adventure games and intricate strategy titles are developed at great cost using cutting edge technology and there is a range of creative games being developed to appeal to a growing game market of middle-aged females.

(*Source*: *Guardian*, Thursday 30 August 2007, ' Will on-line distribution overtake the boxed game?' by Alexander Gambotto-Burke)

Social networking sites are very popular, especially with young people who choose digital platforms as their first choice of communicating with others and for whom the virtual community might be a major main social contact.

■ Case study

Social networking

1 The YouTube homepage describes itself as a community, the home for video on-line, and outlines the opportunities to:
    - watch millions of videos
    - share favourites with friends and family
    - connect with other users who share your interests
    - upload your videos to a worldwide audience.

    Its strapline is 'Broadcast Yourself' and once you sign up it is easy to follow the prompts to upload videos.

2 MySpace bills itself as 'A place for friends' and favourite music, photos and jokes can be shared with others. Sites like this allow the user to follow a menu to edit content and allow or bar contacts and comments on their page.

3 Facebook 'is a social utility that connects you with the people around you'. Facebook is made up of many networks, each based around a workplace, region, high school or college. The site is mainly about communicating via messages to:
    - 'Share information with people you know.
    - See what's going on with your friends.
    - Look up people around you.'

    Facebook was originally created at Harvard University in America to help students deal with the sometimes unfriendly atmosphere and before autumn 2006 was effectively invitation only. The doors were opened to all-comers. Since then its viral power, its elegant design and the flexibility and openness of its features have made it the hot favourite to become the social networking site that would make the leap into the adult world.

    These sites are funded by advertising, and offer the audiences to advertisers.

At the time of writing, Facebook has 27 million 'friends' and is adding more than 100,000 users a day. No wonder big media companies have clamoured to buy it.

■ Link

At A2 you will study the debates about the digital revolution and make a case study of the impact of new/digital media. For AS purposes you need to be aware of the forms themselves and the processes of production and reception. However, from this brief introduction you can see that the internet is changing the ways in which we communicate with each other and the world.

■ Thinking about media

- What is the appeal of social networking sites for audiences?
- What is the appeal of social networking sites for advertisers?

Organisations other than advertisers have seen the advantages of the internet as a way to communicate with audiences. For example, political parties and politicians have their own sites and profiles on social sites so that they can access wide audiences.

Link

See the e-resources for the 10 Downing Street website address or do a search on-line.

Case study

Website 10 Downing Street

The masthead on the home page and its accompanying straplines welcome the user and list the content available. There are five main sections, Prime Minister, Government, Newsroom, Downing Street and Broadcasts, with subheadings that can be clicked through and clear ways of navigating through the pages. Arranged in columns, with an index on the left-hand side of the page, headlines and thumbnails highlight the main features within the pages.

Navigation is by means of clicking through links and arrow buttons, and the home page invites users to read, listen and view content by following the links. The main dynamic content on the home page is Latest News, Other News and Press Briefing. You can engage interactively by touring the rooms in Downing Street, engaging in web chats with politicians, contributing to a petition or starting one up. There are a host of ways of interacting with the site and communicating with the government. The site provides opportunities to watch Prime Minister's Question Time Live, to download podcasts, to subscribe to news updates and a number of other functions. There is a link to the 10 Downing Street space on YouTube and the videos uploaded there include archive material.

It is a very good example of a website with dynamic content and provides access for the ordinary citizen to learn about government and to communicate with government.

Investigating media

Look at the NHS information website (the address can be found on the e-resources or by doing a search on the web).

1 Look carefully at the content and layout of the home page and note the amount and type of the images used.

2 Note that the advertising is provided by Google and is on the right-hand side of the page. This funds the costs of producing and maintaining the site.

3 Note the way in which patients are addressed in a friendly and personal way, using language that is easy to understand and is encouraging users to click through to their regional area.

4 'These official gateway sites include information about NHS organisations, local NHS services, what the NHS does, how it works, and how to use it. You can search for details of doctors, dentists, opticians, pharmacies, walk-in centres, hospitals, etc. You can look at performance indicators to see how your local services are doing, waiting times, etc.'

5 Follow the link to your regional NHS information site. How and why is this different from the home page?

6 Imagine that the home page has a link for under-16s to find advice. Plan some content, including copy and images for a page that would suit their purposes.

Examiner's tip

When studying media forms and texts across the media platforms consider the following:

■ Identify the major generic conventions.

■ Explore how far audience expectations are fulfilled. Are the conventions treated playfully?

■ Keep an eye out for new formats, hybrid genres and synergy between forms and texts across the media.

■ The first question in Section A of the Unit One examination asks you to say how typical the unseen text is of its type. You will need to discuss narrative, iconography and layout using appropriate terminology.

■ For your Cross-Media case study, you will need to investigate forms the products take across the media platforms.

■ For your coursework, Creating Media, you must use appropriate codes and conventions and explain your choices.

Investigating media

You have learned something about the different genres, or forms presented on media platforms. Using what you have learned about media forms:

1. Go to www.nelsonthornes. com\aqagce\media.htm and click on the link to the supporting resources. Watch the extract from the sitcom at least three times.

   - Identify the major generic conventions, including iconography, narrative, and characters and setting.

   - How typical are the codes and conventions of similar media forms?

2. Go to www.nelsonthornes. com\aqagce\media.htm and click on the link to the supporting resources. Watch the extract from the news programme at least three times.

   - Identify the major generic conventions, including iconography, narrative and characters and setting.

   - How typical are the codes and conventions of similar media forms?

Other forms: blogs, wikis, virtual reality...

The internet gives us opportunities to post or respond to news stories. We can wiki, by contributing to a collaborative website. The word wiki comes from *wikiwiki*, the Hawaiian word for quick. It also stands for What I Know Is, emphasising that the view or information is personal, individual and has not been cross-checked or verified by an editor or other authority.

People can create weblogs of their activities, for example school students on an expedition abroad can post comments and photographs for families back home to chart their progress. Like social sites and news sites the internet is the way to keep up to date with events and share views with others. Many of us spend a great deal of our time with e-media, sometimes browsing or surfing for hours at a time, following links at random.

Another way in which people use the internet is through engaging with virtual reality sites like Second Life.

> Second Life is a 3-D virtual world entirely built and owned by its residents. Since opening to the public in 2003, it has grown explosively and today is inhabited by a total of 7,435,729 people from around the globe.
>
> From the moment you enter the World you'll discover a vast digital continent, teeming with people, entertainment, experiences and opportunity. Once you've explored a bit, perhaps you'll find a perfect parcel of land to build your house or business.
>
> You'll also be surrounded by the Creations of your fellow residents. Because residents retain the rights to their digital creations, they can buy, sell and trade with other residents.
>
> The Marketplace currently supports millions of US dollars in monthly transactions. This commerce is handled with the in-world unit-of-trade, the Linden dollar, which can be converted to US dollars at several thriving on-line Linden dollar exchanges.

From Second Life. What is Second Life?

One US dollar is worth 300 Linden dollars, purchased on-line by credit card and fortunes can be made and lost in cyberspace.

End of topic summary:

- Audiences recognise the codes and conventions used in media forms. There are both similarities and differences between the content and conventions of media forms used on the different media platforms.

- Media forms can be grouped into genres according to narrative, iconography, character and setting. Genres are not static.

- Media producers compete for audiences and audience share and reach is measured. Media producers compete for advertisers.

- The practice of delivering media content to audiences involves responding to audiences' lifestyles and pleasures.

- There is specific terminology to describe the features of media forms, for example the terminology for the layout and content of print media.

- Increasingly, through new technology, audiences interact with media forms.

3 Media concepts and ideas

Key terms

Representation: what is presented to audiences is a likeness, an interpretation, a re-presentation or even a symbol of a reality. It is not reality itself. Media texts are artificial versions of the reality we perceive around us.

Readings: the understandings taken from and brought to the text by the audience, the ways the text is understood.

Reading the media

All of us are brought up with the media and from a very early age know, for example, that the television set in the corner is a source of entertainment. For many people there is very little time in a day when they are not consuming or interacting with a media platform even if they are doing something else at the same time. We become very familiar with the sounds that announce news on radio or television, we can understand the language of the newspaper headlines taking in both what the story is about, the angle that the newspaper has on the story and at the same time the jokiness and punning of the headline. By reading the signs and codes in a film or television drama, we form opinions on whether a character is a hero or a villain, whether we are sympathetic with his or her situation or not. No one needs to explain these meanings to us – we understand them through our experiences.

Media Studies offers a framework with which to investigate media texts; a number of questions, ideas and theories to apply. I shall call it a conceptual toolkit and, at this stage, the concepts will be explored separately. The concepts, or ideas, taken together, give you the critical tools you need to be able to read texts.

As students of Media Studies you need to be able to deconstruct media texts in terms of the content in the text, the **representations** within the texts and the ideas behind these representations. You need to think about how audiences interpret these texts and how variables such as age, class, experience, attitudes, beliefs and values affect audiences' interpretation of texts, the ideas they bring to a text and the meanings they take from a text. What is funny for one audience can be offensive to another.

To investigate media texts we need to look in some detail at how meanings are constructed and at the **readings** that different people may take from their consumption of media products. This involves looking at the languages used in the making of media products, the visual and aural signs and codes. We shall examine these in terms of individual texts, bearing in mind that their meaning may be altered depending on where these signs and codes appear.

Media producers might encode specific meanings to be read in a particular way by audiences. Think about an advertising campaign for a luxury car, for example. The producer of the advertising texts want to attract audiences' attention to the benefits of the product portrayed in the advertisement and will employ a range of techniques to get the intended message across. These will include choosing characters, settings, lighting and sound to convey the ideas about what the car represents and which will resonate with the target audience. The distribution of the advertising campaign, the timing within the television schedule, the magazines chosen for the display advertisements will be important considerations too. The preferred reading of the text, the one the producer intended, is that the car is desirable, attainable and suitable for the viewer.

One of the most interesting aspects about the media is that the meaning intended does not always come across. The reader is part of the equation. An example of this was when, about 40 years ago, an advertising agency produced a television advertisement for a brand of cigarettes. The main character was standing alone on a street corner of a city. The night was dark and wet. A man wearing a belted raincoat and trilby hat was lighting a cigarette. This scenario was intended to represent the character as cool, reminiscent of Hollywood *film noir*, and the brand of cigarettes as sophisticated. Viewers read the text in another way, seeing the character as seedy and isolated. They didn't get the message and they didn't buy the cigarettes. Texts that are open to interpretation are called **polysemic**: they can have many different meanings depending upon the time, place and the class, gender, occupation and experience of the reader.

The Harry Potter books and films offer children exciting adventure stories and to many people Harry Potter is a hero, but to some fundamentalist Christians he stands for an example of the occult, and is an evil figure. They strive to ban the books and films from schools and libraries.

To some, wind farms are part of the answer to global warming while to others they are an intrusive eyesore ruining the countryside.

To help you understand how the concepts work you will learn to deconstruct texts and discuss the meanings of the elements within texts that are available to audiences. This is about interpreting the signs that make up the texts. These signs will be made up of visual elements, such as lighting, dress codes, headlines and aural codes, such as the use of music and sound effects. These are the technical codes with which media texts are constructed to form a media language. Other codes can be called cultural codes and these include the whole of the subject matter of a text such as dress, setting, characterisation and narrative. To interpret these signs and understand how they generate meanings to audiences involves a process of decoding through close textual analysis. Every media text constructs meanings through combinations of signs and practices, and to arrive at these meanings we have to deconstruct the text. This involves

Fig. 3.1 *Polysemic texts: is Harry Potter a hero or heretic? Is a wind farm part of the solution to global warming or an ugly monstrosity? Harry Potter using his magic powers from the* Guardian *July 13th 2007, page 7 and a wind farm*

a process we call **denotation** and **connotation** and it is by using this process that we can investigate the communication and reception of meanings about people, places, products, ideas and events through media products across the media platforms.

Thinking about media

Look at these signs: What do they represent? Where would you find them? How much do they look like what they represent?

Fig. 3.2

Key terms

Denotation: refers to the simplest and most obvious level of meaning of sign, be it a word, image, object or sound. For example the word 'red' may signify one among a number of colours. Applying the process of denotation to a media text one identifies what is actually there, on the page, in the frame in a factual manner.

Connotation: this is the second order of meaning in which a wider range of associations may arise. The sign 'red' might signify heat, danger, sexuality, socialism and so on. These meanings are arrived at through the cultural experiences a reader brings to a text.

Semiology or semiotics: the study of the meanings of signs. It derives from linguistics and seeks to understand how languages, as a system of signs or codes, communicate meaning.

Media language

The concept of media languages and the related ideas of narrative and genre are the starting point for examining what meanings the text carries. Once you have identified these elements of the text, the written signs, the visual and aural signs, the ways the narrative is structured, and how the characters, events or ideas are portrayed, the other key concepts come into play. Then you can deepen your exploration by thinking about why the text is so, who made it and distributed it and to whom.

The languages of media can be thought of as the language of the moving image and the language of print. The construction elements used on web-based and e-media platforms are a hybrid of these languages although, of course, the way the text is navigated is very different. The technical terms used about moving image also apply to still images and aural, sound codes apply to broadcast, film and internet.

The study of signs and codes, **semiology**, is the starting point for studying individual texts and making comparisons between them. The technical codes particular to a media form carry with them cultural meanings. You need to learn the skills of denotation – describing accurately what is there and the detail that makes up the language of a text – and of connotation – being able to say what meanings the language may carry about the ways in which we perceive our contemporary world.

In Topic 2 you learned some terms to describe the content of print texts and aural texts and now we will look at the terms used to describe the technical codes of moving image texts that can be applied to broadcast and film texts, including advertisements, and the visual content of websites.

■ Media in action

Roland Barthes, the influential theorist, said that signs have two parts: the signifier, the thing that does the communication; and the signified, that which is communicated. What interests semiologists is the way that words and images help us to make sense of the world, shape or reflect our attitudes and beliefs. The signs, the words and images and the way these are arranged in a media text carry cultural meanings.

Semiotics first asks how meaning is created rather than what the meaning is.

Roland Barthes investigated the cultural ideas and attitudes carried in the images of popular culture and everyday life. He wrote about denotation and connotation and myth, the orders of signification, in *Mythologies* (1973).

■ Key terms

Mise-en-scène: an expression from film studies meaning the composition of the shot. The components are the setting, the subject and the props and include the technical aspects of photographic and design codes.

Anchorage: a fixing device – the text directs the reader through the signifiers of the image towards a meaning chosen in advance by the producer of the text.

A starting point for analysing media languages is to deconstruct the text using denotation and connotation. Of course, readers respond to texts in many different ways; they have different cultural experiences so don't expect to interpret texts in exactly the same way as anyone else. You have to be aware that no meanings are fixed. Think about the different attitudes to a 4 x 4 SUV, such as a Nissan X-Trail. For some mothers this is a highly desirable vehicle, useful and safe for taking the children to school through the contemporary urban jungle. For the environmentally conscious it's a gas guzzling, climate-changing monster.

Three types of codes were typified to provide a framework for the analysis of newspapers and magazines. They were identified by McMahon and Quinn (1988) as:

- ▓ technical
- ▓ symbolic
- ▓ written.

They can be applied to moving image, still image and print media products.

The technical codes relate to the way the camera has been used, the way the subject has been lit and the way the shots have been framed and edited.

The symbolic codes relate to objects, setting, body language, colour and clothing and these all carry cultural meanings. These elements form the **mise-en-scène**, the visual effect of the way they are put together and displayed to tell the story to the viewer, the non-verbal codes of gesture and body language, the colour codes.

The written codes, some of which you have come across already in this book, consist of such elements as headlines, speech bubbles, style of typeface and captions to photographs. Words are often used to fix a meaning, to **anchor** it.

Fig. 3.3 *Into the blue: Prime Minister Gordon Brown during his speech at the Labour Party Conference in Bournemouth. The blue background was part of a deliberate play to woo Tory voters. The* Daily Telegraph, *September 25th 2007.*

Moving image terminology

Here are some of the terms that are useful in describing the language of the moving image. These can be used to explain moving image sequences in film, television or advertising or animation but are by no means definitive.

Framing

This refers to what is included and excluded in an individual shot, and what is chosen to be placed within the four sides of the camera's frame. This covers camera shots and camera position and movement, lighting and mise-en-scene, editing and sound. These are the technical codes used by the producers to carry meaning to audiences.

Technical codes	Artwork	
Very long shot/wide shot		This shot is often used at the beginning of a film or sequence and acts as an establishing shot, showing where the action is taking place. In this shot figures appear small in the landscape. Conventional connotation: *Person is isolated, alone, vulnerable*
Long shot		A shot in which a figure can be seen from head to toe.
Mid shot		Shows the figure from approximately the waist to the head. In a mid shot, you can easily recognise an individual but you can also see what they are doing with their hands.
Medium close-up		From chest to head.
Big close-up		Head only, used when expressions are important.
Extreme close-up		From just above the eyebrows to just below the mouth, or even closer.

Other terms for shots are:

Point of view shot	A shot from a character's point of view.
	Conventional connotation: we are positioned as the character, we identify.
Two shot	Any shot with two people in it.
Reaction shot	A shot showing a character's response to a piece of action or dialogue.
Over-the-shoulder shot	A shot in which we see a character over another's shoulder, often used in interviews or dialogues.

Lens/focus

The type of lens, and how it is used, can make a big difference to the meaning of a shot. The choices made affect the audience's perspective on the events and characters depicted. The focus of the camera is adjusted to keep images clear or to make images a little hazy if required for a particular mood or narrative purpose.

Wide-angle shot	(Taken with a wide-angle lens.) This has the effect of seeming to exaggerate perspective.
Telephoto shot	Like using a telescope, a telephoto lens appears to bring the subject closer and flatten out perspective.
Zoom lenses	These can vary the angle of view, from wide angle to telephoto, so that the subject appears to move closer (or further away) without the camera itself moving.
Focus	Everything in the shot appears to be in focus, which means that we can be looking at action taking place in the foreground, middle ground and background.
Shallow focus	The subject is in focus and the background is not. Conventional connotation: signalling who's important.
Focus pull	Using the zoom lens a person in the foreground in focus becomes out of focus and the focus shifts to a different subject in the frame.

Camera position and camera movement

Where the camera is in relation to the subject.

Low angle shot	Shot taken from below.
	Conventional connotation: making the subject or setting seem important or threatening.
High angle shot (often using a crane or helicopter)	Shot taken from above.
	Conventional connotation: making the subject look vulnerable or insignificant.
Track	Moving the camera itself towards, alongside, or away from the subject, or to follow a moving subject.
	Conventional connotation: might or might not be someone stalking someone.
Hand-held shot (*cinema verité*)	Shaky and wobbly camera, no tripod. Conveys a sense of immediacy, of naturalism.
	Conventional connotation: a dramatic situation, e.g. running from danger.
Pan	Pivoting the camera to the side to scan a scene or follow a moving subject. The camera remains stationary.
Arc	A 360-degree trip around the subject.

Lighting

Lighting can be high or low contrast and can vary in colour and direction.

High-key	The lighting is bright and relatively low in contrast: often used for Hollywood musical comedies.
Low-key	Much more pronounced shadows and dramatic contrasts.
Colour FX	Cold or blueish lighting. *Can connote a sense of cold, alienation or technology,* Warm or yellowish lighting. *Can connote comfort, sunset and so on.* Black-and-white or sepia. *Can suggest sophistication or that a scene is set in the past.*

Editing

How the individual shots are put together.

There are two main types of editing that you will encounter in mainstream films and TV programmes:

Continuity editing	The majority of film sequences are edited so that time seems to flow, uninterrupted, from shot to shot. Within a 'continuity editing' sequence; only cuts will be used. Continuity editing can also involve 'cross-cutting', where a sequence cuts between two different settings where action is taking place at the same time. The aim is for a seamless flow of action so that the audience does not notice the cuts.
Montage editing	In montage, visual images are assembled in a sequence to build up an impression and create meaning. The cuts are often noticeable. Juxtaposition of images can create a contrast rather than a smooth flow.

Editing can vary both in pace (for how long individual shots stay on the screen) and in the transitions between shots. Transitions describe the way in which one shot replaces the previous one.

Cut	One image is suddenly replaced by another, without a visible transition.
Cross-dissolve	One image dissolves into another. This can be used to make a montage sequence – e.g. the title sequence – flow smoothly; it can also be used in continuity editing to show that we have moved forwards in time and/or space.
Fade up	An image gradually emerges from a blank screen.
Fade out	An image gradually fades out. *Fades to and from black usually mean that time has passed.*
Wipe	One image replaces another without dissolving, with the border between the images moving across or around the screen.

Link

The planning and pre-production topic gives advice and examples about how to storyboard and plan for broadcast, print and e-media products.

Key term

CGI: computer generated imagery. 3D computer graphics used for special effects in films, television programmes, commercials and simulations.

Media in action

Usually, machinima productions are produced using the tools (demo recording, camera angle, level editor, script editor, etc.) and resources (backgrounds, levels, characters, skins, etc.) available in a game. For example Sims 2 machinima started with the photo album. You, the player, could create full shows using the resources from the game. This mixing process continues to develop, for example, in using Lego for machinima.

Link

To read about the art of video game design and its relationship with filmmaking, look at *The Tenth Art*, by Steven Poole, author of *Trigger Happy, The Inner Life of Video Games* on Steven Poole's website (see e-resources or do a web search).

Sound

Diegetic sound	Sound that seems to be part of what is going on on the screen, sounds that seem natural to the scene, such as the sound of thunder, the ring of a telephone, the sound of a car engine.
	Adds realism and adds depth to the characters and setting.
	Can signal an action about to happen.
Non-diegetic sound	Sound that we know is not part of what is on screen, such as music and voiceover. The music soundtrack, sometimes especially composed, to match the visuals and convey a mood.
	Typical conventions are that fast music accompanies chases, solemn music for sad occasions etc. These can be overturned, e.g. in Kubrick's *Clockwork Orange* classical music accompanies extreme violence.
Sound bridge	This is used to link two scenes, by having the picture and the diegetic sound change at different points. Usually the sound from the second scene is heard before we start to see the picture from that scene.
Sound effects (SFX)	In media terms this means all sounds in a media text apart from dialogue and music. Sounds are intensified and others added in the post-production state by Foley artists.

'New' media language

The language of the moving image is the vocabulary of the cinema and television but in the contemporary media landscape and with new graphic technologies the possibilities are ever expanding. The art of creating a video game is very young and is limited only by the designer's imagination. Animation and gaming has been at the cutting edge of the development of the visual languages of media products. With sophisticated software available to home users we can create high quality audio/visual material with digital cameras, MP3 players and computer editing packages.

Recent accessibility of **CGI** software and increased computer speeds has allowed individual artists and small companies to produce professional grade films, games and fine art from their home computers. This has brought about an internet culture with its own set of global celebrities, clichés and technical vocabulary.

A collection of production techniques, machinima, has become a film genre in itself. Started by game players putting game tools to use to make films, it is a mixture of traditional film techniques reapplied in a virtual environment. This can be done in real time using the computer of the creator or the viewer.

Film and broadcast products have drawn on the video game technologies and used CGI. Early CGI was used by George Lucas in *Star Wars* in 1977. The last 10 years has seen a great change in animation from the drawn cells of Disney and Hollywood to the use of CGI animation from *Toy Story* onwards. *The Matrix*, in 1999, was a film that was appreciated for its special visual effects as much as for its story about virtual reality. A large proportion of its $60 million budget was spent on the CGI element, and the ways in which technology was used in the making of the film was one of its selling points. Using CGI in movie making is now common. It is more controllable than processes such as constructing miniatures for effects shots or hiring extras for massive crowd scenes, and allows the creation of images that would not be feasible using any other technology.

It can also allow a single artist to produce content without the use of actors, expensive set pieces or props so it works for independent and individual film and video game makers as well as for the big companies with big budgets.

Practising readings

We can identify the technical codes and identify the types of shot, lighting, editing and the use of sound but we mustn't stop there. We must look at how, when and where these codes are used, their connotations, and sometimes the way they have been subverted in our post-modern world.

You need to make detailed readings of whole texts like advertisements, film and video game trailers and music videos and also of texts that use the visual conventions used across the media platforms. Much of the terminology above can be applied in your readings of newspaper photographs, magazine illustrations, movie posters and print advertisements. Don't forget sound, not just in broadcast products and films but also on the internet. Some e-media advertisements attract users' attention by sound, animation and other movement on the screen. It is difficult to ignore the buzzing of a mosquito on your computer screen; a mosquito that has to be silenced by your mouse.

Alongside the technological elements of a text, you need to consider the significance of the symbolic codes within it: facial expression, body language and gesture, clothing and objects.

In Topic 2 you read about the graphology of print texts and the significance of the layout and choice and presentation of copy. Most print texts have a visual element and these images need your attention too. Photographs in newspapers may have been graphically edited, possibly cropped, airbrushed, layered or manipulated in some other way to give the impression of the subject that the editor wants. They can be captioned in such a way as to anchor a preferred reading of the picture.

- How has this picture been cropped?
- What meanings does the framing carry?
- What meaning does the anchorage – Last man sitting – convey?
- What intertextual references are used and how does the humour work?

Print advertisements are a rich source for analysis. Producers need to communicate immediately to catch the attention of the reader and get them to look at the advertisement rather than turn the page.

Fig. 3.4 *Photograph from www.guardian.co.uk/politics, the caption reads 'Last man sitting I want to be alone. A lively response from Prescott to the all-female platform during the health debate.'*

Fig. 3.5 *Advertisement for XLEAGUE TV in SciFiNow, Image Publishing, Issue 3*

■ Investigating media

Use the following ideas to examine the graphology of this advertisement. Use the correct terminology and think in terms of symbolic, technical and written codes used.

Symbolic codes: the mise-en-scene: setting, body language, colour, objects:

1 Has the advertisement an identifiable setting? If not, why?

2 What does the gender, age, ethnic group tell you?

3 What do the clothing codes tell you?

4 What is the posture? Why?

5 Does the product appear in the advertisement? If not, why?

Technical: framing, lighting, editing:

1 How does the advertisement use colour and black and white? Why?

2 How have the images been framed? Does it look as if it has been cropped? Why?

3 Are all elements of the image in focus? If not, why?

4 Has anything been left out of the illustration? Why?

5 How has the image been lit and what is the camera angle? Are these important?

Written: typeface, word choice:

1 What kind of typeface(s) is used? Why?

2 What is the significance of the colours used?

3 What is the relationship between the copy (words) and the image(s)? Why?

4 Who is being addressed?

Narrative

The process of denotation and connotation involves being able to identify and discuss all the signs within a text and how they communicate with audiences, how they tell the story and put across the message. All texts, even single print advertisements, have a narrative. An advertisement like the one you've looked at shows what could be interpreted as a snapshot of the life of the character. We can imagine what might have happened before and after that frozen moment in time even though there is no evidence. We understand implicitly the ongoing narrative.

You will need to be able to identify the ways in which narratives are constructed in individual texts and across the media. The way in which, on digital platforms, we click through at our own pace, following links that interest us, or engage in a virtual reality computer scenario, is different from the experience of sitting in the cinema and seeing the story unfold. The way in which information is presented influences our responses to it. We can be positioned by the way the narrative is structured to identify with a particular **protagonist** in a film or broadcast text and to take a particular side in an issue presented in a newspaper or other source.

Events can be packaged differently and filmed or print material can be reorganised and reused over and over again. Think of a news story about a dramatic event, such as a kidnapping, which is covered on print, broadcast and internet and other e-platforms as the story breaks. This is the beginning of the narrative. As the story continues, perhaps over days and months and new audio/visual material and written comment becomes available, the story will be told differently. Early ideas and images may be rejected; fresh ones will be included to support the narrative of the unfolding story. There will have been background research into places and characters, interviews and expert opinion, added to the mix. When the whole incident comes to a conclusion, perhaps with the trial and conviction of the kidnapper, the material will be restructured into a summary of all the major stages of the story. Now the producer knows the whole story.

Key term

Protagonist: the main character in a play, story or film or any person at the centre of a story or event. Think about James Bond or Uma Thurman's character, The Bride, in *Kill Bill*.

Case study

A major sporting event will be broadcast live, as it happens, in real time.

The producers and the viewers are in the same position as the spectators, they don't know what will happen, and they don't know the end of the story, the result. There will be a number of cameras and the choice of shots selected by the producer and the commentary is part of the shaping of the story. The half-time interval will be filled by talk from experts and at the end of the match the players and their managers will be interviewed as they go off the pitch. The same event, shown later in the day, will have been re-shaped to fit into a shorter time and will show only parts of the match, the highlights. The production team, now knowing how the story ends, will have selected sequences of images to shape the tale of a victory, a loss, a draw, concentrating on the dramatic moments, fouls, goals, penalties, injuries and off-the-ball incidents involving the referee. The match has been edited and cut-away shots of the crowd or bench are inserted where editing has taken place. Other shorter versions of the original broadcast material will be used in news programmes. The match will also have been covered live on the internet and

Link

In Topic 2 you read about how audiences like elements of surprise and change and how producers are aware of this and will build repetition and difference into narratives.

Link

To remind yourself of Roland Barthes' theories, see the Media in Action box on page 44.

Media in action

A special feature on the DVD of *Memento*, The Beginning of the End, retells the story in a re-edited version of the narrative.

Thinking about media

- Consider a number of enigmas involved in the Channel 4 make-over programmes, *10 Years Younger*, *You are What you Eat* and *How Clean is Your House*, and *How Not to Decorate Your House* on Five.
- What enigma are we left with at the end of each programme?

Thinking about media

Watch a half-hour episode of a familiar soap opera:

- What are the clues from the characters' behaviour that make you aware that something is going to happen?
- Which technical codes indicate impending developments of the narrative?

bulletins of scores will have been available over a range of forms. People who watch a live match will often claim to see more of the match when they watch the highlights on television. The cameras may catch all the action and the organisation of the mass of material into a slick narrative puts it into a sequence that is easy to follow.

Different media forms, especially conventional generic texts, have recognisable narrative structures, although in the contemporary media landscape this is less obvious.

Enigma and action codes

A useful way of looking at how audiences become engaged with a moving image text is to use the narrative codes of enigma and action and how they structure our understanding and response. These terms, coming along with the terms denotation and connotation from the work of Roland Barthes, relate to developments within a story and the ways in which audiences respond to the flow of information.

The enigma code generates and controls what and how much we know in a narrative and holds our interest. What is going to happen? Enigmas are puzzles waiting to be solved and are present in a wide range of media. The central enigma in *Life on Mars* 'Is Sam mad ... in a coma ... or back in time?', a mystery that kept Sam himself and the audiences interested for 16 hours.

Within a film there is usually a central enigma that is resolved at the end of the story and a number of other enigmas or false solutions to the central mystery during the course of the narrative. Audiences take pleasure in being kept guessing, in anticipating what might happen.

In the film *Memento* (2001), written and directed by Christopher Nolan, the narrative starts at the end of the story and follows in a linear style to the beginning. The enigma for the audience is to follow the protagonist, who has amnesia, as he tries to remember what happened the night his wife was killed.

Action codes are those events within a story that we know will be significant in the development of the narrative that we understand and recognise immediately from other narratives. The metallic sound of a gun being cocked signifies that a shooting will take place, that there will be scenes of violence. They are often used like this as a shorthand way of advancing the action. An action signifies another action and so the narrative progresses. The narrative could be broken down into a series of titles signifying the sequence of events. This is made explicit on DVDs when the chapter titles are usually based on events or actions.

Beginnings and endings

The opening of a media product is a fruitful place to start an analysis of a text. This is where the text has to grab our attention, engage our interest and start off the story. It is the same for the first 10 minutes of a romantic comedy film or the first paragraph of a news story in a newspaper. Our attention is grabbed, our interest is engaged and we become involved in the narrative.

Conventionally, films and one-off media products have closed endings. The problem is resolved and all the ends are tied up and the action is completed. Other texts have more open endings, when the reader is left with a range of possibilities.

Conventionally, narratives follow a linear pattern, in other words they have a plot that moves forward in a straight line without flashbacks or digression. They follow a simple time line with the story moving through beginning, middle and end, with the flow of the information to the audience being strictly controlled.

Multi-strand narratives are a feature of many contemporary films and broadcast texts. In *Babel*, a film of 2006, there are four parallel narratives, different scenes going on at the same time but in different places with characters speaking in different languages. The camera cuts between the different strands and the audience is engaged in the process of discovering the link between them.

Some documentaries might cut between three or more separate characters or groups of characters. The story cuts between the groups, showing their problems, the development and finishing with the resolution of these problems. Factual programmes might contain separate narratives connected by a central theme, trying to buy a house, for instance, or having troublesome neighbours. A wildlife documentary might be structured to follow, for instance, several different types of animal waking in the morning, hunting and feeding and finally settling down to sleep. The footage for this will have been filmed separately over possibly a long period of time and edited to form a logical and pleasing sequence of events. We are helped to follow these complex narratives by a presenter or a voiceover providing continuity and acting as a narrator.

Long-running series such as *Lost* or *Prison Break* have one major narrative, in this case, escape! Alongside the story line, there are personal narratives concerning particular characters. Some of these mini-narratives might be resolved within one programme but the final resolution may not even come at the end of the series. In series one of *Prison Break*, Michael Schofield, his brother and a number of others finally escaped only to be hunted by the authorities. This open ending led, of course, to another series.

Different forms of media products lend themselves to different narrative structures.

> ■ **Link**
>
> In Topic 2 you learned about the production and reception of different genres and different format. The codes of media language, genre and narrative are closely related and should be considered at the same time.

■ Media in action

Here are two theories concerning the structure of narratives. These were originally developed to examine printed stories and novels rather than moving image or other modern media texts. They help us understand how narratives can be structured.

It must be emphasised that these are not formulas that media producers themselves follow.

Tzvetan Todorov saw a recurring pattern in narrative structure.

Equilibrium	Disequilibrium	New Equilibrium
An existing state of harmony	Equilibrium is disrupted by an unfortunate event or evil character that leads to a chain of events involving conflict of some kind	The forces of evil are overcome, the conflict is resolved and harmony exists once more

Vladimir Propp, analysing Russian fairy tales, classified their narrative structure in terms of character roles and the functions

Media in action

Binary opposition: a theory of meaning that can be used to look at some of the cultural beliefs built into texts.

In the mid-20th century, two major European academic thinkers, Claude Levi Strauss and Roland Barthes, realised that the way we understand certain words depends not so much on any meaning the words themselves directly contain, but much more by our understanding of the difference between the word and its 'opposite' or, as they called it, 'binary opposite'. They realised that words merely act as symbols for society's ideas and that the meaning of words, therefore, was a relationship rather than a fixed thing: a relationship between opposing ideas.

For example, our understanding of the word 'coward' surely depends on the difference between that word and its opposing idea, that of a 'hero'.

these roles play in a narrative. The functions, 31 in all, are comparable to Todorov's and each develops logically from the one before. It is the characters' actions that move the narrative along.

The Seven Spheres of Action	What character does in the narrative
The villain	Creates the narrative complication
The donor	Gives the hero something that helps in the resolution of the narrative
The helper	Gives help to the hero in restoring equilibrium
The princess	Has to be saved by the hero
The dispatcher	Sends the hero on his task
The hero	Saves the day and restores equilibrium; sometimes he's been on a quest to find something. The central protagonist in the action of the narrative
The false hero	Appears to be good but it is revealed at the end has been bad all along (rare)

Case study

This is an adapted extract from a student analysis. Notice how the essay combines denotation and connotation and uses the terminology of the moving image to discuss the themes, characters and settings. The subject is the documentary film *Touching the Void* (2003) in which two mountaineers recall events from 1985 in Peru.

'*Touching the Void* highlights the dangers present in nature and the courage displayed by humans. The documentary shows a re-enactment of the events which actually occurred. We see the actual people involved talking both to camera and as voiceover during the re-enactment of the situation on the mountain. The sequences of the reconstruction of the climb are inter-cut with visuals of the men talking. The mountain ranges are shown as a beautiful, vast landscape; using natural lighting the camera pans across the mountains to emphasise the expansive environment. There are overhead and high angle shots used to show how minute the men are in comparison to the landscape and also their vulnerability. It represents humans as being vulnerable in the presence of nature.

The audience is shown the danger of mountains and mountain climbing and the strength required physically and mentally. The men are represented as strong willed and courageous. Through the mise-en-scene the audiences can see the clothing and equipment used for mountain climbing and learn about the activity itself. Big close-ups show the feet and hands of the mountaineers in the process of climbing and the audience is positioned as a climber struggling behind the protagonist.

This documentary shows the hard decisions that people have to face in life. One point of view shot shows the man who was cut loose lying and looking up at the crevasse with the light at the top. He is in a dark place, the darkness perhaps has connotations of trouble, and the light is what he needs to aim for, to have a chance to survive. This is a binary opposition with the dark that surrounds him standing for misfortune and despair, and the light above symbolising the freedom, which needs extraordinary human effort to attain.

Touching the Void was made for the cinema. As in a feature film, the narrative gets the audience emotionally involved with the characters. The man who had to cut the rope on his partner, his best friend, can at times be seen as a Proppian villain but the audience learns through the voiceover that he did what he had to do, he had to make a hard decision. The audience can empathise with the man and understand what he did.'

This piece shows understanding of media language, narrative and the generic conventions of the documentary. There is reference to media theory, which is supported by reference to the text. The concept of representation is present in the discussion of the way nature and the mountaineers are portrayed.

Thinking about media

Mountaineering and other extreme sporting activities are, of course, not compulsory. The mountaineers in *Touching the Void* survived a life-threatening situation and lived to tell the tale. The commonly shared **ideology** of Western culture is that indulging in potentially life threatening adventures displays courage and bravery and that these human attributes are admirable.

- Do you agree?
- What would be an alternative belief about these activities?

Fig. 3.6 *Extreme sports*

AQA Examiner's tip

- In Section A of the examination you will be asked to respond to an unseen stimulus text. You need to show that you understand the concept of media language, but describing what is there without showing the possible meanings conveyed will not earn many marks.
- You will be creating media products using the codes and conventions of media language including narrative and genre in Unit 2.

Key term

Ideology: the opinions, beliefs and ways of thinking characteristic of a particular person, group or nation. Ideology as a media concept underpins the concepts of media representations, media audiences and media institutions.

Media representations

You've come across a definition of representation already and know that most media products have been intentionally composed, lit, written, framed, cropped, captioned, branded, targeted and sometimes self-censored by their producers and that they are artificial versions of the reality we perceive around us. Nearly everything in the traditional media has been produced by an institution and its personnel, and their experiences, attitudes and ideology will affect how they represent their subject. We may not be aware of this but when someone writes a web log, e-mails or texts to a broadcast programme or gets a letter printed in a newspaper or magazine it is obvious that it is a view, an opinion that is being presented.

We all know that a television drama is written and acted and that the characters in *Coronation Street* are fictional, that special effects and CGI add to the 'realism' of the action in a blockbuster movie. It is less obvious that factual media products, for example an item on a news broadcast, or

Investigating media

When you look in detail at texts from across the media platforms, you should apply the vocabulary you have learned and perform the processes of denotation and connotation to explore the following questions:

1 Which technical codes help to create meaning(s)?

2 What possible readings are available in the text?

3 How is narrative used to control the flow of information?

4 How is the audience positioned in relation to the narrative?

5 What media genre(s) are at play in the text?

6 Are there aspects of this text which remind you of other texts?

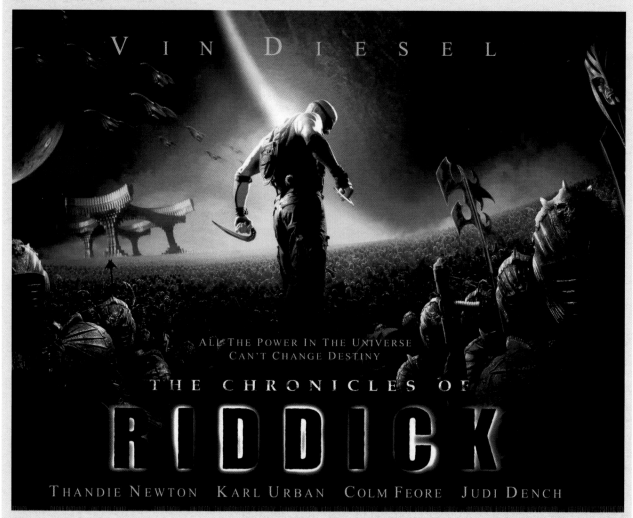

Fig. 3.7 Chronicles of Riddick *poster*

1 Use the questions above to analyse the poster, which was distributed free in cinema foyers by United International Pictures in 2004.

2 **Practical activity**
Create a synopsis, using a maximum of six still images, to show how enigma and action codes control the narrative flow of an episode of a television crime series.

an article in our local newspaper, while based on facts, has been shaped. Processes of selecting and editing make something fit into a fixed amount of space in a newspaper or a fixed amount of time in a broadcast text. The same processes are used to show a particular person, place or idea in a certain light. Morgan Spurlock's documentary film, *Supersize Me*, about McDonald's, represents the company in a negative light by showing the effects of a diet of fast food.

Media texts are a construction of reality. There is no single 'reality', rather a range of definitions of 'reality'. Reality as presented by the mass media is therefore not a picture or reflection of 'reality', but, rather, a constructed interpretation of reality. In the view of 'radical' critics of the media in particular, the mass media play a crucial role in constructing 'reality' for the rest of us.

The reality has been subject to **mediation**, and the nature of the production process will have changed the meaning in some way. It is media practice to represent a topic, types of people, an event or a situation and you need to be aware of how this process works. Audiences receive products that have been subject to the process of selection and organisation.

Representation is concerned with how media texts present and mediate ideas of the following:

- People: How are they represented? What activities are they doing?
- Places: How is this place 'given' to its audience?
- Events: In the represented event, what is included and what parts are left out?

Thinking about media

Assuming that you have no first-hand experience of these places, write down four ideas, words and/or images, about each one:

- images of Africa
- images of Scotland
- images of Pakistan
- images of Spain
- images of USA.

Now, write down four ideas that you think people who have not been in the UK would say about each of the following aspects:

- British people
- British weather
- British food
- British lifestyle.

Media in action

Chambers 21st Century Dictionary definition of 'Representation', noun:

1. The act or process of representing, or the state or fact of being represented
2. A person or thing that represents someone or something else
3. An image
4. A picture or painting
5. A strong statement made to present facts, opinions, complaints or demands.

The *Oxford English Dictionary* gives two definitions of 'Representation':

1. To represent something is to describe or depict it, to call it up in the mind by description or portrayal ...; to place a likeness of it before us in our mind.
2. To represent also means to symbolise, stand for, to be a specimen of or to substitute for; as in the sentence, 'In Christianity, the cross represents the suffering and crucifixion of Christ.'

Key term

Mediation: the process by which an institution or individual or a technology comes between events that happen in the world and the audience that receive this representation.

Impact of representations

When we study representations we should look at how the technical language of media images helps communicate a view of how the world is. The technical, symbolic and written codes construct the representation.

The process of representation often involves the use of **stereotypes**. In a very short space of time or in a few words the character, situation and narrative have to be communicated to the audience. A stereotype is a kind of short-hand, where one word or image stands for a lot more. Think about the national stereotype of a German and you may think of efficiency. This common stereotype can have a humorous use, for example in advertisements for German cars. Many stereotypes can be offensive, prejudiced and even racist. The stereotype of the dumb blonde suggests that a blonde-haired woman – it's always a woman – is stupid. We value their appearance but not their brains. In a post-modern way we

Investigating media

Plan and make three photographic representations of yourself for different audiences. Use captions under each photograph to anchor its meaning.

Ideas: a photograph of yourself to send to a potential employer to show you as reliable and studious; a photograph to send your grandma to show you as young and carefree; a photograph to send up to *Big Brother* or *The X Factor* to get an audition.

In pairs, shoot a short sequence of film or make a sound recording of the place where you live. Each pair should represent it differently, perhaps for a YouTube Crap Towns item or as a part of a tourism package to attract foreign students.

Key term

Stereotype: a standardised, usually oversimplified, mental picture or attitude that is held in common by members of a group towards a person or group, place or event.

AQA Examiner's tip

- You will be researching and constructing representations in Unit 2.
- In your evaluation you will need to comment on your use, or not, of stereotypes.

Thinking about media

- Does watching violence produce violence?
- Does swearing in television drama lead young people to think that swearing is acceptable behaviour?
- Do the images of skinny models have an impact?

can joke about this but by saying in normal conversation that we 'had a blonde moment' we are carrying on the potentially offensive stereotype.

We, as individuals, classify and stereotype by considering:

- appearance – this can include physical appearance, clothing and sound of voice
- behaviour – typical things people in a group might do.

Media stereotypes use appearance and behaviour and will emphasise them through:

- construction – this is how the camera is used, the soundtrack and the music. Think about emotive headlines, choice of photograph in print media
- contrast – often there will be an 'opposition' with what is 'normal'.

The question of whether audiences are influenced by the representations they see in the media is an old one but you need to think about it. The attitudes and ideology encoded in a text, when repeated over and over again in a number of texts may come to seem 'normal' to audiences. Media representations – and the extent to which we accept them – are a political issue, and it has been said that the influence the media exerts has a major impact on the way we view the world.

At one time many people believed that audiences accepted everything the media said to be true, that producers and the owners of production platforms pumped ideas into the minds of the population, but that view is not held today. We in the Western world are media savvy and we do not consider ourselves to be passive. We don't just accept that what is represented within a text is true; our reading is active and our cultural experience and our situation result in a negotiated reading (see Media in action – Readings, above).

There is often heated discussion, including in the media itself, about the dangers of exposure to the media. David Gauntlet, media theorist, thinks that those who believe that the media has bad effects on people are wrong. His paper *10 Things Wrong with the Effects Debate* explains why this is so.

Any media representation is a mixture of:

- the thing itself
- the opinions of the people doing the representation
- the reaction of the individual to the representation
- the context of the society in which the representation is taking place.

Over the years representations are accepted or rejected by the majority of people and the dominant ideology is gradually changed. Views change, for instance on women's role in society, smoking, youth, different ethnic or religious groups and the environment. We would probably all agree though that some views about appropriate behaviour remain fairly constant. People should put their families first, people should work for their money and not show off too much about how much they have, and people should marry for love. Mainstream media texts, both factual and fictional, contain these values, generally assuming that they re-present to us our shared cultural beliefs.

The media industries are aware of the effect that representations or lack of them have had. In the past minority groups felt under-represented in the media and felt they did not have a voice. These days, women, gay people, people of colour and ethnicity have a visible presence in the

Thinking about media

Earlier in this topic you read about binary opposites and how they show something about the beliefs a culture holds about meanings.

The chart below shows some 'traditional' binary opposites.

Youth	Old age
Masculine	Feminine
Good	Evil
Hero	Coward
Light	Dark
Strong	Weak

In early Western films it was a convention that the goodies wore white stetson hats while the baddies wore black ones. In *film noir* it was the woman who was the *femme fatale* and who led the man into crime. Old people have often been the subject of news stories where they have been portrayed as weak and vulnerable victims of crime or in television comedy as grumpy or comically forgetful. The road sign warning of old people crossing the road stereotypes them as weak and frail, ignoring the fact that many people over 60 run countries and businesses and sail around the world.

- How far do you think any of these oppositions are re-enforced by contemporary media texts?
- What other pairs of opposites might you add to the chart?

media, both in front of the camera and behind the scenes, but it was not always so. With Web 2.0 there is a decentralisation of production; individuals and groups can represent themselves when, where and as they choose. The broadcast and print platforms also afford opportunities for audience participation and interaction and the public service broadcasters are concerned to represent everyone.

Media in action

Representation theory

The reflective view
According to this view, when we represent something, we are taking its true meaning and trying to create a replica of it in the mind of our audience – like a reflection. This is the view that many people have of how news works – the news producers take the truth of news events and simply present it to us as accurately as possible.

The intentional view
This is the opposite of the reflective idea. This time the most important thing in the process of representation is the person doing the representing – they are presenting their view of the thing they are representing and the words or images that they use mean what they intend them to mean. According to this theory, if you see a picture of an attractive person drinking a can of Coke in an advert, it will have the same meaning to you as the advertiser intended – go away and buy some!

Fig. 3.8 *Shared cultural ideology*

Link

The website of the BBC World Service on Globalisation has an article Global Music Machine; you can find the address by looking in the e-resources or doing a web search.

Key term

Globalisation: *Encyclopaedia Britannica* defines globalisation as 'the process by which the experience of everyday life ... is becoming standardised around the world.'

Link

More ideas about the ways in which audiences respond to texts are in the Audiences section of this topic.

AQA Examiner's tip

There is a question specifically on representation in section A of the examination.

Be sure that your discussion is rooted in how these representations are constructed and how audiences might read and respond to them.

Investigating media activity

Look again at *The Chronicles of Riddick* (Fig. 3.7) and use the framework above to analyse the representations available in the film poster.

Link

Investigate Pearl and Dean's website for more information on market data. You can find the address in the e-resources, or do a web search, then follow the links to business, then market data.

The constructionist view

This is really a response to what has been seen as a weakness in the other two theories. Constructionists feel that a representation can never just be the truth or the version of the truth that someone wants you to hear since that is ignoring your ability as an individual to make up your own mind and the influences of the society that you live in on the way that you do so.

In our Western culture and especially through the newer media platforms, we have access to alternative representations. We can access different views on topical issues, for example we are no longer reliant on Western broadcasters for reportage on events in war zones. We, in the developed world, have the technology to access media texts from other cultures and can listen to news from other countries.

Increasingly, the media transmits representations all over the world. There is increasing global connectivity as well as integration and interdependence in economic, social, technological, cultural, political and ecological spheres. This situation, known as **globalisation**, attracts increasing interest and importance in contemporary world affairs.

The convergence of patterns of production and consumption result in a mixing together of culture and the wider spread of media texts. Western popular music, broadcast and film products are listened to, watched and sold throughout the world.

People around the world are responding to texts and their representations of ideas, events and groups of people from Western culture. The most translated books in the world are the books of the Disney animation films. These books and films carry certain ideologies relating to male and female roles and come from European folk tales.

Information and discussion of the implications of globalisation comes under close focus at A2, but if you are aware that images, especially visual images, are privileged in late modern culture and are saturating the world, it will help you understand the importance of the concept of representation.

In order to fully appreciate the part representation plays in a media text you must consider:

1 Who produced it?
2 Which individuals/groups/issues appear?
3 How are they portrayed?
4 Why was this particular representation (this shot, framed from this angle, this story phrased in these terms, etc.) selected?
5 What frame of reference does the audience use when responding to the representation? Age, nationality, social class, lifestyle, experiences of other media representations.

Media audiences

Researching audiences

The idea of audience is built into the production of a media text. At the very least, the producer has thought about a specific target audience and how they might make sense of the text. Traditional media texts are usually expensive to produce and therefore most productions do not begin unless the people who control the money have some confidence that the appropriate audience exists. Research is used to see if there is a market, and audiences are classified and measured accordingly.

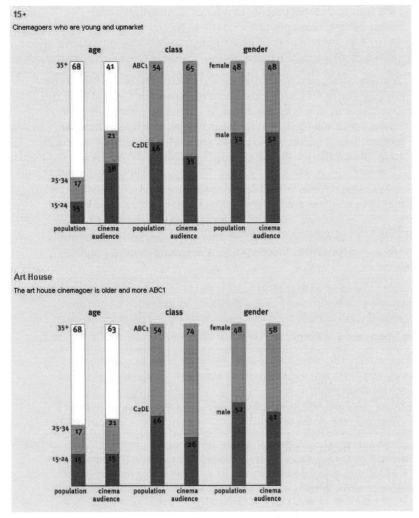

Fig. 3.9 *Bar charts showing cinema audiences from Pearl and Dean's website*

Demographics

Audiences can be classified into groups using quantitative data about age, gender and socio-economic group. They can be segmented further into groups and sub-groups by identifying professional status, geographical location, religion, ethnicity and so on. This is demographic research. This data is used by media producers in two ways. It influences future production and perhaps, more importantly, can be used to gain advertising revenue by selling audiences to advertisers.

You have already read about how companies like BARB and RAJAR measure broadcast audiences. National newspaper circulation is measured by ABC (Audit Bureau of Circulation) and hits on web pages are rated too. For example, the number of user visits to a video on YouTube is counted and displayed.

Psychographics

Psychographics is a system for measuring consumers' beliefs, opinions and interests. It's like demographics but instead of counting age, gender, race, etc., it gathers psychological information (opinions on abortion, religious beliefs, music tastes, personality traits, etc.). These are also called IAO variables, standing for Interests, Attitudes and Opinions. Groups can be classified in terms of variables like personality, values, attitudes, interests or lifestyles.

Media in action

Definitions of socio-economic groups

- AB: Professional, business and white collar
- C1: Higher skilled manual
- C2: Lower skilled manual
- DE: Semi and unskilled manual

Earning potential and ability to spend is identified but attached to this are notions of 'taste' and expectations about it. Devised originally to allow advertisers and marketers to target their audience by using certain media outlets, this model is crude and pigeonholes people, often inaccurately, and should be used sparingly alongside other analytical audience models that look at aspirations and lifestyle rather than income.

Media in action

The scope of demographic research has been extended in the case of research into cinema audiences to cover the film consumption of disabled people and people from ethnic minority groups. This is in line with the policy of the UK Film Council to promote full access and participation in film audience.

Media in action

Early psychographic research described consumers or audience members on the basis of psychological characteristics usually gathered from standardised questionnaires.

One system of classifying lifestyles is VALS (Value Life Styles).

Four main categories were subdivided into nine life-styles:

- groups driven by needs – survivors and sustainers
- groups who are outer-directed – belongers, emulators, achievers
- groups who are inner-directed – I-am-me, experientals, societally conscious
- groups who are both outer and inner directed – integrated.

Research into audiences usually combines demographic and psychographic information.

■ Case study

A study conducted several years ago, Youth Facts, claimed to be not just statistics about kids' spending power but an aid to help advertisers understand their rapidly maturing personalities and behaviour. They identified 6 distinct types of young people, or profiles, based on responses to 48 attitude statements. This is an extract from the profile description.

Free spirits	These guys are laid back. They are almost new-age hippies, into sex and drugs and rock and roll. Just over half are male, and they are the oldest of the clusters; with an average age of 16 and 3 months they spend the most money.
	Free spirits reject marriage, children, shopping, cosmetics and capitalism. They are interested in social matters and care about the environment. They buy environmentally friendly products and would never use anything tested on animals. One in eight is vegetarian.
Nesters	Far removed from Free spirits. They want to get married as soon as possible and to have children, in that order. Very little sex before marriage, these nesters believe in family values. They disagree with abortion and don't think marriage is outdated. They are against legalising soft drugs and would never try any drugs themselves.
	They are tidy, virtuous, hard-working, concerned and worry a lot. Six out of 10 are girls.
Funseekers	These kids work hard, play hard and spend hard. They were born to shop. Fewer are in higher education than the other groups. Physical appearance is very important and being trendy equally so. They display labels and believe most strongly that brands say a lot about you.
	Funseekers consume more media than the other groups. Over three-quarters read a daily newspaper, they prefer magazines to books and love sports and soap on the telly.
Leaders	These kids look the stuff of today's gang leader or school captain. They are independent, concerned, responsible, hard-working, competitive and gregarious. Career success is very important as is earning money and enjoying work. Although they save well, they enjoy spending money. They like shopping for clothes and are sufficiently aware of their appearance to be heavy users of cosmetics. The boys use after-shave, and other men's products.
	They are not overly influenced by their friends, yet they spend a lot of time in their company and frequently go out to a pub, cinema or live music.
Followers	In just about everything they think and do they want to be 'normal'. They want to be like their friends. Wanting more responsibility and standing out from the crowd is not for them.
	Friends are their great comfort. Having friends round, visiting their homes or just hanging out is central. When friends visit the TV is always on in one room and chart music in the others.
	After Funseekers they consume the most media, reading lots of magazines, the boys computer magazines and the girls TV and gossip magazines. Soaps are unmissable.
Armchair rebels	These kids have attitude. They are the youngest of the clusters with an average age of 15, which may well excuse their negative, apathetic natures.
	Armchair rebels are more likely to try drugs than other kids, and they think soft drugs ought to be legalised. Crime, they believe, would not increase if sentences were lighter.
	They don't think keeping fit or eating sensibly is important. They believe less than anyone else that smoking harms others or that drinking can be bad for people. They don't worry about anything.

■ How far do these groups fit in with your ideas about youth today? Expand the descriptors to include:

- How does each group get and listen to music?
- How does each group use the internet?
- How does each group use mobile telephony?

Niche audiences

In the contemporary media landscape with much on offer on a variety of inter-connecting media platforms and a growing number of places where media can be produced and received, it is quite rare for any one media product to attract a mass audience. National sporting events and television soap operas still gain viewing figures of 10 million or more but many media products are created for **niche audiences**. The major broadcasters have expanded their portfolio of channels, with some channels like Sky Arts and BBC Four in the knowledge that they attract relatively small audiences. The niche audiences for these channels have interests that are catered for by the programming. If you look at a list of the digital broadcast channels, many cater for a variety of niche audiences.

On the internet, when blogging, uploading audio/visual material, communicating socially or participating in a virtual reality scenario we have an idea of our likely audience and how they will respond to the text and we can check on how many hits we have had.

Case study

The *Daily Telegraph* website has pages devoted to readers' blogs.

Called My Telegraph it provides the opportunity 'to read, write and share your opinions with other *Telegraph* readers'. The homepage of My Telegraph invites users to 'Join in the conversation. Become a member of the *Telegraph*'s reader community'. The community of users posting comments is a sub-group of a larger number of readers of the on-line newspaper, which is in turn a smaller group than those reading the print version of the newspaper.

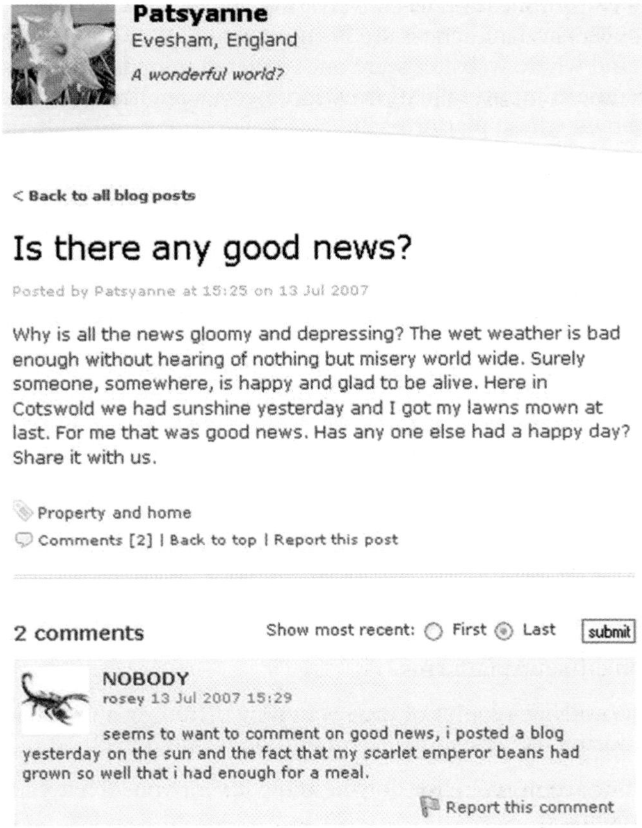

Patsyanne
Evesham, England
A wonderful world?

< Back to all blog posts

Is there any good news?

Posted by Patsyanne at 15:25 on 13 Jul 2007

Why is all the news gloomy and depressing? The wet weather is bad enough without hearing of nothing but misery world wide. Surely someone, somewhere, is happy and glad to be alive. Here in Cotswold we had sunshine yesterday and I got my lawns mown at last. For me that was good news. Has any one else had a happy day? Share it with us.

Property and home
Comments [2] | Back to top | Report this post

2 comments Show most recent: First Last submit

NOBODY
rosey 13 Jul 2007 15:29
seems to want to comment on good news, i posted a blog yesterday on the sun and the fact that my scarlet emperor beans had grown so well that i had enough for a meal.
Report this comment

Fig. 3.10 *Patsyanne's blog with accompanying comment, on* My Telegraph

AQA Examiner's tip

- Practise analysing media products that you come across. Seek information about how the audiences are described. This can often be found in the information given to potential advertisers. Look back at [FIG.1.9] for the information about the readership of *Woman's Weekly*.
- In your pre-production research for Unit 2 you will need to research audiences using a mixture of demographic and psychographic information. Your products themselves must be designed to position and address the intended audience appropriately.

Key terms

Niche audiences: the separation of the media audience into segments, each of which have different tastes and concerns.

Media in action

BBC Digital Radio was set up initially to cater for an Asian audience, which had been underrepresented on the national airwaves. Thus, the Asian Network provides 20 hours of music, discussion and news to serve this audience. In spring 2007 0.20 per cent of the population listened for an average of 5 hours, approximately 450,000 people.

■ Investigating media

Visit the My Telegraph website (for address, see the e-resources or do a search on the web) and make a note of the subjects that have been commented on today.

Visit the website of another on-line newspaper, for example the *Sun* (for address, see the e-resources or do a search on the web). Go to the Have Your Say feature. Make a comparison of subjects raised by *Sun* on-line readers.

Account for the similarities and/or differences from what you have learned about audiences.

■ Link

See the Uses of Television section in Topic 2, page 16.

■ Thinking about media

Think of some television programmes, magazines and websites where 'ordinary' people are featured.

■ Why do they participate?

■ How are they represented?

■ How do audiences respond to these texts?

■ What is the appeal of these programmes for audiences?

Patsyanne's comment started the thread and received two comments within half-an-hour.

■ What does the initial blog and the following comment tell you about the attitude of these users to the news?

The leading page of my.telegraph has blogs on current affairs. The tags at the top of the page for 13 July 2007 grouped the blogs into the subjects that had interested users that day. They are listed in alphabetical order: Animals and Pets, Arts, BBC, Blair, Books, Brown, Comedy and Humour, Current Affairs, Cycling, Education, Entertainment, Expat Life, Health, History, Humour, Islam, Life, Politics, Queen, Travel.

■ What information do these interests tell you about the members of this website community?

The power of the audience

The relationship between the media and their audiences has always been a matter of debate and there have been shifts in ideas about the relative power of the media and the audience. In the early 20th century, behavioural theorists saw the media as a hypodermic needle, injecting the ideas held by the powerful groups in society into passive individuals. Since then, opinion has shifted, recognising that audiences already have well-developed attitudes, that their identity is formed by the many social groups to which they belong and, most importantly, that they actively select and interpret media texts.

Audiences can be thought of as using the media for a variety of purposes and pleasures, both as responders to content and as producers of content. No longer are they passive receivers, they participate. The new media platforms see communication as conversation and the distinctions between producers and audiences are breaking down. It is a culture of sharing data and where websites were once isolated information sites they have become computing platforms serving web applications to users. And those who use these platforms are both institutions and audiences.

This has overturned the old culture of owners and producers providing and distributing media content. It has decentralised the authority of traditional media producers and produced a platform for open communication. However, we must not forget that the new platforms are used by retailers and advertisers as a powerful way of selling products and services to users.

You read in Topic 1 how, thanks to new technology, audiences can interact with media products. Let's think about the opportunities for participating directly in the media. In recent years 'ordinary people' have appeared in the talk shows of daytime television, makeover shows and reality TV programmes.

Attracting an audience

You know that audiences participate in media texts and have opportunities to interact with the media. You know how people can produce audio/visual and print products themselves that can be shared with others on e-media platforms.

But most of us still spend a lot of time watching, listening and reading on all media platforms. We consume far more than we produce.

What grabs your attention? How do you know it's for you? That you are the target audience?

Consider these reasons:

■ You know and like the form, the genre of text and want more. You like Bollywood musicals, US cop shows, gossip magazines, snooker, trance music.

■ You like the star, celebrity, presenter, band, sportsperson and always follow their work.

■ You have heard about it from another source, a person (word of mouth) or promotional material that has reached you through another media text that you like.

One or more of these reasons might designate you as a potential audience and have called to your attention the desirability of the film, magazine, website or whatever it is.

The text itself needs to connect with you to hold your interest. It speaks to you. You can identify with it in some way. It **interpellates** to us, calls us as if it wants to speak to us. For example, the cover of a magazine like *Stuff* addresses us or hails us as young men who are interested in technology and viewing the bodies of young women. It thus contributes to the identities of young men as having these as two of their core interests.

How does this work? By the media language used, visual, aural and written – and this brings you, as a media student, back to the technical, symbolic and written codes that operate in media texts.

You need to investigate the elements in texts that position the audience to respond in a certain way.

What elements are designed to make you laugh, for example? Often, in a television comedy show there will be canned laughter or a studio audience to signal us to find a joke, an expression or an incident funny.

Every text has a mode of address, a way of speaking to its reader. Look back to the pictures on pages 42 and 44 and the choices of words, colours and stylistic elements used to interpellate with the readers. The image(s), sound and/or visual, will create a point of view for you. In a charity appeal advertisement, for instance, the technical choices will have been made in order to provoke a strong reaction from you. For example, the camera angle and shot size may be looking down on a malnourished child via a long shot that shows the child as small and isolated. A strategic edit may cut to a close-up of a number of flies pestering and landing on the child's face that is passive and resigned, unable to fight the insects off due to a lack of strength.

■ Key terms

Interpellation: term used by Louis Althusser to describe how the media hail us as an individual who has a shared understanding of the ideology within the text.

■ Investigating media

1 Look back to Fig. 3.7 on page 56 – *The Chronicles of Riddick* film poster – and analyse it in terms of audience(s). Remember that it was distributed to cinema goers in advance of the release of the film:

■ Who is the target audience?

■ How is the audience addressed?

Use details of the text to support your answers.

2 Use the same questions to explore radio audiences. Record a section of two commercial radio stations that includes advertisements and music. Choose two stations with different audiences such Classic FM and Virgin Classic Rock or a local radio station.

AQA Examiner's tip

There is a question specifically on audiences in relation to the unseen text in section A of the examination.

■ Be sure that your discussion is rooted in how the text is constructed to address the potential audience.

■ Give textual evidence to support your discussion of likely audience and how the audience is positioned.

■ Media institutions

The word institution can be interpreted in a number of ways. In Topic 1 we defined it as 'The organisation or company, public or privately owned that produces and/or distributes media products' and organisations in the traditional media industries, broadcasting, cinema and music fitted that description. An institution is formed by the relations of production, distribution, consumption and regulation, all of which have been covered earlier in this book.

As we said earlier we live in a world where Western media products are sold worldwide. Individuals such as Rupert Murdoch have built up media empires that cover a large part of the world. His political influence and right wing agenda is well known and considered to be most evident in the US Fox News Channel, which is available all over the world.

■ Visit the website for News Corporation and see how many communication outlets Murdoch owns (for address, see the e-resources or do a search).

Italian media magnate Silvio Berlusconi is an example of how media owners can use personal power. Like Murdoch he owns newspapers and television channels but unlike him, he is the leader of the Forza Italia political movement, a centre right party he founded in 1993 in Rome, and has twice held office as prime minister of Italy. His ownership of an Italian television network has been controversial. According to Berlusconi's adversaries, his television channels played a crucial role in his political success by airing propaganda during news or other information-oriented programming. After Berlusconi's election as prime minister, the left accused him of abusing his position as premier to control the publicly owned RAI TV channels.

As media students you need to be aware that values and ideologies are transmitted through the representations in media texts and therefore powerful institutions, such as those mentioned above and worldwide content transmitters like Hollywood and the BBC for example, could influence the attitudes, interests, beliefs and desires of people on a world scale.

When looking at any media text you need to ask yourself the following questions:

■ What is the institutional source of the text?

■ In what ways has the text been influenced or shaped by the institution that produced it?

■ Is the source a public service or commercial institution? What difference does this make to the text?

■ How has the text been distributed?

Regulation about media content, fairness and balance varies across countries and across the different industries. The statement for the British Government Department for Culture, Media and Sport sums up the government position regarding broadcasting: 'We want to ensure that we foster fair and effective competition, promote high quality broadcasting from a diverse range of sources, provide a high level of consumer protection, and safeguard freedom of expression.'

There have always been smaller, independent media institutions, so-called because they are free from the financial or organisational influence of the large-scale media institutions. They tend to create 'indie' products, low budget films, broadcast or print products, often appealing to smaller

■ Media in action

Manuel Alvarado in *Learning the Media* lists seven features that shape media institutions:

■ Finance

■ Production practices

■ Technology

■ Legislation

■ Circulation

■ Audience construction

■ Audience use.

Investigating media

■ Apply the above questions to *The Chronicles of Riddick* poster (Fig. 3.7, on page 56).

■ Pair activity or class research activity: examine the similarities and differences in the views expressed in the coverage of a headline news story, one that leads to editorial content. Choose newspapers that have different owners and different readerships. The *Daily Mirror*, *Daily Mail* and *Independent* would work well.

Investigating media

Research activity: what legislation covers the internet?

niche audiences. Larger film and broadcast institutions often support the work of the independents, sometimes by financing or part-financing production and sometimes by marketing or distributing. Independent movie-making has resulted in the proliferation and repopularisation of short films and short film festivals. Full-length films are often showcased at film festivals such as the Sundance Film Festival or the Cannes Film Festival. Award winners from these exhibitions often get picked up for distribution by major film studios and go on to worldwide releases.

With digital technology, the actual creation of media products is easier, cheaper and quicker than ever and individuals and independent companies can make media texts and put them out on the internet. The internet played an important part in bringing public attention to bands like the Arctic Monkeys. One of the main differences between the institutional processes of old media and new media is that the new media gains public attention more quickly and this speed of delivery has transformed the media, particularly in the production and consumption of music and news.

With digital technology and, arguably, since 9/11/2001 when everyone was taken by surprise by the events in New York, there has been an increased demand for hot news. We have come to expect Martini news; anywhere, anyplace, anytime. It is now the convention for war journalists to be embedded with troops sending personal reports on video phone via satellite. The development of broadband has given us the opportunity for even more first-hand news, often from people directly experiencing the situation.

One notable instance was shortly before the invasion of Iraq. In 2003, Salem Pox (a pseudonym combining the Arabic and Latin words for 'peace') wrote a web log, a diary of events, from his home in Baghdad, to his friend Raid. These blogs were picked up eventually by Reuters, the press news agency, putting him and his family in a dangerous position in Saddam's Iraq.

Media in action

Marshall McLuhan, a media sociologist, said 40 years ago that we live in 'a global village' where we can communicate with each other instantly; and that time and space as restrictions on access to information were vanishing.

Case study

The Baghdad Blogger

This is an extract from an article about how Salam Pax became the Baghdad Blogger, published in the *Guardian*, 9 September 2003:

'My name is Salam Pax and I am addicted to blogs. Some people watch daytime soaps, I follow blogs. I follow the hyperlinks on the blogs I read. I travel through the web guided by bloggers. I get wrapped up in the plots narrated by them. I was reading so many blogs I had to assign weekdays for each bunch, plus the ones I was reading daily. It is slightly voyeuristic, especially those really personal blogs: day-to-day, mundane stuff which is actually fascinating; glimpses of lives so different, and so much amazing writing. No politics, just people's lives. How they deal with pain or grief, how they share their happy moments with anybody who cares to read.

'And I cared. We had no access to satellite TV, and magazines had to be smuggled into the country. Through blogs I could take a peek at a different world. Satellite TV and the web were on Saddam's list of things that will corrupt you. Having a satellite dish was punishable with jail and a hefty fine because these channels would twist our minds and make us do bad things. They spread immoral values.

Of course he and his buddies were incorruptible so they could watch all the satellite TV they wanted.

'This was the case with internet as well. While the world was moving on to high-speed internet, we were being told it was overrated. So when in 2000 the first state-operated internet centre was opened, everybody was a bit suspicious, no one knew if browsing news sites would get you in trouble. When, another year later, you were able to get access from home, life changed. We had internet and we were able to browse without the minders at the internet centres watching over our shoulder, asking you what that site you are browsing is.

'Of course things were not that easy, there was a firewall. A black page with big orange letters: access denied…

'We also had no access to sites offering free web mail or web space. You had to use the mail account provided by the ISP and you can bet your wireless mouse this mail was being monitored. But the beauty of the internet is that it is not static, it changes all the time. There are always new sites offering all sorts of services and the people who run the firewall were not always that clued-up. They were just as new to this as we were and it was a race… You had to be creative with your search terms and have lots of patience… They knew it was happening. It was a cat and mouse game.

'It was on one of these searches that I found blogs. With blogs the web started talking to me in a much more personal way. Bits of news started having texture and most amazingly, these blogs talked with each other. That hyperlink to the next blog – I just couldn't stop clicking. And the best thing about it was that Mr Site Killer had absolutely no clue.

'To tell you the truth, sharing with the world wasn't really that high on my top five reasons to start a blog. It was more about sharing with Raed, my Jordanian friend who went to Amman after we finished architecture school in Baghdad… So 'Where is Raed?' started. The URL used to be where_is_raed.blogspot.com, just a silly blog for me and Raed. I never worried about the people monitoring the web finding out, it was just silly stuff. The first reckless thing I did was to put the blog address in a blog indexing site under Iraq. I did this after I spent a couple of days searching for Arabs blogging and finding mostly religious blogs. I thought the Arab world deserved a fair representation in the blogsphere, and decided that I would be the profane pervert Arab blogger just in case someone was looking.

'Putting my site at that portal (eatonweb) was the beginning of the changing of my blog's nature. I got linked by the Legendary Monkey and then Instapundit – a blog that can drive a stampede of traffic to your site. I saw my site counter jump from the usual 20 hits a day to 3,000, all coming from Instapundit – we call it experiencing an Insta-lanche (from avalanche) and if I remember correctly it was a post I wrote on October 12 in which I called the American plan to invade Iraq just a colonialist plot. I just flicked the rant switch on, wrote for half an hour and was surprised that the world took notice…

'Things got worse when the Reuters article got picked up by other news outlets. My brother saw my agitation and I had to tell him. He thought I was a fool to endanger the family, which was true. I was kicking myself in the butt for the next couple of days. Then Blogger did get blocked. This was the end. My brother and I kept checking on Blogger.com every couple of hours. But the 'access denied' page still did not come up. I signed in, deleted the archives and stopped blogging for a couple of days...

'By the end of January war felt very close and the blog was being read by a huge number of people. There were big doubts that I was writing from Baghdad, the main argument being there was no way such a thing could stay under the radar for so long in a police state. I really have no idea how that happened. I have no idea whether they knew about it or not. I just felt that it was important that among all the weblogs about Iraq and the war there should be at least one Iraqi blog, one single voice: no matter how you view my politics, there was at least someone talking...'

www.guardian.co.uk/world/iraq (and follow the Baghdad blogger link)

Convergence of new and old media

'If you can't beat them join them.' Old media companies have not stood still in the face of competition for audiences and advertisers from internet platforms. All terrestrial broadcasters and newspaper owners have bought into the internet. Rupert Murdoch's News Corporation has bought MySpace to add to his new media assets.

Convergence of technology works both ways. Eric Schmidt, chief executive of Google was ranked number 1 in the 2007 Media Guardian Top 100 powerful people in the British media Industry. Google, which started as a search engine, has since bought YouTube, the on-line advertising group DoubleClick, and is expanding its advertising business into TV, print, radio and mobile. Number 2 in the list is Rupert Murdoch with a broadcasting, publishing and new media empire. Number 3 is Mark Thompson, director general of the BBC broadcasting, new media and publishing industry.

Case study

Virgin Media

Richard Branson, an English entrepreneur, started the Virgin brand. He published a magazine at the age of 16 and set up a record mail order business and then a chain of record stores. He set up Virgin Atlantic Airways and Virgin Trains and a wide range of successful businesses. Always keeping up with or ahead of the times he moved into financial services, holidays and publishing. Virgin Media has a strong profile in radio, mobile phones, broadband and cable television.

Well known for his lively personal style, gaining publicity through activities such as round the world air ballooning and cameo appearances in movies, he has created and maintained a brand image that is admired and respected.

Virgin.com explain what the brand is about:

'We believe in making a difference. In our customers' eyes, Virgin stands for value for money, quality, innovation, fun and a sense of competitive challenge. We deliver a quality service by empowering our employees and we facilitate and monitor customer feedback to continually improve the customer's experience through innovation.'

Fig. 3.11 *The Virgin brand logo*

AQA Examiner's tip

Section A in the Unit 1 examination will give you brief information about where the stimulus material comes from. You will have to answer a question on institution. You will need to consider how far the text may have been shaped or influenced by the institution that produced it and what details in the construction of the text reflect the values and brand of the product.

Investigating media

Visit the Virgin Media website (for the address, see the e-resources, or do a search):

1 Note the content of the website including the logo.

2 Navigate through the website noting the use of the logo and the way the user is positioned and addressed.

3 Watch the Why Choose Us part of the site, http://allyours.virginmedia.com/whychooseus/index.html and comment on the:
- media language
- representation
- slogan – Watch it, surf it, talk it, walk it – to discuss how the presentation matches the brand as described.

4 What can you assume about the audience/consumer of Virgin Media?

In this topic you have practised the skills of reading the media in order to draw conclusions about how the media products from across the media are understood and interpreted by audiences. In Section A you will need to apply all the concepts to one text. It may be a moving image, website or print text.

These are the sort of questions that will be asked in the examination:

1 Media Forms (this means genre, narrative and the media language codes) Discuss the use of codes and conventions in the construction of this text.

2 Media Representations Consider the representations of people (places and/or events, where relevant) in this text.

3 Media Institutions What does this website tell us about the media institutions involved?

4 Media Audiences Explore some of the ways in which this text communicates with its target audiences.

Try them out on different forms of texts: websites, print materials including advertisements and moving image extracts from a variety of forms.

End of topic summary:

- The key concepts and ideas that underpin the study of media texts across the media are media languages, media representations, media audiences and media institutions.
- Audiences make active readings of media products through their understanding of the codes and conventions within a text and across types of text.
- The representations of people, places and events in media products carry cultural meanings.
- Ideology is carried through the representations in texts, the institutions producing the texts and the audience readings of texts.
- By looking closely at texts and applying the key media concepts, you can understand the processes involved in their construction and audiences' interpretation of the media.
- The understanding and application of these concepts and ideas is fundamental to the Unit 1 examination and the Unit 2 coursework.

4   The cross-media study

AQA   Examiner's tip

The technology of production and reception does not stand still. Keep as up to date as you can. For example at the time of writing a new internet protocol is being developed to cope with the billions of users and it's become the norm to download broadcast products and watch whenever you like. New technology is being continually developed to improve the speed and quality of transmitting data electronically.

AQA   Examiner's tip

Forty per cent of the marks for the AS exam are awarded for the case study:

▪ Your essay will require you to show knowledge and understanding by analysing media products and processes to show how meanings and responses are created.

▪ You need to have made a detailed analysis of at least three media products within your topic in order to show this knowledge and understanding in your essay.

Now you know about the media platforms, the types of media products that appear on these platforms and how to analyse the meanings in the media products. You've been introduced to some media ideas and theories and are aware of the debates around how audiences respond to the media. You know something of the industries that make and distribute media products and of the big changes happening through developing technologies. In this new information age, information can be shared, and so can entertainment and conversation. What you have learned is the nuts and bolts of media studies and your critical understanding of media texts and the contexts in which they are presented will be put to the test in your response to Section A of the examination.

You are going to develop this knowledge and understanding by making a detailed case study in which you will undertake an analysis of a topic in more depth, which could be termed loosely as a genre. To make your case study:

▪ you will examine media products within the topic and the processes and technologies used to create them

▪ you will look at how, where and when your chosen topic appears on each media platform and understand the reasons for this

▪ you will study the ways in which audiences consume the media products within the topic

▪ you will explore the ways in which audiences respond to the topic across the media.

As media students you don't need to be techies but you need to know about the changes in how content is produced and presented. You also need to be aware of the changes in how audiences respond to the media content available on broadcast, print, the internet and emerging media platforms.

There are six suggested topics for the cross-media study and you will have to study at least one. They cover a range of media forms and each topic has a presence on each media platform. Some of them will feature predominantly on one media platform but you must investigate how it is presented on all of them. It is possible to study a topic that is not listed here but your tutor will need to check on its suitability first.

Whatever topic is chosen, you must study it using the media studies perspective, which means applying the concepts and ideas to texts, forms and platforms. For example, if you are studying Music as a topic and you intended to focus on country, pop or world music, your concern should be the presentation of the genre in broadcasting, print and the e-media and the ways in which audiences respond to music products on each of those platforms. Just studying a music genre, the bands, the fans, the songs and the festivals would not be a media studies perspective.

In this topic you will be guided through the four stages of the case study.

Link

Topic 2, Television Genre, Broadcast Fiction and Radio Forms. You've looked at broadcast fiction as a genre in Topic 2 and already know something about its different fictional forms.

The topics

Broadcast fiction

To study this topic you will need to investigate how audio/visual broadcast fiction is presented and consumed across the media.

To gain an overall view of the types of broadcast fiction you must look at a range of broadcast fiction texts and their presence across the media.

💡 Where broadcast fiction is presented across the media (some ideas to get you started)

Broadcast	Print	e-media
Scheduled on television or radio – series, one-off dramas... Catch-ups, repeats, spin-offs – e.g. *Dr Who/ Torchwood, Buffy/Angel...* Talk shows, news, arts and review programmes Red button interactivity	Previews and reviews – newspapers/magazines Stories and features on themes, characters or production. Interviews with writers, directors, actors Special publications News coverage of events and issues around the text Comments from audiences	Clips, previews and reviews, extra scenes: official sites, fan sites, social networking sites Individual websites of actors, writers, directors Blogs Listen again/watch again/ downloads/podcasts Games Opportunities for interaction and dialogue
Trails, sponsorship, advertising	Promotions/ advertisements	Trails, advertising

Stage 1 – The topic

- Look at texts across different genres and different institutions. For example, a US drama series might be studied alongside a British mini-series, a continuing drama on radio might be studied alongside a television soap opera, a popular sitcom aimed at a family audience could be compared with a more edgy, comedy drama targeted at a different audience.

- Apply the media concepts you learned about in Topic 3 to a variety of texts. For example, you could compare the representations of characters and settings in a Hollywood-produced series such as *Desperate Housewives* and a British soap such as *Emmerdale*. Account for any similarities or differences.

- Don't forget radio, where fictional forms include specially written radio plays, stories and serials.

- See how a text is presented across the media. Choose one text and investigate it over the places where it appears. For example, look at the way in which *Dr Who* figures across the BBC channels, in magazines, on the internet as games, mobile ring tones and other interactive facilities.

Stage 2 – Focus your study

Choose at least three texts that have features in common. Each must have a presence in broadcast, print and e-media.

- Examine them in close detail, closely studying the content of each text and the way the semiotic, narrative and generic codes are used.

- Examine the representations available and how these are constructed and construed.
- Find out who produced the texts.
- Investigate the target audience(s) across the media.
- Investigate cross-media connections, for instance, synergy, intertextuality…
- Investigate how the texts are promoted to audiences within and across the media.

You might wish to choose programmes from a specific genre or programmes that link in some other way, appealing to younger audiences, for example.

Who are the institutions?

The primary producers, in the case of most broadcast fiction products, will include large organisations such as the BBC and independent production companies making material to be broadcast. However, other institutions might be involved, especially in the print and e-media. Think about the institutional relationship between the channel, the programme and the sponsor, as found in commercial television, for example, Cadburys chocolate, which used to sponsor *Coronation Street* and ITV (Granada). If you look at the end credits of the medical drama *House*, the institutions NBC Universal, United Network Television, Bad Hat Harry Productions, Heel & Toe and ShoreZProductions all have an involvement in the production. Spontex gloves sponsor the programme when it is broadcast on British television on Five.

Find out the institutional details for each text in your case study.

 Investigating media

Broadcast fiction's primary presence is audio/visual. However, to help you understand the differences in the content and form in non-broadcast platforms, try this planning exercise.

A new character is going to be introduced into a popular teen-adult continuing drama broadcast on Channel 4. The character will be played by an actor who is already known to the audience.

1 Plan the layout of a page in *Heat* magazine about the actor and his/her character in the drama, which will include an interview and a photograph.

2 Plan some additional content for the programme's fansite to promote the event.

3 Plan a viral advertisement for the event to be sent by mobile phone.

Explain the differences in content and form and your reasons for making them.

Link

Go to the Production Process and Audience reception sections later in this topic. These show you how to complete the further two stages of your case study.

Film

You have looked at film genre in Topic 2 and in other parts of this book you have seen that feature films have a global appeal. You have read a little about the cinema industry and for your case study you need to learn more.

For your case study you will need to investigate how films are presented across the media. This will involve looking at the presence on broadcast, print and e-media.

Link

For more information on films, see Topic 2, Film and Genre.

Case study

Transformers

Traditionally, the process of making a film began with a story, perhaps an adaptation from a novel. In the contemporary media landscape, feature length films can start from other sources, for example, computer games as in the case of Lara Croft. Transformers, a summer release for the 2007 school holiday period, is a live action movie version of the 1985 animated movie, The Transformers: the Movie, which itself was a development from a television series. The makers of Transformer toy robots have been trying to sell their properties to film makers since 2002. They co-operated with the design of the movie and General Motors and the US military also lent their support. The movie was produced by Steven Spielberg and two other producers. Another of the producers, Tom DeSanto, stated his intention for the film. 'I think it's going to be something the audience has never seen before. In all the years of movie-making, I don't think the image of a truck transforming into a 20-foot tall robot has ever been captured on screen. I also want to make a film that's a homage to 1980s movies and gets back to the sense of wonder that Hollywood has lost over the years. It will have those Spielbergian moments where you have the push-in on the wide-eyed kid and you feel like you're 10 years old even if you're 35.'

The marketing included the following:

The first teaser trailer was released on the internet on 29 June 2006, depicting a Transformer attacking the Beagle 2. A second trailer was released on 20 December, breaking Spider Man 3's record for the number of internet hits. A third trailer was released on-line on Yahoo's movie website on 17 May 2007. Another trailer was attached with Shrek the Third. The director, Michael Bay, originally intended that '[The audience] never really get a good look at the robots until the release' but by the third trailer he had abandoned this idea. The Sector 7 viral marketing website featured several videos recording supposed evidence of Transformers on earth. These featured cameos by Generation 1 Transformers, including Grimlock destroying a construction site, and a security video showing a robot resembling Generation 1 Bumblebee transforming in a parking garage.

Hasbro made deals with 200 companies across 70 countries to promote the film.

Their toy line for the film was created over two months over late 2005/early 2006, collaborating heavily with the filmmakers. A pair of preview toys, Protoform Optimus Prime and Starscream were released in the USA on 1 May 2007, before the first wave of figures was released on 2 June. Characters that do not appear in the film are also featured in the film's style. The toys feature 'Automorph Technology' in which moving parts of the toy allow other parts to shift automatically. Michael Bay directed tie-in commercials for General Motors, Burger King and PepsiCo while props including the 1977 Chevrolet Camaro used for Bumblebee were put up for charity on eBay. In the third quarter of 2007, Nokia released a special Transformers edition of their N93i.

(source Wikipedia Encylopedia : Transformers, film)

The film itself was previewed and reviewed in the print media and advertisements for the film and the toys featured in print and e-media forms. The critics enjoyed the special effects but criticised the characterisation.

Where feature films are presented across the media (some ideas to get you started)

Broadcast	Print	e-media
Cinema, scheduled on television DVD on TV/player Themed on TV channels – by director, by actor, by genre Talk shows, arts and review programmes News items: awards, festivals, premieres	Previews and reviews – newspapers and magazines Stories and features on themes, characters or production. Interviews with writers, directors, actors Film magazines Spin-off publications News coverage of events around the film, issues around the film, people involved in the production Comments from audiences	Production company website Dedicated film website Websites of stars, directors… Blogs Excerpts and previews and reviews – official sites, fan sites, social networking sites Extra scenes and information Opportunities for interaction and dialogue Games Downloads, podcasts
Trailers (cinema and TV), sponsorship, product placement	Promotions, advertisements	Trailers, advertisements, promotions

Stage 1 – The topic

- Broaden your knowledge of what types of feature films are available to audiences. By looking at some films that come from different institutional backgrounds you will gain a wider understanding of how films are presented and received. A film made by a well-known director of auteur status such as Tarantino will be presented and received differently across the media than a first-time filmmaker who's won a prize at a festival.

- Although you will not have to contrast texts in your exam, studying differences helps you better understand the elements that go into a fiction film. A good pairing might be a mainstream US big-budget production, with a big marketing budget that includes tie-in merchandise contrasted with a smaller budget British or independent film, which might have an art-house showing or go straight to television. Another example might be studying a film that is part of a well-known franchise with familiar characters and narratives, a James Bond film, for example, alongside a world cinema film, not made in English or with a non-Western director.

- Apply the concepts you learned about in Topic 3 to one or two films you know well. Think about representations and ideology.

- Be aware how a film is presented across the media. For example, the way in which Harry Potter films appear in the cinema, on television and DVD, in magazines, on the internet, as games, other interactive facilities and merchandise.

Stage 2 – Focus your study

When you have a sound understanding of the different processes at work, narrow your study to an investigation of three films. Each must have a presence on broadcast, print and e-media platforms.

Choose your three texts and for each text:

- examine in close detail the content of each text and the ways that the semiotic, narrative and generic codes are used across the media
- examine the representations available and how these are constructed and construed
- find out who produced the texts
- investigate the target audience(s) across the media
- investigate cross-media connections, for instance, synergy, intertextuality…
- investigate how the texts are promoted to audiences within and across the media.

You might want to choose films that are from a specific genre, horror or science fiction, for example, or you might want to choose films that link, in some other way, British films, alternative films, family films and so on.

Who are the institutions?

Many films made outside the big corporations are co-productions and the finance comes from a variety of sources, some commercial, some from subsidies and grants. Many films are financed from more than one country. The actual creative production of a film is just one aspect of the process. The DVDs and the soundtrack CDs, the merchandise, the computer games and the sale of the rights to television channels can involve a number of institutions. The marketing strategy in terms of direct advertising via trailers, a poster campaign and other promotional strategies is another feature of the film production business, sometimes handled by a separate institution and sometimes dealt with in-house.

Find out the institutional details for each text in your case study.

Investigating media

Film's primary presence is audio/visual. However, to help you understand the differences in the content and form in non-broadcast platforms, try this exercise.

An independent film set in a British city and aimed at a young adult audience, the film features the first acting appearance of a pop star. Plan some texts for the marketing campaign:

1. design a poster
2. plan a radio advertisement or a spoken word podcast
3. plan the layout for an article about the film in pre-production to go in a music magazine
4. plan some content for a film database such as www.totalfilm.com
5. plan a viral advertisement for the opening to be sent by mobile phone.

Explain the differences in content and form and your reasons for making them.

Documentary and hybrid forms

You looked at documentary forms and techniques in Topic 2 and thought about the appeals of documentaries for audiences. For a case study you will need to make a more thorough study of the documentary genre and how it is presented and consumed across the media.

■ Link

In Topic 1, Films, you read about the film industry and how films form an important part of broadcasters' schedules.

In Topic 2, Film and Genre, you read about film franchises.

AQA Examiner's tip

You will need to adapt what you know to the focus of the examination. Merely reproducing facts about institutions will not earn you many marks. However, understanding the contexts of production helps you investigate the meanings within the text.

AQA Examiner's tip

This exercise is helpful for your understanding of cross-media forms and as practice for your Unit 2 pre-production skills. Do not use this imaginary material in your examination.

■ Link

Go to the Production Process and Audience Reception sections later in this topic. These show you how to complete the further two stages of your case study.

All documentaries have a function. Classic documentaries have primarily informative functions that have been classified as expository, observational or reflexive. All documentaries are about real people but some contemporary documentaries, often designed more for entertainment than for information, choose people via auditions. All documentaries are about real events but in reality TV documentaries the events are often contrived and happen in an artificial setting. Some codes and conventions of classic documentaries are used (see Conventions of the Documentary in Topic 2) but many contemporary television documentaries can be described as hybrid forms.

Link

For more information, see Topic 2, Factual Television.

Media in action

There are different ways of classifying documentaries into groups. A simple one is to see documentaries as having a specific function: expository, observational or reflexive.

Expository mode
These documentaries aim to explain or expose something to audiences. Traditionally about a topic that was unfamiliar to audiences, the documentary aims to inform and educate. There is usually a narrator who can be a presenter or a voiceover (this technique is sometimes referred to as Voice of God) that explains the accompanying images to the audience. Wildlife programmes, historical documentaries, science documentaries follow this tradition.

Observational mode
These documentaries attempt to let events unfold before their cameras; they do not attempt to interpret their subject by using voiceover. Hand-held cameras, lack of staging and extra lighting characterises this format. The term 'fly-on-the-wall' describes observational documentaries and undercover/investigatory texts have observational functions. The camera is observing what happens as it happens. In reality, all the observed material is subject to editing: selection, shaping and adding a soundtrack and this process is in itself an interpretation.

Reflexive mode
These documentaries are generally ones in which the documentary maker gives us his or her thoughts, his or her angle on a subject. He or she makes a case for a particular perspective. Documentary makers such as Nick Broomfield, Michael Moore and Morgan Spurlock intervene and take a part in the action in front of the camera. Documentary formats are constantly evolving and there are many hybrids.

Modern documentaries, including hybrid forms, can be described as observational. There is constant development within this fluid genre and contemporary formats often include participants addressing the camera and interacting with the programme makers. Within these documentaries we see people talking in front of their own 'camcorder' about their lives or their feelings. Technology has changed the ways in which documentaries are produced and consumed. Observational documentaries made by individuals can be uploaded to the internet. Documentary records of events made on mobile phones by ordinary people can be shown on other media.

💡 *Where documentary forms are presented across the media (some ideas to get you started)*

Broadcast	Print	e-media
Made for and scheduled on television or radio – one-offs, series…	Previews and reviews – newspapers and magazines	Dedicated websites. Tags from other websites: subject matter, television channel, production company
Made for cinema, then on television and DVD	Stories and features about the issues, participants, audiences	Clips, previews and reviews, official sites, fan sites, social networking sites…
Live formats		
Repeats, catch-ups, follow-ups, out-takes	Discussions and complaints about the production process – editing…	
Spin-offs and tie-ins		Extra scenes and information – follow ups on issues, participants
Talk shows, news programmes, preview and review programmes about the documentary or related issues	News coverage of issues raised by documentaries – investigation and further information and opinion	Opportunities for interaction, dialogue with producers, participants
Red button interactive	Comments and opinions from producers, participants, audiences	Participants' websites
Opportunities to comment, vote, participate by phone, text, e-mail	Spin-offs for participants – weekly column in magazine or newspaper	Blogs
		Updates of action on mobile
User generated content	Campaigns connected with the documentary	
Trailers, sponsorship, advertising	Promotions, advertisements	Trailers and promotional material

Stage 1 – The topic

■ First you need to broaden your knowledge of the documentary genre by looking at a range of texts.

■ Look at a documentary made for cinema release, perhaps about an event or a person or group of people or an issue. Examine the codes and conventions and the filmmaker's intentions. Look at a documentary where the filmmaker is making a strong point that s/he wants to get across to the audience.

■ Move on to broadcast documentary formats and look at some documentaries that have different functions that position audiences in different ways. This way you will come to understand the processes of documentary production.

■ You will find it useful to look at the listings that classify factual and documentary programmes. Don't forget radio.

■ Apply the media concepts you learned about in Topic 3 to a variety of texts. See how editing techniques and other aspects of moving image language mediate the 'reality' portrayed.

■ See how a text is presented across the media. For example, even before a documentary about the Queen being photographed by Annie Leibovitz was to be screened on BBC, a trail, produced by independent production company RDF, showing a moment of contrived conflict, created a stir. A still photograph of the Queen apparently stalking out of the photo session featured in all the daily newspapers and on all news platforms. The resulting furore about fakery by editing and who might be to blame featured across the media for several days and the issue of documentary 'truth' drew comments and opinions for some time after.

Stage 2 – Focus your study

When you have a sound understanding of the different formats that can be classified as documentaries and the processes that are at work, narrow your study and make a detailed conceptual analysis of at least three documentaries. Representations and ideology are particularly important for this topic. All your chosen texts must have a presence on broadcast, print and e-media platforms.

Choose your three texts and for each text:

▪ examine in close detail the content of each text and the ways that the semiotic, narrative and generic codes are used across the media

▪ examine the representations available and how these are constructed and construed

▪ find out who produced the texts

▪ investigate the target audience(s) across the media

▪ investigate cross-media connections, for instance, synergy, intertextuality...

▪ investigate how the texts are promoted to audiences within and across the media.

You might want to choose documentaries that share a function: expository, observational and reflexive for example, or you might want to choose texts that link in some other way. Subject matter would be one link (family life, the environment, for example); using 'ordinary' people another (seeking fame, at work, for example); point-of-view on society might be another (trying to change a law, pointing out something about contemporary society).

Who are the institutions?

The primary producers, in the case of most film and broadcast fiction products, will include large organisations, independent production companies and co-productions.

Find out the institutional details for each text in your case study. Consider, the point the documentary institution (filmmaker or other) intends to convey to audiences, and the techniques used to do this.

Investigating media

Documentaries are primarily audio/visual. However, to help you understand the differences in the content and form in non-broadcast platforms, try this exercise.

Channel Five is showing a series of half-hour documentaries featuring five individuals who are living a 'green' life-style:

1 Plan a full-page advertisement for a Sunday newspaper advertising the programme.

2 Plan the layout and navigation of a website offering follow-up advice and information.

3 Plan a web log by one of the subjects and the follow-up comments.

Explain the differences in content and form and your reasons for making them.

▪ What changes have you made and why?

AQA Examiner's tip

This exercise is helpful for your understanding of cross-media forms and as practice for your Unit 2 pre-production skills. Do not use this imaginary material in your examination.

Link

Go to the Production Process and Audience reception sections later in this topic. These show you how to complete the further two stages of your case study.

Life-style

What is life-style and why is it a topic?

In sociology a life-style is the way a person lives. This includes patterns of social relations, consumption, entertainment and dress. A life-style typically also reflects an individual's attitudes and values. In the contemporary media landscape where there are so many channels of communication that need to be filled with content, one of the growing categories of content are texts about what we consume and how we live.

Life-style media products, in broadcast, print and e-media, can be grouped into two areas.

Link

When learning about the importance of audience to media producers in Topic 3, we looked at some of the ways market researchers measure and classify audiences. One method, psychographics, looks at consumption patterns, attitudes and values, in other words life-styles.

1 The first area could be said to give advice and information on:
   - homes, cooking and cleaning
   - houses, DIY, buying and selling
   - gardens and gardening
   - marriage, relationships, children, finance, security
   - holidays
   - hobbies
   - fashion, health, beauty.

   These texts tell us how to manage our lives better, often with the help of an expert, and in our consumer society there are commonly shared aspirations for success in all of the areas of life listed above.

2 The second area in which life-style features in the media is the focus on celebrities and their lives. A celebrity is someone who is well known to the public, is recognised and, therefore, to some degree famous. Celebrity can be achieved by talent but celebrities can also be constructed by the media itself. Think, for a moment, about the different ways in which an outstanding footballer or rock star achieves recognition as compared to one of the contestants on *Big Brother*. People can become famous by just being on television and this in itself can open other media opportunities. In 1968, American artist and filmmaker, Andy Warhol said that, 'In the future everyone will be world famous for 15 minutes.' He meant that celebrity as created by the media could not last long and that the attention span of the public was short and that interest would move on to a new media-created celebrity.

   The media loves celebrities because they need to keep in the public eye and are happy to be featured in an article in a life-style magazine or appear on a talk show.

Media in action

It is commonly thought that the media has a role in making and breaking celebrities. It loves to catch them off guard, to expose them and to disclose details of their personal lives. A celebrity from the entertainment world, if discovered showing unacceptable views or behaviour or if involved in a criminal investigation, can lose reputation and career if they lose the support of the media, particularly the press.

The subject matter in celebrity life-style texts is often about their houses, beauty hints and relationships, but audiences respond to them in a different ways. They might feel admiration for the celebrity and aspire to be like them in some way. They might try to emulate them by choosing a similar hairstyle or buying a pair of shoes or after-shave that has been endorsed by them. There is a voyeuristic pleasure for audiences in looking behind the scenes, learning something of the life-styles of the famous. Some celebrity life-style media products position us to scorn or condemn the subject of the piece, giving us a feeling of superiority.

Where life-style products are presented across the media (some ideas to get you started)

Broadcast	Print	e-media
Made for and scheduled on television or radio programmes – series, magazine format…	Life-style, celebrity life-style, gossip, celebrity gossip, consumer magazines.	Magazine and newspaper websites
Specialist channels – UKTV Bright Ideas…	Features in newspapers, often on special pages or special supplements	Dedicated websites for broadcast products, tags from other websites giving extra information, extra scenes – follow-ups on issues and advice
Shopping channels	Broadcast texts previews and reviews in newspapers and listings magazines.	Opportunities for interaction, dialogue with producers, participants
Repeats, catch-ups, back-stories and follow-ups, out-takes	News coverage of issues raised – investigation, information, opinion…	User generated content
Talk shows, news programmes, preview and review programmes about related issues	Stories generated in the press	Blogs
Phone-in programmes	Comments from producers, participants, audiences	
Red button interactive	Subject of text has column in newspaper or magazine	
User generated content		
Trailers, sponsorship, advertising	Promotions, advertisements	Trailers and other promotional material
		Advertising

Stage 1 – The topic

- Investigate a range of these media products to reveal the shared attitudes and values that underpin the subject, style and narrative of the texts.
- Look at texts across genres and across institutions.
- Apply the media concepts you learned about in Topic 3 to a variety of texts.
- See how a text is presented across the media. For example, a documentary about Victoria Beckham moving to the US, an article in a celebrity magazine showing her new house and her blog on the Beckham Brand website.

Stage 2 – Focus your study

When you have a sound understanding of the different formats that can be classified as life-style, narrow your study and make a detailed conceptual analysis of at least three texts. Representations and ideology are particularly important to this topic.

Choose your three texts and for each text:

- examine in close detail the content of each text and the ways that the semiotic, narrative and generic codes are used across the media
- examine the representations available and how these are constructed and construed
- find out who produced the texts
- investigate the target audience(s) across the media

- investigate cross-media connections, for instance, synergy, intertextuality…
- investigate how the texts are promoted to audiences within and across the media.

You might want to choose from a specific genre, practical advice, personal improvement stories or celebrity gossip for example, or you might want to choose texts that link in some other way. Whatever texts you choose, they must have a presence on broadcast, print and e-media platforms.

Who are the institutions?

Apart from the major cross-media institutions producing media content about life-style, advertisers, too, are closely associated with life-style products. Some celebrities themselves can be seen as brands, institutions in themselves.

Find out the institutional details for each text in your case study.

■ **Link**

You will learn more about celebrities and brands in Topic 5, Advertising and Marketing.

AQA Examiner's tip

This exercise is helpful for your understanding of cross-media forms and as practice for your Unit 2 pre-production skills. Do not use this imaginary material in your examination.

■ **Link**

Go to the Production Process and Audience Reception sections later in this topic. These show you how to complete the further two stages of your case study.

■ **Link**

You learned a little about music radio in Topic 2 where there was a case study of Radio 2.

■ **Investigating media**

Celebrity media products have a presence across all media platforms. However, to help you understand the differences in the content and form, try this exercise.

Invent a piece of celebrity news concerning a footballer:

1. Plan the content and layout for *OK!* magazine.
2. Plan the content and layout for the piece in BT Yahoo! entertainment section.
3. Plan the story for a *Five News* bulletin at 10pm.
4. Plan a multi-media message from a mobile phone network to subscribers.

Explain the differences in content and form and your reasons for making them.

Music

Music features across the media platforms and the production and reception of music texts makes an interesting case study. The processes by which it is transmitted and consumed have changed a great deal due to the advance of technology.

■ **Thinking about media**

- How many categories of music can you think of?
- How would you classify the audience for each genre?

Music festivals, such as Glastonbury and The Proms get a lot of coverage, including live broadcasts across the mainstream media on television and radio. The major broadcasting channels cover music events and competitions across all genres of music. Digital and satellite broadcasting television and radio channels include a number of video music and music only channels. Some of these are interactive, with viewers and listeners requesting plays.

FRIDAY 27 July

FRIDAY

Radio

ROCK, POP & CLASSICAL MUSIC

BBC Radio 1
97.6–99.8 FM

Freeview 700 Sky 0101 Virgin TV 901
or via www.bbc.co.uk/radio1

News and **Newsbeat** as Tuesday except no news at 10.00pm and no **Entertainment News** at 6.30pm

7.00 AM **Scott Mills**
10.00 Jo Whiley
1.00 PM **Edith Bowman**
4.00 Sara Cox
6.00 Friday Floor Fillers With Sara Cox.
7.00 Pete Tong
Club sounds, live at Global Gathering.
9.00 The 1Xtra Takeover
10.00 Annie Mac's Mash-Up
12.00 Fabio and Grooverider
2.00 AM **In New DJs We Trust**
4.00 Radio 1's After Show

Radio 1: Get in touch by phone on 0870 010 0100 (calls from land lines cost no more than 8p per minute) or text 81199 (standard rate). Write to Radio 1, BBC, London W1N 4DJ

1Xtra

Freeview 701 Sky 0137 Virgin TV 907
or via www.bbc.co.uk/1xtra

6.00 AM **Jason and Iyare**
9.00 Rampage Club vibes.
12.00 Max
2.00 PM **TXU**
With Charlene White and G Money.
4.00 Ace and Vis
7.00 Semtex
Hip-hop from both sides of the Atlantic.
10.00 Mistajam Hip-hop.
12.00 DJ B
Soul- and R&B-influenced recordings.
2.00 AM **The M1X Show** With DJ Q.

BBC 6 Music

Freeview 707 Sky 0120 Virgin TV 909
or via www.bbc.co.uk/6music

7.00 AM **Shaun Keaveny**
10.00 Gideon Coe
The Indie Disco A to Z Special revisits the letter P, from Placebo to Pigbag.
1.00 PM **Nemone**
4.00 Steve Lamacq New music.
7.00 Tom Robinson's Evening Sequence
With live sets and guest interviews.
10.00 Bruce Dickinson's Rock Show
Focus on Rage Against the Machine.
12.00 Don Letts Eclectic selection.
1.00 AM **Jen Brister** Music and chat.

BBC Proms 2007 *7.30pm Radio 3* Mark Elder conducts the Hallé Orchestra in a rousing programme of Strauss, Britten and Nielsen

BBC Radio 2
88–90.2 FM

Freeview 702 Sky 0102 Virgin TV 902
or via www.bbc.co.uk/radio2

News and **weather** as Wednesday except no news at 8.00pm and 9.00

6.00 AM **Sarah Kennedy**
Including at **6.20 Pause for Thought** with Jess Wilde.
7.30 Johnnie Walker
Including at **9.15 Pause for Thought** with the Rev Ruth Scott.
9.30 Ken Bruce
12.00 Jeremy Vine
Topical phone-in show.
2.00 PM **Steve Wright**
5.00 Chris Evans
7.00 Mad about the Boy: the Songs of Noel Coward
2/3. Pet Shop Boy singer and songwriter Neil Tennant recalls the prolific and influential musical career of actor, playwright and composer Noël Coward (1899–1973). Tennant explores Coward's formidable legacy in musical theatre, with input from performers indebted to the creative giant. Veteran stage actress Elaine Stritch – who starred in the 1962 London production of Coward's *Sail Away* – pays tribute to the prolific writer, whose verbal wit and incisive lyrics graced more than 400 songs in a career spanning five decades.
7.30 Friday Night Is Music Night
Robin Stapleton conducts the BBC Concert Orchestra with tenor Juan Diego Flórez, Opera Babes and the Mandolinquents. Presented by Ken Bruce at the Mermaid Theatre. (R)
9.15 Rebecca
New series 1/8. Actress Alex Kingston reads an abridged version of Daphne du Maurier's masterful and ambiguous tale of romance and suspence. In this first instalment, elegant widower Maxim de Winter targets a holidaying young beauty.
Abridged by Neville Teller
Producer Neil Gardner (R)
9.30 Listen to the Band
Frank Renton presents a studio performance by the Black Dyke Band, conducted by Nicholas Childs.
10.00 The Weekender
Matthew Wright with a survey of contemporary arts and culture, including the current cinema.
12.00 Mark Lamarr
New music and banter. His guest is reggae veteran Alton Ellis.
3.00 AM **Pete Mitchell**
Including at **3.30 Pause for Thought**.

Virgin Radio

Freeview 727 Sky 0107 Virgin TV 915
or via www.virginradio.co.uk

6.00 AM **Christian O'Connell**
10.00 Greg Burns
1.00 PM **Leona Graham**
4.00 Neil Francis
7.00 Sarah Champion
10.00 Robin Burke
2.00 AM **John Osborne**

Planet Rock

Sky 0110 Virgin TV 924
or via www.planetrock.com

6.00 AM **Breakfast with Alice**
9.00 Rob Birnie
1.00 PM **Rock Blok** Listeners' picks.
2.00 Mark Jeeves
Including tracks by Black Sabbath.
7.00 Ian Anderson – under the Influence A show devoted to hippy-dippy musical madness. (R)
8.00 Nicky Horne
11.00 Planet Rock Non-stop rock.

BBC Radio 3
90.2–92.4 FM

Freeview 703 Sky 0103 Virgin TV 903
or via www.bbc.co.uk/radio3

News and **weather** as Monday

7.00 AM **Rob Cowan**
Music includes:
7.00–8.30: Janiewicz *Divertimento* Polish Chamber Orchestra, conductor Jerzy Maksymiuk
Wagner *Good Friday Music (Parsifal)* Houston SO, conductor Leopold Stokowski
Bach *Cantata No 66: Erfreut euch, ihr Herzen*
8.30–10.00: Bizet *Symphony in C* RPO, conductor Charles Munch
Korngold *Gluck, das mir verblieb (Die tote Stadt)* Pilar Lorengar (soprano), Vienna Opera Orchestra, conductor Walter Weller
Dvorak, arr Dennis Russell Davies *Bagatelles, Op 47* Orchestra of the Bonn Beethovenhalle, conductor Dennis Russell Davies
10.00 Classical Collection
With Sarah Walker.
Britten *Prince of the Pagodas (Act 2, Scene 2)*
10.12 Debussy, arr Grainger *Pagodes (Estampes)* City of Birmingham SO, conductor Simon Rattle
10.19 Stravinsky *Les Noces* Alison Wells (soprano), Susan Bickley (mezzo), Martyn Hill (tenor), Alan Ewing (bass), Simon Joly Chorale, International Piano Quartet, Tristan Fry Percussion Ensemble, conductor Robert Craft
10.44 Dohnanyi *Violin Concerto No 2* James Ehnes, BBC Philharmonic, conductor Matthias Bamert
11.16 Cage *Third Construction* Amadinda Ensemble
11.27 Perotin *Sederunt Principes* Hilliard Ensemble
11.40 Reich *Music for Mallet Instruments, Voices and Organ* Pamela Wood Ambush, Rebecca Armstrong (voices – long tones), Jay Clayton (voice – melodic patterns), Bob Becker, Tim Ferchen, Russell Hartenberger, Steve Reich (marimbas), Garry Kvistad, Thad Wheeler (glockenspiels), James Preiss (vibraphone), Nurit Tillis (electric organ)
12.00 Composers of the Week: Alessandro and Domenico Scarlatti
5/5. Donald Macleod concludes the story of the Scarlattis and examines the enormous influence that they exerted on European musical life.
D Scarlatti *Sonatas: in D, Kk492; in F minor, Kk239* Scott Ross (harpsichord)
Pur nel Sonno Almen Cyrille Gerstenhaber (soprano), Musique des Lumières, director Jean-Christophe Frisch
A Scarlatti *Concerto da Camera No 7 in D* Judith Linsenburg (recorder), Musica Pacifica
D Scarlatti *Sonatas in D, Kk430; in G, Kk13* Glenn Gould (piano) (R)
1.00 PM **Afternoon on 3**
Introduced by Louise Fryer.
Radio 3 Lunchtime Concert
Cheltenham Festival 2007
A recital by Radio 3 New Generation Artists the Pavel Haas Quartet given in the Pittville Pump Room.
Mozart *Adagio and Fugue in C minor K546*
Dvorak *String Quartet in F, Op 96 (American)*
Janacek *String Quartet No 2 (Intimate Letters)*
2.10 BBC Proms 2007
Another chance to hear Sunday's concert, presented by Christopher Cook.
Gondwana Voices, BBC Symphony Chorus, BBC Symphony Orchestra, conductor David Robertson
Brett Dean *Vexations and Devotions (BBC co-commission with Perth Festival; first European performance)*
Beethoven *Symphony No 7 in A* Rptd from Sunday 7.30pm
4.00 From the Bath Festival 2006
Carolin Widmann (violin), Simon Lepper (piano)
Bach *Chaconne (Partita in D minor, BWV1004)*
Xenakis *Dikhthas*
Stravinsky *Divertimento* (R)
5.00 In Tune
Sean Rafferty presents music and arts news.
7.30 BBC Proms 2007
LIVE Presented by Martin Handley, live from the Royal Albert Hall in London. The Hallé and their charismatic chief conductor bring together two of this year's themes: Shakespeare and the Auden centenary.
Lisa Milne (soprano),
Hallé Orchestra, conductor Mark Elder
Strauss *Macbeth*
Britten *Our Hunting Fathers*
8.20 Twenty Minutes: This Green Plot
Michael Dobson begins his two-part history of outdoor Shakespeare performance with a look at professional productions across the land.
8.40 Nielsen *Symphony No 4 (Inextinguishable)*
Repeated on Wednesday 1 August at 2pm

9.45 Meetings of Minds
3/3. *Fourth International Congress of Modern Architects – Marseille and Athens 1933.*
In July 1933, Le Corbusier and 90 other delegates boarded a boat in Marseille. Architects, engineers, writers and artists from 18 countries spent the next 15 days, on board and in Athens, discussing ideas for the city of the future. Though they didn't know it, the delegates were creating a blueprint for the rebuilding of Europe's cities, about to be destroyed by the Second World War. Today many argue that the utopian ideas that came to dominate architecture after the 1933 Congress have led to misery and social breakdown for the inhabitants of those new towns and buildings. Frances Stonor Saunders explores how this meeting in 1933 changed the way people live today and how, as cities continue to expand, it will go on to influence the way they live in the future.
Producer Kirsty Pope (R)
10.30 Jazz Library
In the first of what will eventually be several editions devoted to the music of Duke Ellington, bandleader and Ellington expert Pete Long joins Alyn Shipton to propose the essential recordings from Ellington's output between 1940 and his death in 1974. These include the long symphonic work *Black, Brown and Beige*, as well as versions of the *Nutcracker Suite* and the Second Sacred Concert.
Producers Simon Poole and Alyn Shipton
EMAIL: jazzlibrary@bbc.co.uk
11.30 Womad Festival 2007
LIVE Twenty-five years after the very first Womad, the world music festival moves to the green and pleasant fields of Charlton Park in Wiltshire. Andrew McGregor and Verity Sharp begin a weekend of broadcasts with live performances and recorded highlights from the two main stages, the Open Air and the Siam Tent. Artists include Congolese rumba maestro Samba Mapangala, Mexican singer Lila Downs, and Egyptian band El Tanbura. And from Radio 3's own stage in Charlton Park's arboretum, Fiona Talkington introduces a live set from Malian ngoni virtuoso Bassekou Kouyate.
Producer Roger Short
1.00 AM **Through the Night**
Presented by Susan Sharpe. **Schumann** *Overture: Manfred* **Beethoven** *Violin Concerto in D* **Mendelssohn** *Symphony No 3 in A minor (Scottish)* Christian Tetzlaff (violin), BBC Symphony Orchestra, conductor Jiri Belohlavek
2.36 Prokofiev *Romeo and Juliet* **3.16 Beethoven** *Piano Trio in B, Op 97 (Archduke)* **3.56 Leclair** *Violin Concerto in D* **4.11 Mendelssohn** *Overture: The Hebrides (Fingal's Cave)* **4.22 Steve Martland** *Three Carols* **4.32 Szymanowski** *Variations in B flat minor, Op 3* **4.46 Sibelius** *Valse Triste* **4.52 Grainger** *To a Nordic Princess* **5.00 Wagner** *Overture: Tannhauser* **5.15 Grieg** *Wedding Day at Troldhaugen (Lyric Pieces, Op 65 No 6)* **5.22 Couperin** *Treizième Concert à deux violes* **5.33 Nystroem** *Tre Havsvisioner* **5.44 Debussy** *Première Rapsodie* **5.53 Escher** *Ciel, Air et Vents* **6.06 Moyzes** *Symphony No 6* **6.36 Thomson** *String Quartet No 2*

Radio 3: Get in touch by phone on 0870 010 0300 (calls from land lines cost no more than 8p per minute) Or write to BBC Radio 3, Broadcasting House, London W1A 1AA

Classic FM
99.9–101.9 FM

Sky 0106 Virgin TV 922 or via www.classicfm.com

6.00 AM **Easier Breakfast** With Jane Jones.
8.00 Simon Bates
Classical hits, including at **9.00 The Hall of Fame Hour** and just after **10.00 CD of the Week.**
12.00 Classic FM's Most Wanted
1.00 PM **Classic FM Requests** With Jamie Crick.
4.00 Drivetime With Mark Forrest.
6.30 Classic Newsnight With John Brunning.
7.00 Smooth Classics With John Brunning.
9.00 Evening Concert Presented by Nick Bailey.
Wagner *Overture: Tannhäuser*
Berlin Philharmonic Orchestra/Claudio Abbado
Handel *Water Music Suite No 1 in F*
English Baroque Soloists, conductor John Eliot Gardiner
Weber *Clarinet Concerto No 1 in F minor*
Sabine Meyer, Dresden State Orchestra, conductor Hans Vonk
Dvorak *Symphony No 7 in D minor*
LSO, conductor Colin Davis
11.00 Classic FM Magazine With Mark Forrest.
12.00 Chill on Classic FM Relaxing classics.
4.00 AM **Nicola Bonn** Classic FM favourites.

THIS WEEK'S RADIO highlights on page 128

Latest updates *Radio Times* has the details on www.radiotimes.com

Key (R) Repeat

142 RadioTimes 21–27 July 2007

Fig. 4.1 Radio Times, *Friday 27th July 2007. What do you notice about the relative radio coverage for rock, classical and pop music?*

Media in action

The Freeview broadcasting platform carries a range of music stations:

BBC Radio 1, BBC 1Xtra, BBC Radio 2, BBC Radio 3, BBC 6music, Virgin Radio, Heat, Heart, The Hits Radio, Kerrang!, KISS, Magic 105.4, Mojo, Q Radio, Smash Hits Radio, Smooth

The Hits is also a television channel that carries music videos and advertising.

Some of the radio stations are multi-platform brands. For example, *Heat* is a consumer magazine and a radio station. '*Heat* is emap's market defining celebrity weekly. It has spawned a generation of celebrity, life-style and gossip fanatics and offers the best in entertainment and celebrity news every week.'

Taken from the emap website

Investigating media

Listen to Heat radio and look at *Heat* magazine.

- What synergy is there between the two products?
- How far does the content of the radio station interpellate to the readers of the magazine?

Radio stations are available on e-platforms as are opportunities to share music, to upload your own music and music videos and to download music. A popular video at the time of writing is a machinima version of Lily Allen's *Smile*, which was put on YouTube by EA, a video games producer.

CD sales have been steadily going down as more of us buy our music tracks on-line, creating our personal library of music and videos to consume on portable electronic devices. The technology of the internet as a place to listen to music, to upload music and videos and to download music in MP3 format, to listen to on a variety of devices, has revolutionised the reception and consumption of music.

Media in action

Buying music

For a long time the record business was conducted by a traditional process. The record company took up a band or performer, produced the recording in a studio, distributed it to record stores and arranged air play on radio stations. As in other media industries there were big institutions such as EMI and Sony and smaller, independent labels. Income from the plays and sales of the records went to performers and producers. If we buy CDs from shops or on-line stores the distribution of income is the same.

With the World Wide Web came the possibility of sharing music files as MP3. In 1999 Shawn Fanning launched a new program that was to change how many people used the internet: Napster. The software enabled music fans to swap songs stored on their computers with each other and to find each other through a central directory. Napster users could trade in bootlegs, rare tracks and current releases by major artists. The music industry regarded this as piracy and took legal action against Napster for 'engaging in, or facilitating others in copying, downloading, uploading, transmitting, or distributing copyrighted musical compositions and sound recordings' and in 2001 they were forced to withdraw files with copyright attached, which effectively shut them down. Napster was re-launched as a pay per track organisation in the UK in summer 2004 by which time it was up against Apple's iTunes and a wide range of other paid-for music sites. As a result income from the sales of tracks goes to performers and producers.

In Topic 3 you read about how non-diagetic music is an important aspect of the production of film and broadcast texts. It establishes the setting and the mood and sometimes the lyrics themselves anchor the meaning of the sequence. Cinema, television and radio advertising uses recorded music and has often stimulated a revival in sales of songs from earlier decades. Music soundtracks in films may be specially composed or existing songs and music are chosen.

Moving image sequences have been made to complement music. Walt Disney's *Fantasia*, 1940, is a full-length animation of classical music; the music came first as the inspiration for the filmed material. During the 1940s and 1950s short films of singers and musicians performing their work were made. In the 1960s the BBC's *Top of the Pops* began to use short films made by bands to accompany their songs. These became known as pop videos. In the 1980s music station MTV based the format of their programming around the pop video. Since then it has often been the case that the video sold the song.

💡 *Where music products are presented across the media (some ideas to get you started)*

Broadcast	Print	e-media
Scheduled radio and television: recorded and live – DJ shows, genre programmes, profiles of individuals or bands, chart shows... Series or one-offs – music documentaries... Appearances on talk shows, music quizzes, charity events Specialist music television and radio channels Red button interactive Voting, texting, e-mailing	Specialist music magazines Previews and reviews in newspapers and magazines: music releases, concerts and events News and magazine coverage of music personalities Fanzines Music personalities' columns in newspapers and magazines	Web and internet radio Record company and artists' websites Fans' websites Blogs Podcasts iTunes and other music purchase websites Downloads including to mobile and MP3 players UGC – videos on YouTube and similar sites
Trailers, sponsorship, advertising, promotions (including gigs)	Promotions, advertisements	Trailers and promotional material

Stage 1 – The topic

■ For this case study, first gain an overview of the presence of music across the media platforms. In the multi-channel television and radio landscape there are music channels that cater for niche audiences. The same is the case on the internet, where many radio stations worldwide can be accessed.

■ Listen to different music radio stations and investigate their target audiences. Do this by your personal knowledge about certain music genres and by research. Commercial radio stations provide information to give to advertisers about the demographic and psychographic breakdown of their audiences.

■ Watch some music programmes, including non-stop music channels. Note how far audiences are involved in the choice of track.

■ Look at listing magazines and use the internet to see the range of music genres available. A web-browser such as BT Yahoo! has tags to radio stations that are classified under music genres. The music that appeals to the largest audience is pop or rock music which itself is sub-divided into sub-genres (see Figure 4.2 below).

■ Be aware of how a text is presented across the media. Choose one text, which could be a recording artist, and investigate it over the places where it appears.

Stage 2 – Focus your study

When you have a sound understanding of the different formats in which music is packaged, narrow your study and make a detailed conceptual analysis of at least three texts. Each one must have a presence in broadcast, print and e-media.

Choose your three texts and for each text:

■ examine in close detail the content of each text and the ways that the semiotic, narrative and generic codes are used across the media

■ examine the representations available and how these are constructed and construed

■ find out who produced the texts

■ investigate the target audience(s) across the media

■ investigate cross-media connections, for instance, synergy, intertextuality…

■ investigate how the texts are promoted to audiences within and across the media.

You might want to choose from a specific genre of music or you might want to choose texts that link in some other way. The launch of a new single or album would be a media rich text, the tour of a music artist and his or her presence in the media. Whatever texts you choose, be sure that you keep a media studies conceptual approach to the analysis of the production and reception processes.

Who are the institutions?

You've learned a little about the institutions involved in recording, playing and distributing music. Publicity and promotion involves more institutions and much expenditure.

Find out the institutional details for each text in your case study.

■ **Link**

In the Advertising and Marketing topic, the illustration 'The high cost of selling out' from the *Guardian* of 29 June 2007 gives a picture of just where about half a million pounds might be spent for a band to get its first hit.

■ **Investigating media**

Music products have a presence across all media platforms. However, to help you understand the differences in the content and form, try this exercise.

You are the publicist for a new band. Choose the type of music and decide on the target audience. You have arranged a couple of local gigs for the band and have recorded a couple of songs:

1 Plan the publicity photos to represent the band's desired image.

2 Plan a MySpace piece for one or two of the band members.

3 Plan the cover for the 7-inch vinyl with artwork, title and track listing.

Explain the differences in content and form and your reasons for making them.

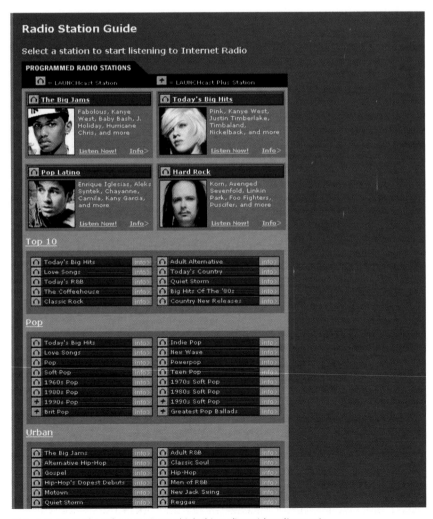

Fig. 4.2 *Note the subgenres into which this radio guide splits music (Reproduced with the permission of* Yahoo! Inc. ® 2007)

News

To study this topic you will need to investigate how news is presented and consumed across the media.

You have learned something about the newspaper industry in Topic 1 and read a case study of broadcast news and listened to some radio news in Topic 2.

You will need to remind yourself of the newspaper layout terminology and about the role of Ofcom and the Press Code of Practice. In Topic 3, you read about how 'old' media companies have developed e-media platforms for the delivery of news and looked at how news is no longer in the hands of the institutions. News can be produced by ordinary people, using new technology, both on the internet and by contributing UGC to news on the more traditional broadcast and print platforms. Technology has transformed the processes of news gathering and news presentation.

Where does news come from?

News content comes from a variety of sources:

1 The diary – this lists all the major events taking place on each day that are likely to be worthy of coverage: court cases, Parliamentary debates, royal visits. All newsrooms have one.

2 Organisations – organisations such as the government, political parties, the police or a pressure group want to communicate policy, proposals and ideas and send their news through:

   - press releases
   - press briefings
   - news conferences
   - public relations
   - publicity stunts.

3 Agencies – news is also provided by national and international news agencies such as Reuters and Associated Press. Often provide breaking news and reports on events.

4 Journalists – report on events for specific news organisations.

5 Members of the public – might contribute content to a story, providing photographs, videos, first-hand experiences and reactions.

What makes the news?

The news media has an agenda, which varies depending on the institution producing the news and the audience that consumes it. The news agenda is traditionally managed by a gatekeeper or editor (usually more than one person) whose responsibility is to decide what should go into the news and what should be ignored and the running order or layout of the news.

Newspapers, and also broadcast news organisations, are said to operate a system of news and entertainment values, which are different for different organisations.

The simplest division is that hard news is primarily concerned with hard facts and information and soft news covers less substantial or serious items such as stories about entertainment.

Depending on the form of news, different factors will influence news selection. There is a need for pictures, a visual imperative, for moving image news programmes and this affects whether a story is included or

Link

Go to the Production Process and Audience Reception sections later in this topic. These show you how to complete the further two stages of your case study.

Media in action

Public relations consultants try to obtain positive news coverage for an organisation or individual. They send out press releases, appear on the news and arrange parties and events to which journalists are invited. Commercial organisations, public bodies and individuals need to keep themselves in the public eye and need a positive media profile.

Media in action

Galtung and Ruge in 1965 produced a taxonomy of hard news values based on detailed analysis of newspapers. They used 12 categories and found that the more categories an event matched the more likely it was to be included in the news. Their work has been drawn on by other academics and tested by, among others, Tony Harcup, at present, senior lecturer in the Department of Journalism at Sheffield University. You will apply his 10 categories to your news texts.

not. Sometimes a story will run but with older visuals, so called 'library footage'. A dramatic piece of visual material will often determine the positioning of a news item.

After a tragedy or disaster, journalists have to file follow-up reports from the location giving details of how the event has influenced people's lives. The July flooding in England saw days of coverage of the floods themselves and weeks and months of stories about the after-effects.

Where news is presented across the media (some ideas to get you started)

Broadcast	Print	e-media
Scheduled live television and radio programmes 24-hour rolling news Scheduled live television and radio bulletins Interactive red button Phone-in programmes User generated content: e-mails, texts, sending phone photos and videos…	Newspapers: national and local paid-for and free specialist news magazines Readers' letters, e-mails, photographs	Newspapers on-line News through browsers Blogs Podcasts Personalised news feeds Updates through mobile phones – headlines, sports, weather, traffic… Limited web news through phone provider UCG
Trailers, sponsorship	Promotions, advertisements	Advertising

Stage 1 – The topic

- Look at news products across the media. Include television and radio news, newspapers and on-line newspapers, news blogs and places to share news and views about the news. Include news products that are aimed at different audiences. Think about different types of news – don't forget sports news, local news, weather news.
- Apply the media concepts you learned about in Topic 3 to a variety of news texts. Account for any similarities or differences.
- Choose one story and investigate it over the places where it appears. For example, an international sporting event.

Stage 2 – Focus your study

When you have a sound understanding of the different formats that can be classified as news, narrow your study and make a detailed conceptual analysis of at least three texts. Representations and ideology are particularly important in this topic.

Choose at least three texts that have features in common. Each must have a presence in broadcast, print and e-media:

- examine them in close detail, closely studying the content of each text and the way the semiotic, narrative and generic codes are used
- examine the representations available and how these are constructed and construed
- find out who produced the texts
- investigate the target audience(s) across the media
- nvestigate cross-media connections, for instance, synergy, intertextuality…

Thinking about media

Broadcast news has a responsibility to be fair and unbiased; newspapers do not have this obligation but must avoid breaking the law. Traditional media institutions check stories for accuracy. However, news put up on the internet is not regulated or checked.

- Is it possible for news to be truly objective and unbiased?

Think about the coverage of the Middle East from the point of view of the BBC, Fox News and Al Jazeera.

- investigate how the texts are promoted to audiences within and across the media.

You might wish to choose news events or stories about a specific subject, or news stories that link in some other way.

Investigating media

Tony Harcup revisited Galtung and Ruge's news values by looking at a thousand lead stories in three national newspapers. The categories he suggested will be very useful for your study of News as a topic. You should apply it to the texts you choose for your case study.

Stories that fall into a number of these categories are more likely to feature as news and more likely to have a higher place on the news running order:

1. The power elite – stories concerning powerful individuals, organisations or institutions
2. Celebrity – stories concerning people who are already famous
3. Entertainment – stories concerning sex, show business, human interest, animals, an unfolding drama, or offering opportunities for humorous treatment, entertaining photographs or witty headlines
4. Surprise – stories that have an element of surprise and/or contrast
5. Bad news – stories with particularly negative overtones, such as conflict or tragedy
6. Good news – stories with particularly positive overtones, such as rescues and cures
7. Magnitude – stories that are perceived as sufficiently significant either in the numbers of people involved or in potential impact
8. Relevance – stories about issues, groups and nations perceived to be relevant to the audience
9. Follow-ups – stories about subjects already in the news
10. Newspaper agenda – stories that set or fit the news organisation's agenda.
    - How many of these categories can be applied to each of the stories in your case study?
    - Do these categories apply across the media?
    - Why or why not? Consider the production and consumption processes.

Investigating media

News is presented and consumed across the media. However, to help you understand the differences in content and forms try this exercise:

Scientific research has found that eating too many carrots may be unhealthy.

1. Plan a leading article, including headline, photograph and caption for the *Sun* newspaper.
2. Plan a two-minute package for *Newsbeat* on Radio 1.
3. Plan an article for *Parenting* magazine for mothers of young children.

Explain the differences in content and form and your reasons for making them.

AQA Examiner's tip

This exercise is helpful for your understanding of cross-media forms and as practice for your Unit 2 pre-production skills. Do not use this imaginary material in your examination

Link

Go to the Production Process and Audience Reception sections later in this topic. These show you how to complete the further two stages of your case study.

Sport

To study this topic you will need to investigate how sport is presented and consumed across the media.

To make a case study of sport in the media you will need to take a media studies approach and consider the texts in terms of the processes that convey meanings about the sport and the way audiences respond to these processes rather than the content of the actual sporting event itself.

Thinking about media

1 Which sports are most represented on broadcast media? Why?

2 Which sports would you expect to find represented in your local newspaper? Why?

3 Where would you find coverage of minority sports? Why?

Link

In Topic 2 you read a case study about the broadcasting of a major sporting event and the way the narrative structure varies according to the format of the programme.

Investigating media

Make a case study of the sports coverage in a daily national newspaper. This may be a separate section of the newspaper or the traditional sports pages at the back:

1 What sports are predominant?

2 What minority sports are presented? How much space do they take up?

3 What women's sports are presented? Are any women visible?

4 What sporting events other than national events are presented?

Look carefully at the Sky Sports homepage (for the web address, see the e-resources or do a search). Watch a 15-minute extract from *Sky Sports News*, available on Freeview, Sky and cable.

1 What sports are predominant?

2 What minority sports are presented and how do you access them?

3 What women's sports are presented? Are any women visible?

4 What sporting events other than national events are presented?

Where sport is presented across the media
(some ideas to get you started)

Broadcast	Print	e-media
Live on television and radio	Reports in newspapers – predictions, results…	Live coverage on internet or other device
Scheduled sports programmes on television and radio	Stories and features about people and issues	Live updates
Dedicated channels	Specialist magazines	Dedicated websites – tags to other websites
Phone-ins on radio	Fanzines	On-line newspapers
News items, previews and reviews about sport	Sports personalities' newspaper and magazine columns	Blogs
Sports talk and quizzes…		Opportunities for interaction and dialogue
Red button interactive	Comments and opinions from participants and the public	
Opportunities to comment, vote, participate by phone, text, e-mail		
Trailers, sponsorship, advertising	Promotions, advertisements	Trails, advertisements and promotional material

Stage 1 – The topic

- For this case study, firstly gain an overview of the presence of sport generally across the media platforms. In the multi-channel television and radio landscape there are dedicated sports channels, but sport appears on nearly all television and radio channels, in some shape or form. Where does sports news appear?

- Figures from the sporting world appear in sections of the media not dedicated to sport. Many sporting heroes act as ambassadors for charity and health campaigns, and make personal appearances that are unrelated to sport. Think of Kelly Holmes, for instance. There are features about the relationships, marriages, holidays and homes of sports stars. Many sports stars appear in advertisements. Most of them employ public relations staff to manage their media image. Focus on such a person and investigate their presence across the media. Some of them are brands in themselves and make money from celebrity endorsement and sponsorship.

- Apply the media concepts you learned about in Topic 3 to a variety of sports texts. A text could be a report on a tennis match with a photograph in a newspaper or magazine, the homepage of a football club, the live coverage of test match cricket. Account for any similarities or differences.

- Choose one story and investigate it over the places where it appears. For example, an international sporting event.

Stage 2 – Focus your study

When you have a sound understanding of the different formats that can be classified as sport, narrow your study and make a detailed conceptual analysis of at least three texts. Representations and ideology are particularly important to this topic.

Choose at least three texts that have features in common. Each must have a presence in broadcast, print and e-media:

- examine them in close detail, closely studying the content of each text and the way the semiotic, narrative and generic codes are used
- examine the representations available and how these are constructed and construed
- find out who produced the texts
- investigate the target audience(s) across the media
- investigate cross-media connections, for instance, synergy, intertextuality…
- investigate how the texts are promoted to audiences within and across the media.

You might wish to choose texts about a specific sport or texts that have another type of connection with each other.

Find out the institutional details for each text in your case study.

💡 The cross-media study – the production process

In Section B of the Investigating Media examination you will be given a choice of two essays. One option may ask you to consider your case study from the point of view of its producers.

When you make your case study across the media you must investigate the processes used to create and distribute the products. This means seeing the production process from the point of view of the institutions involved.

AQA Examiner's tip

This exercise is helpful for your understanding of cross-media forms and as practice for your Unit 2 pre-production skills. Do not use this imaginary material in your examination.

Link

Go to the Production Process and Audience Reception sections later in this topic. These show you how to complete the further two stages of your case study.

Sport is presented and consumed across the media. However, to help you understand the differences in content and form try this exercise:

Sport England want to promote bowls as a sport for young people. You, as a bowls player, have been asked to help present the sport as accessible, inexpensive and fun.

1 Plan a video to upload to MySpace.

2 Plan a two-minute package for *Newsbeat* on Radio 1.

3 Plan an article to feature in *Heat* magazine.

4 Plan an item for the Sport England website

Explain the differences in content and form and your reasons for making them.

In Topic 3 you learned that institutional factors influence the representations, values and ideology carried within the text itself. Here is a reminder of how to question the origin of a text. For each of the texts in your case study find out the answers to these questions:

■ What is the institutional source of the text?

■ In what ways has the text been influenced or shaped by the institution that produced it?

■ Is the source a public service or commercial institution? What difference does this make to the text?

■ How has the text been distributed?

Stage 3 – Production issues

Consider how any of the following factors might affect the production and distribution processes of your chosen case study:

■ media ownership – level of independence or convergence

■ cross-media presence

■ public service and other obligations

■ censorship and control

■ the technologies used

■ how, where and to whom the products are transmitted

■ scheduling

■ the role of advertising or sponsorship

■ relationship with audience.

↘ 💡 The cross-media study – the reception process

The second optional question in Section B of the Investigating Media examination may ask you to consider your case study from the point of view of audience consumption and reception.

When you make your case study across the media you must investigate how audiences select each text and how they respond to it. In Topic 2 you learned about how audiences have certain expectations of media texts, the ways in which they use media texts and specific media forms. In Topic 3 you learned about how audiences can be classified and how they are addressed and positioned by media texts. Apply this knowledge and understanding to your case study.

Stage 4 – Audience issues

For each text in your case study find out:

- Who is the primary audience?
- Is there a secondary audience?
- How, when and where is the text consumed by audiences?
- How does the audience respond to the text? What elements of the text appeal to the audience (narrative, themes, values, uses and gratifications)?
- What are the differences in the type of audience and the conditions of reception across the media?

End of topic summary:

- To make a case study you start by making a general investigation of a particular topic looking at a range of different forms and genres across the media platforms and how meanings and responses are created and received.

- The second stage is to narrow your focus to at least three texts and examine them in closer detail looking at the similarities and differences in the production processes used across the media and the reasons for these.

- The third stage involves finding out about the institutional contexts including the relationship with the advertising industry and any issues of regulation that affect the specific case study topic.

- At the fourth stage of your case study, you will investigate the ways in which audiences receive and respond to these texts across the media and give reasons for any similarities and differences in the consumption pattern.

- This study involves looking particularly at opportunities for interaction with and participation in the production process.

Link

In Topic 6 you will have the opportunity to write a practice essay about your case study taking the point of view of the media producers.

Link

There are tools in the e-resources to help you research, plan and structure your case study.

Thinking about media

- How do audiences respond to texts presented on different platforms?
- Which platform offers most interactivity for audiences?

5 Investigating advertising and marketing

🔍 What is marketing?

Marketing, in media terms, is about building relationships with audiences, the consumers and users of media products. In the contemporary media landscape and in a social climate in which there are plenty of choices to be made by consumers, marketeers are responsible for identifying, anticipating and satisfying consumer requirements. Marketing attempts to determine how an organisation competes against its competitors in a marketplace and how to attract, keep and satisfy consumers. This involves research into audiences and planning strategies to attract consumers' attention and interest in their products. ITV1 and BBC One still compete for Saturday night audiences; rival newspapers give away DVDs and so on.

Marketing is often centred on a brand rather than a one-off product. A brand can be a media institution that produces a range of media products such as Sky, Yahoo! or Orange Network. Marketeers want consumers to recognise their brand as being different from others. They want to encourage brand loyalty so that, for example, when considering an update of a product or service consumers will not consider any other make. They want their brand values to be understood and shared by their consumers. Media institutions have public relations, publicity and marketing personnel to manage their brand and communicate with audiences and users. Commercial media institutions have marketing departments that deal with selling time and space to advertisers and organising other marketing opportunities such as sponsorship, sports and music events.

Marketing consists of a number of strategies and one of these is the use of advertising. Marketeers plan a number of promotional tactics and decide what sort of advertising to commission and where best to place the advertising, across the media, to engage with the target audience for their product or service. Traditional outlets are television, cinema, radio, newspapers and magazines; and outdoor advertising such as billboards and posters. We have become familiar with buses bedecked with advertising. The current media environment has resulted in many small, niche audiences who are difficult to reach and are quite resistant to direct advertising. Attempts to capture attention in unexpected places has led to ambient advertising, which covers the projection of messages on to large buildings, messages on the back of tickets or coat hangers in clothing stores and a range of other messages imported into our everyday environment. Advertising on the internet is another challenge for marketeers and advertisers.

Increasingly marketeers seek to capitalise on the take-up of technology. Some current examples of this are the following:

- Plans to offer free mobile phone calls and texts to teenagers provided they are willing to receive adverts on their phone. Younger audiences have grown up with advert-supported free services such as MySpace and Bebo on the internet. Advertisers that use or intend to use the mobile phone platform include Microsoft, for its Xbox games console, Coca-Cola, L'Oreal and Buena Vista. Some of the adverts let customers download free content such as games, wallpaper and video.

▪ Marketeers seek to connect with users of alternative reality games, for example, Microsoft sponsored a game, Vanishing Point, in order to promote their Windows Vista operating system. This involved a cross-media collaborative treasure hunt with people around the world scanning newspaper classifieds, watching television ads, analysing websites, making phone calls, sending emails and piecing together clues littered across the international landscape to win a prize. The buzz created by this activity, the social interaction and the chat would, it was hoped, generate sales of Vista. (Source: 'The game genre that could not exist without the net' by Aleks Krotoski in the *Guardian* on 8 February 2007.)

▪ Recording artists giving away free CDs. In August 2007, rock musician Prince did a deal with the *Mail on Sunday* and released his latest album as a covermount. This led to more papers being sold, a burst of publicity for the fading rock star, a potential rise in ticket sales and merchandise for the Prince tour and free publicity for both Prince and the *Mail on Sunday*. The issue of a new album being released free was newsworthy enough to gain news coverage in the press, broadcast and online media.

For your cross-media study you will need to consider how media products and services are marketed within and across the media. An example of cross-media promotion would be a marketing campaign to promote a new film that might include a series of trailers in the cinema, on television and on the internet; articles and advertisements in newspapers and magazines; organising events that gain publicity and **viral marketing** techniques such as sending messages to mobile phones and posting blogs on social websites to create a buzz around the launch of the film and make people want to see it. If your case study is concerned with celebrities or a particular sport, for instance, you will need to consider the marketing strategies used to create the image and manage information about the celebrity. Look carefully at how the different media platforms are used to reach audiences.

Media products are promoted in a variety of ways. In your case study you will investigate these ways and the advertising and marketing texts themselves.

Promotional tactics used by marketeers or the producing institution itself include:

Broadcast – cinema, television, radio…	Print – newspapers, magazines, posters…	e-media – including telephony, games…
Trailers	Promotional features and offers	Trailers
Sponsorship	Previews and reviews	Promotional articles and offers
Paid-for advertisements	Paid-for advertisements	Previews and reviews
Appearances on talk shows		Paid-for advertisements
Review programmes		Viral marketing
Coverage of promotional events		Blogs
		Ringtones…

🔍 What is advertising?

The purpose of advertising is to sell products and ideas, and to do this an advertisement or advertising campaign must tap into its audience's sense of need. Advertising, in its simplest form, is the way in which

---

Thinking about media

▪ Why did Prince choose the *Mail on Sunday*? Think about readers, circulation, Prince's fans.

Media in action

AIDA is an acronym used in the marketing and advertising industry to summarise what a marketing text should do.

Any text should:

A – attract attention and awareness

I – create interest

D – create desire

A – lead to action on the part of the consumer.

An addition to the acronym to consider is:

S – satisfaction and a desire to return to the brand and consume more products.

💡 Key term

Viral marketing: the spreading of a message, like a virus. Similar to 'word of mouth' or 'network marketing', it applies to any strategy that encourages individuals to pass on a marketing message to others, creating the potential for growth of exposure and influence. This technique uses images, texts, web links, Flash animations, audio/video clips and emerging forms, passed from user to user chain letter style, via email and often through mobile telephony.

AQA Examiner's tip

In your cross-media case study you must investigate the opportunities available on each media platform for promotional opportunities.

i Key term

Product placement: the inclusion of a product in sound or vision in return for cash or services.

■ Link

See the e-resources for websites that explain the advantages of product placement and give examples of where this has been used, for example, specific branded cars in *The Bill*.

■ Media in action

Advertisers' lines of appeal

Gillian Dyer in *Advertising as Communication* (Routledge, 1988) shows how advertisers use specific lines of appeal that tap into our desires and our fears. Images and references put into advertising connect with our social needs.

Advertisements often feature some of the following:

- happy families
- rich, luxurious lifestyles
- dreams and fantasy
- successful romance and love
- elite people or experts
- glamorous places
- nature and the natural world
- beautiful people
- comedy and humour
- childhood.

AQA Examiner's tip

For the unseen text in Section A of the examination, whatever the form of the text, you will need to identify and comment on the persuasive techniques used by the producers to convey the brand image and values of the institution.

■ Thinking about media

- What advertisements can you remember and why?
- Which of the above techniques and tools were included? Any others?

the promise of a product is communicated to consumers. Products are promoted in such a way as to offer the promise of satisfying consumer needs and aspirations.

Advertising texts can take the form of direct advertising, which is paid-for slots that take up time or space on media platforms. Other forms of advertising are covert and include the sponsorship of programmes or events, the use of celebrities to promote products and **product placement.** Product placement is often present in films, television, music videos and games. It is a way of getting messages across to an increasingly sophisticated audience that skips or ignores direct advertising.

In Section A of the examination you may be presented with an advertising text to analyse in terms of media form, media representations, media audiences and media institutions. The advertising text may be from broadcast, print or e-media platforms. Advertisements and promotional products, like trailers for instance, are persuasive texts and designed to attract the attention and interest of audiences.

Techniques that attract audience attention to the message within an advertising text include:

- humour
- repetition
- shock tactics
- sex.

Tools that are used to get the message across effectively in a short time or space include:

- intertextuality – using references to other texts creates and adds additional meaning
- special language – persuasive words, puns, slogans, rhyme
- direct address – referring to the audience as 'you'
- stereotypes – this is a quick way of carrying a lot of meaning
- music – connotes a mood and attitude
- elite persons – celebrities carry prestige and additional meanings.

These techniques and tools are used in all persuasive texts, including public service campaigns to promote, health, social or charitable issues.

When producing promotional texts such as the trailers or advertisements required for Unit 2 products, incorporate some of these techniques where appropriate.

Advertisements appear across the media. In Topic 3 you analysed a print advertisement in terms of symbolic, technical and written codes. For moving image, radio or e-media advertisements you would need to adapt this framework to fit the form of the text.

When making readings of advertisements you should apply the media concepts. Don't forget to consider the text in the context of other advertisements, noting the use of generic conventions. How far does it relate to different advertisements of the same type? Identify the roles and stereotypes, life-styles and desires built into the text and the values conveyed to the audience.

■ Investigating media

Examination practice

(AQA Past paper Med 1 January 2007)

Look carefully at the advertisement for a series of television programmes about cookery considering the media concepts and what you have read in this chapter. Then answer the following questions:

■ Discuss the use of codes and conventions in the construction of this advertisement. TIP: this question tests knowledge and understanding of the generic conventions of advertisements (features to discuss include: use of colour, framing, relationship of image and information, narrative).

■ Consider the representations of people and places in this advertisement. TIP: this question tests knowledge and understanding of how representations are constructed and conveyed within media products (features to discuss include: Jamie, Italy, Italian cooks and kitchens, cookery).

■ What does this advertisement tell us about the media institutions involved? TIP: this question tests knowledge and understanding of how the institution(s)' brand image and brand values are created and conveyed by visual, narrative and technical codes (features to discuss include: Jamie Oliver, Channel 4, *Radio Times*, cookery).

■ Examine some of the ways in which this website communicates with its target audience. TIP: this question tests knowledge and understanding of the concept of audience, identifying target audiences and how they are hailed and addressed by the advertisement (features to discuss include: possible target audiences, prior knowledge, intertextual references, mode of address).

■ **Link**

For more information on Moving Image terminology and on Representation, see Topic 3.

Fig. 5.1 *Advertisement for* Jamie's Great Italian Escape, *published in the* Radio Times *15–21 October 2005. Published by* Radio Times/*BBC*

■ Media in action

The Advertising Standards Authority (ASA), which represents the main industry bodies of advertisers, agencies and media owners, regulates the content of advertisements, sales promotions and direct marketing in the UK. It investigates complaints made about ads, sales promotions and direct marketing. The advertising standards codes are separated out into codes for TV, radio and all other types of ads. There are also rules for Teletext ads, interactive ads and the scheduling of television ads. Adjudications are published on the website every Wednesday.

The main principles of the advertising standards codes are that ads should not mislead, cause harm or offend. The codes are the responsibility of two industry Committees of Advertising Practice – CAP (Broadcast) and CAP (Non-broadcast) and are independently administered by the ASA.

Sponsorship is not covered by the ASA and is the responsibility of Ofcom.

The ASA carries out research, including research into people's attitudes towards advertising and compliance with the advertising standards codes within specific sectors and media.

■ Link

Figures 1.6 and 1.7 show how advertising works in the print media.

■ Thinking about media

House, a US-made medical drama series, is sponsored by Spontex Comfy Gloves. At the start of each programme and after each advertising break the glove puppets do comic routines, each one followed by the phrase, 'Sponsored by Spontex Comfy Gloves'.

Choose three broadcast texts, one could be radio, and note:

■ Who the sponsors are and how the sponsorship is presented.

■ What is the connection between the sponsorship, the presentation and the programme?

Marketing and advertising in the media

You already know that a great deal of the income used to create products across the media comes from advertising.

Advertisers need audiences and media institutions sell their audiences to advertisers: most media institutions rely on direct advertising, sponsorship and to a growing extent product placement income. The BBC, of course, is barred from these practices and promotes its own products across its broadcast, print and e-media platforms while its business arm, BBC Worldwide, sells its products.

■ Case study

Promoting a band

Teenagers form the primary audience for new music and teenagers spend much time on the internet but also listen to radio, watch television and read magazines. Cross-media promotion is seen as essential and a band and its record company will seek publicity using a range of strategies and media outlets. Dave Simpson gives a hypothetical account of how a band signed to a record company might be launched. For our purposes, the actual figures used are unimportant, but a careful study of the processes involved will give you insight into what marketing across the media entails.

To summarise the illustration: alongside the actual writing, playing and recording of the album, which might take around eight months, goes the making of the video, the shooting of publicity photographs and the organisation involved with touring to promote the album, typically three UK tours a year.

The type and quality of the music is, of course, an important element of appeal, but the image of the band as conveyed through clothing, photographs and the video must be right for the target audience and the media platforms that carry the publicity.

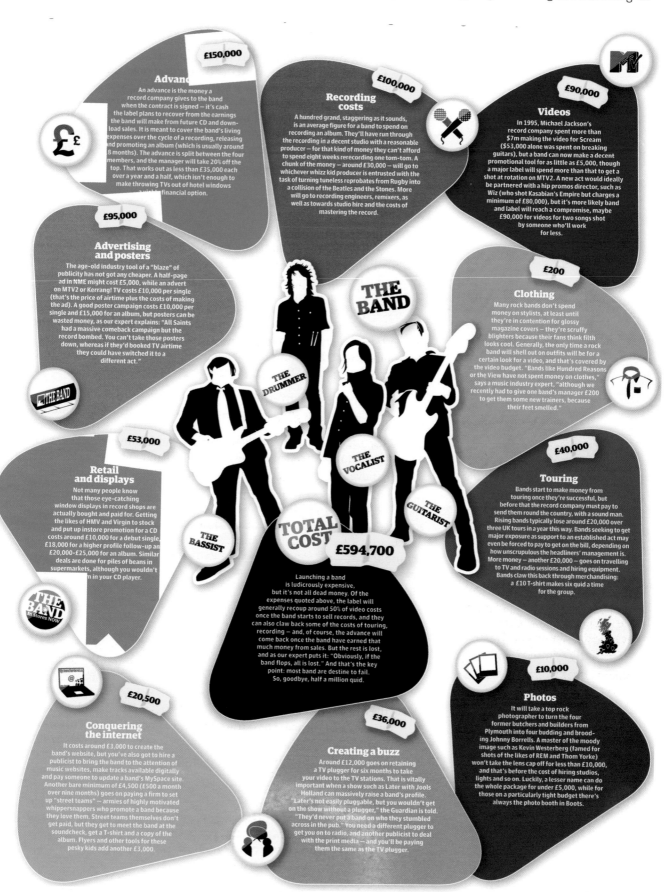

£150,000

Advance

An advance is the money a record company gives to the band when the contract is signed — it's cash the label plans to recover from the earnings the band will make from future CD and download sales. It is meant to cover the band's living expenses over the cycle of a recording, releasing and promoting an album (which is usually around 18 months). The advance is split between the four members, and the manager will take 20% off the top. That works out as less than £35,000 each over a year and a half, which isn't enough to make throwing TVs out of hotel windows a viable financial option.

£100,000

Recording costs

A hundred grand, staggering as it sounds, is an average figure for a band to spend on recording an album. They'll have run through the recording in a decent studio with a reasonable producer — for that kind of money they can't afford to spend eight weeks rerecording one tom-tom. A chunk of the money — around £30,000 — will go to whichever whizz kid producer is entrusted with the task of turning tuneless reprobates from Rugby into a collision of the Beatles and the Stones. More will go to recording engineers, remixers, as well as towards studio hire and the costs of mastering the record.

£90,000

Videos

In 1995, Michael Jackson's record company spent more than $7m making the video for Scream ($53,000 alone was spent on breaking guitars), but a band can now make a decent promotional tool for as little as £5,000, though a major label will spend more than that to get a shot at rotation on MTV2. A new act would ideally be partnered with a hip promos director, such as Wiz (who shot Kasabian's Empire but charges a minimum of £80,000), but it's more likely band and label will reach a compromise, maybe £90,000 for videos for two songs shot by someone who'll work for less.

£95,000

Advertising and posters

The age-old industry tool of a "blaze" of publicity has not got any cheaper. A half-page ad in NME might cost £5,000, while an advert on MTV2 or Kerrang! TV costs £10,000 per single (that's the price of airtime plus the costs of making the ad). A good poster campaign costs £10,000 per single and £15,000 for an album, but posters can be wasted money, as our expert explains: "All Saints had a massive comeback campaign but the record bombed. You can't take those posters down, whereas if they'd booked TV airtime they could have switched it to a different act."

£200

Clothing

Many rock bands don't spend money on stylists, at least until they're in contention for glossy magazine covers — they're scruffy blighters because their fans think filth looks cool. Generally, the only time a rock band will shell out on outfits will be for a certain look for a video, and that's covered by the video budget. "Bands like Hundred Reasons or the View have not spent money on clothes," says a music industry expert, "although we recently had to give one band's manager £200 to get them some new trainers, because their feet smelled."

£53,000

Retail and displays

Not many people know that those eye-catching window displays in record shops are actually bought and paid for. Getting the likes of HMV and Virgin to stock and put up instore promotion for a CD costs around £10,000 for a debut single, £18,000 for a higher profile follow-up and £20,000-£25,000 for an album. Similar deals are done for piles of beans in supermarkets, although you wouldn't want them in your CD player.

£40,000

Touring

Bands start to make money from touring once they're successful, but before that the record company must pay to send them round the country, with a sound man. Rising bands typically lose around £20,000 over three UK tours in a year this way. Bands seeking to get major exposure as support to an established act may even be forced to pay to get on the bill, depending on how unscrupulous the headliners' management is. More money — another £20,000 — goes on travelling to TV and radio sessions and hiring equipment. Bands claw this back through merchandising: a £10 T-shirt makes six quid a time for the group.

THE BAND

THE DRUMMER

THE VOCALIST

THE GUITARIST

THE BASSIST

TOTAL COST

£594,700

Launching a band is ludicrously expensive, but it's not all dead money. Of the expenses quoted above, the label will generally recoup around 50% of video costs once the band starts to sell records, and they can also claw back some of the costs of touring, recording — and, of course, the advance will come back once the band have earned that much money from sales. But the rest is lost, and as our expert puts it: "Obviously, if the band flops, all is lost." And that's the key point: most band are destine to fail. So, goodbye, half a million quid.

£20,500

Conquering the internet

It costs around £3,000 to create the band's website, but you've also got to hire a publicist to bring the band to the attention of music websites, make tracks available digitally and pay someone to update a band's MySpace site. Another bare minimum of £4,500 (£500 a month over nine months) goes on paying a firm to set up "street teams" — armies of highly motivated whippersnappers who promote a band because they love them. Street teams themselves don't get paid, but they get to meet the band at the soundcheck, get a T-shirt and a copy of the album. Flyers and other tools for these pesky kids add another £3,000.

£36,000

Creating a buzz

Around £12,000 goes on retaining a TV plugger for six months to take your video to the TV stations. That is vitally important when a show such as Later with Jools Holland can massively raise a band's profile. "Later's not easily pluggable, but you wouldn't get on the show without a plugger," the Guardian is told. "They'd never put a band on who they stumbled across in the pub." You need a different plugger to get you on to radio, and another publicist to deal with the print media — and you'll be paying them the same as the TV plugger.

£10,000

Photos

It will take a top rock photographer to turn the four former butchers and builders from Plymouth into four budding and brooding Johnny Borrells. A master of the moody image such as Kevin Westerberg (famed for shots of the likes of REM and Thom Yorke) won't take the lens cap off for less than £10,000, and that's before the cost of hiring studios, lights and so on. Luckily, a lesser name can do the whole package for under £5,000, while for those on a particularly tight budget there's always the photo booth in Boots.

Fig. 5.2 *The high cost of selling out by Dave Simpson, the* Guardian/*Friday June 29 2007*

As you can see from the illustration, advertisements on MTV or *Kerrang!* and in I, video on MTV, a written piece in *NME* and a poster campaign are all part of the marketing mix. Creating a website for the band, making the tracks available and even using fans to promote the band over social networking sites for the reward of band merchandise and other freebies seeks to communicate with internet users. Finally, the marketing would involve using paid 'pluggers', separate ones for each medium, to get the band on radio and television programmes and coverage in the print media.

Media in action

Plugs and pluggers

In marketing terms, plugging means to gain favourable publicity for a product or programme. Many talk programmes on radio and television offer the opportunity for participants to plug their film, new programme, book or tour in conversation with the host. Newspapers and magazines do the same. Stars in films are required, as part of their contract, to do the rounds of the media, providing interviews and reawakening awareness and interest in potential audiences. This is mutually beneficial, providing content for the text and publicity for the new media product.

Plugging on the internet

We hear a lot about how bands and artists are discovered through the internet, one of the first stories being that of the Arctic Monkeys who were supposedly publicised by fans uploading the demo CDs that had been handed out at gigs by the band. This created a buzz that eventually drew the attention of *NME* and Radio 1 and in January 2006, their debut album became the fastest selling debut album in UK chart history.

Thinking about media

■ How much of the plugging on the internet is genuine sharing and how much is paid for covertly by marketeers?

Investigating media

To help you focus on the range of opportunities for marketing across the media, consider the following scenario:

As part of a government health campaign to encourage college students (18–22) to learn to cook and eat healthy food, Jamie Oliver has been approached to front a series of television programmes, to be broadcast on Channel 4, which will also be available as vodcasts.

Plan the marketing campaign:

■ Where would you place broadcast (television and radio) advertisements?
■ How would you use e-media?
■ Where would you place print advertisements?
■ Where would you use posters?
■ How might you create a buzz?

If you think that Jamie Oliver might need re-branding to appeal to a college student audience, choose another presenter.

Case study

Maintaining a brand

O_2 UK is part of Telefónica O_2 Europe which comprises mobile network operators in the UK, Ireland and Slovakia along with integrated fixed/mobile businesses in Germany and the Czech Republic.

Since its launch in 2002, the UK's leading mobile operator O_2 has always maintained a consistent vision for its brand. Its mission 'To put customers at the heart of everything we do' and brand values are central to all marketing and communications.

Fig. 5.3 O_2 logo

Brand

O_2's brand values, which are reflected through all marketing activity, are listed as:

'*Bold*
We are fresh, surprising and distinctive
We are confident, but not arrogant, continually coming up with new and exciting ideas that are practical and relevant to customers.
We are an energetic brand, full of life.

Open
We are candid in communications – we tell it like it is.
We are never secretive.
We communicate openly and explore new opportunities for our customers.

Trusted
We understand customers.
We are accurate and truthful and never over-claim.
We have an inseparable relationship with our customers and always aim to be helpful, supportive and responsive.
We are never strident, but instead we listen to customers.

Clear
We make highly complex technology simple to understand and easy to use.
We are clear and straightforward in communications, avoiding industry jargon.'

Advertising

Of course, the key brand assets (the logo, blue graduation and bubbles) are present in the vast majority of communication channels. O_2 pays for direct advertising across the media to promote its product portfolio. From the start, customers rather than products have been at the heart of O_2's approach. Rather than treating products as technical gizmos, or tariffs as tactical one-offs, O_2's communications wrap them in the brand idea. This is intended not only to create consumer-focused propositions that are of genuine interest and relevance, but also to drive positive associations with the brand. Each proposition is developed by marketing and carried into other areas – so the same idea and creative materials are used across the board.

At the time of writing, BBC Worldwide has announced a deal with O_2 allowing O_2 to add to its O_2 Active Portal as mobile content highlights from BBC shows such as *Alan Partridge*, *Doctor Who* and *Little Britain* to O_2 customers in the UK. The deal will shortly add highlights from the shows, along with branded wallpapers and ringtones, to the O_2 Active portal, which already offers customers news services, games, chat tools and music downloads, charged by the cost of the data used.

Sponsorship

O_2 engages in dynamic sponsorship partnerships, such as The O_2. The former Millennium Dome was previously regarded as a white elephant but has since been turned into the most successful sponsorship project in the UK. The O_2 enables O_2 to reach its 18 million customers and turn them into fans through engaging entertainment experiences.

O_2 also cites Arsenal football club and the England and Ireland Rugby Teams on its impressive sponsorship portfolio. In addition, the O_2 Wireless Festival and other grass-root activities have brought national and international exposure for the O_2 brand. With its past and existing sponsorships, O_2 has gone beyond simply 'logo badging' and has created more interactive experiences for its customers.

O_2 UK is an example of a brand that has a powerful and trusted consumer presence in our daily lives. It is a leading mobile communications company, which provides services, games and downloads in addition to traditional network offerings. Through its marketing activity, O_2 maintains a visible presence in popular music and sporting events.

- In what ways do their activities reflect their brand values?
- Research and view some advertisements for O_2 and some of their films and podcasts. What audience(s) are they targeting?
- How do the trademark O_2 logo, bubbles and the colour blue reflect their brand?

Media in action

O_2 understands the importance of protecting its brand, which extends to its brand imagery – the O_2 bubbles – and also its brand values (see Case study and O_2 website – the address for O_2's website can be found on the e-resources).

Investigating media

Choose another mobile provider, Orange, Vodafone, T-Mobile, Virgin Mobile or another of your choice and research their brand values, advertising, sponsorship and any other promotional activities across the media. Watch some of their advertisements.

- How far are they different from O_2?
- What audience(s) are they targeting?
- What is their trademark imagery and how does this reflect their brand values?

The advertisement opposite for Orange appeared in the *Guardian Guide* to entertainment in the music section.

- What does this advertisement tell us about the media institutions involved?
- Explore some of the ways in which this texts communicates with its target audience.

🔍 *End of topic summary:*

- Advertising is an element of a marketing strategy that involves a range of strategies, techniques and tools to attract and appeal to audiences.

- Media institutions seek to promote the positive values of their brand.

- Unit 2 briefs often call for promotional productions. Marketing and advertising techniques and tools should be both researched and applied creatively.

Fig. 5.4 *Orange advertisement in* The Guardian Guide *August 25–31 2007*

6 Approaching the examination

AQA Examiner's tip

Remind yourself about:

- Media Languages, including the codes and conventions of narrative and genre
- Media Representations
- Media Audiences
- Media Institutions.

You also learned that ideology and values are associated with representations, audiences and institutions and are carried within texts by the media language.

Approaching the unseen text

You will be assessed on your ability to demonstrate knowledge and understanding of media concepts and contexts. This means that you will be marked on how well you can analyse any media text, from any media platform.

You learned about the media concepts in Topic 3 and about the contexts in Topics 1 and 2 and you used your understanding of concepts and contexts when you researched, produced and evaluated your practical coursework.

The contexts are the platforms on which a text is presented and you have studied the similarities and differences between these in terms of how they are produced and the ways in which the audience respond to different forms of media.

You won't be asked to do anything you haven't done before but there are two big differences. You are dealing with an unfamiliar text, one you are unlikely to have ever seen and you are dealing with it in a specified time in examination conditions.

Questions you should ask

What sort of text will it be and how will it be presented?

The unseen text could be a moving image text, an audio based text, a print text or an e-media text. At the moment a website will be presented in a printed form but in future it may be possible that websites and other interactive media will be made available electronically. Moving image and audio texts will be provided by AQA in DVD format.

How much time should I spend on my responses to the unseen text?

The Investigating Media examination lasts for 2 hours with 1 hour 15 minutes spent on Section A, response to the unseen text. This section accounts for 48 marks of the total of 80 for the whole paper. You should spend 15 minutes on reading time during which you observe, read or listen and make notes, and 1 hour answering the questions, 15 minutes on each one.

If the unseen is a moving image text it is likely to be between 30 seconds and 3 minutes in length and will be shown three times. You are advised not to make any notes during the first viewing. There will be pauses for making notes between the viewings.

How should I approach the questions?

The questions follow a familiar pattern, each one encouraging you to show your understanding of a media concept by applying it to the text. It is important to read through all the questions before starting to plan your answers, as you don't want to repeat your ideas or use the same examples more than once. Each question is marked out of 12 so make sure that you divide your ideas and examples evenly. An examiner cannot give more than 12 marks for a question so make sure that you are not using too many ideas and examples in one answer and not enough in another.

When you are sure what you want to include for each question and have made some notes, start writing in the examination booklet.

The markscheme is divided into four levels with level four being the highest. To get into this level your answers must show that you thoroughly understand each concept and can discuss it in relation to the unseen text. You must give detail from the text to show evidence of your understanding. You will use media terminology when expressing your ideas and giving examples from the text. To get the highest marks in this level you must be able to explore a little further than the actual text by moving beyond it to discuss further media ideas and issues.

What is meant by media terminology, ideas and issues?

Terminology: key words relating to the key concepts and the technical terms that relate to media language.

Ideas and issues: theories of semiotics, narrative, genre, representation and audience. Information about the media industry.

What questions will I be asked?

These are the questions for Section A on the AQA specimen paper. Actual examination questions are likely to be identical or very similar in wording.

1 Media Forms – Discuss the codes and conventions in the construction of this text.

2 Media Representations – Consider the representations of people and places in this text.

3 Media Institutions – What does this text tell us about the media institutions involved?

4 Media Audiences – Explore some of the ways in which this text communicates with its target audiences.

■ **Link**

You have seen these questions before at the end of Topic 3. All the Thinking and Investigating activities in Topic 3 were preparation for these questions.

AQA Examiner's tip

There is no 'right' answer to each question as there are different readings available in media texts. What you should do is support your own reading with examples from the text. Be bold and explore the text and any ideas around it.

■ Case study

Study each of these texts and make notes for each question. The first one is the text for the specimen paper and is from the e-media platform. There is also one moving image text and one print text.

Here are some ideas about the content you could use in your answer to each question. None of the answers is complete. You should improve them in the ways suggested.

1 Media Forms – Livelistings

Figure 6.1 is a screenshot of the homepage of a website that shows the codes and conventions of this form. To see the latest version of the full home page, go to www.livelistingsmag.com/. This will be well worth your time as there are many other interesting features to notice as you scroll down the page. The technical codes used include the title and the strapline for Livelistings, the producer of the text. The layout consists of columns of content and one of advertisements on the right-hand side of the page. It has the conventions of a homepage with headings, headlines and thumbnail photographs relating to each item with navigation opportunities to further pages and information that continues the narrative. This narrative form is typical of homepages and it shares similarities with the contents pages of magazines. The column at the left-hand side gives a summary of the content of the Livelistings website with links to take

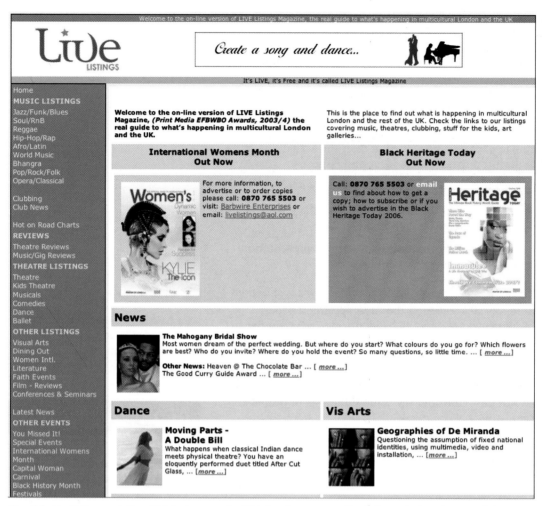

Fig. 6.1 *Livelistings website which features on the AQA Specimen paper. Carefully study the print-out of the Livelistings website homepage for March 2007. Instruction on the examination paper. 'You should bear in mind that the website is interactive, enabling the user to follow hyperlinks to further pages.'*

the user straight through to specific content, for example music or theatre listings. Colour and different fonts are used and the copy for each thumbnail can pose an enigma to interest the user in following the narrative. The page is busy with information showing the variety of activities available in London. There are direct advertisements placed by London venues in the right- hand column and images of the covers of Livelistings print magazines that can be purchased. There is information for potential subscribers to print magazines and for advertisers on how to contact the institution. This is typical of an online version of a print magazine.

■ Choose examples from Fig. 6.1 or the current Livelistings homepage illustrate each point made about the content of the page.

■ What terminology and media ideas have been used in the tests.

■ What other websites does the Livelistings homepage remind you of?

2 Media representations – *Blackpool*

Go to www.nelsonthornes.com\aqagce\media.htm and click on the link to the supporting resources. Watch the opening sequence to the series, which shows representations of a family, a couple and their teenage children and of Blackpool, a seaside town in Northern England. The representation of Blackpool is one of glamour, conveyed by the clothes, the limousine, the bright lights, the casino and the song, *Viva Las Vegas*, which links to Las Vegas, the US gambling city by association. This gives the idea that Blackpool is like, or trying to be like Las Vegas, reinforced by the family singing along to the Elvis Presley song. We see fairly conventional representations of the two women, getting ready for a big night out, putting on nail varnish and checking their appearance. The father is shown as rather flashy and pleased with himself, dressed in a white suit, admiring his appearance in the mirror and leading the singing party down the stairs to the waiting limousine. The teenage girl is on her mobile and the teenage boy goes outside to smoke. These are examples of conventional representations of young people. The family seem happy together as they run down the steps of their house and sit together in the chauffeur-driven limousine drinking champagne on the journey to the casino. Blackpool landmarks are shown during the journey to the casino, which establishes the location as a place for enjoyment and amusement. The mise-en-scène for most of the extract is light, bright and happy with the characters almost dancing to the soundtrack and the neon-lit and colourful Blackpool. The mood changes when the family arrive for the party. There is a group of people, dressed in dark clothes, with stern faces that contrast with the family's evening wear and high spirits. They are demonstrating about the casino. This contrast represents the beginning of a conflict between different people. We have seen that the hedonistic values and the ostentatious consumption of the style of the four leading characters are not shared by all.

Choose examples from the text to illustrate each point made about the representations available in this sequence.

- What terminology and media ideas have been used here? What else might you include?

- What other texts does it remind you of?

Fig. 6.2 *The representation of Blackpool in the BBC musical drama series* Blackpool

3 Media Institutions – *The Memory Keeper's Daughter*

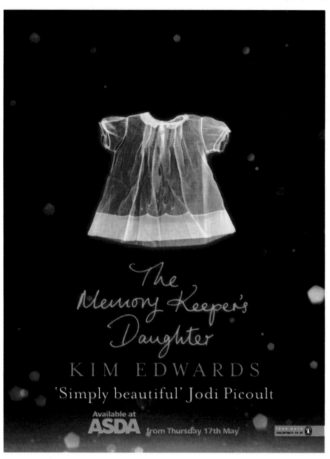

Fig. 6.3 *A full page advertisement for a Penguin book,* The Memory Keeper's Daughter *in Saga Magazine, August 2007*

This is an example of synergy between institutions as the advertisement draws attention to and promotes four different commodities. One is the book itself with the dominant image and copy being the book title, the author's name and the central image of the transparent child's dress representing a possible theme of the book, some memory of childhood perhaps. (The connotations of the dress, its transparency and the dark background with its hazy planets/bubbles could be discussed further.) The logo of the publisher, the orange penguin, stands for tradition and modernity combined. The wording, which would be on the book itself indicates that the book must be worth reading as it has been recommended by the best-selling author Jodi Picoult. The advertisement also includes a suggestion that readers should buy their copy from Asda. Whilst the advertisement is for a certain book, it also promotes Asda supermarket, Jodi Picoult's novels, and other Penguin books to readers. Interestingly, something that this book and Jodi Picoult have in common is that they have both featured on *Richard and Judy's* book club, which is part of their Channel 4 afternoon television show. Perhaps this advertisement, which appears in *Saga* magazine, aimed at the over 50s, assumes that the readers watch afternoon television?

■ What other texts does this advertisement remind you of?

■ What terminology and media ideas have been used here? What else might you include?

4 Media audiences – notes for livelistings, *Blackpool*, advert in *Saga*

Livelistings

Target audience(s): Londoners, ethnic groups, people with a multi-cultural outlook, singles and parents, consumers of arts and cultural events.

Style of address: friendly and welcoming; intertextual references; rhetorical questions; clear, brief information with navigation links for more; range of events to appeal to different tastes; second-person informal address; neutral unsensational mode of address.

Blackpool

Target audience(s): BBC One drama audiences, weekday audience more experimental than weekend audiences, audiences for British drama , familiarity with actors' or writer's work, young adults to middle-aged audiences who enjoy humour and quirky genres, audience familiar with the Elvis song.

Style of address: conventional openings with title and the writer's and leading actors' names; unusual style with the characters singing along to the soundtrack; song is familiar and helps audience by unfolding the narrative; exciting and fast-moving; easy to follow narrative with the location and the characters established clearly.

Advertisement in *Saga* magazine

Target audience: *Saga* readers – over 50s, probably retired; readers of novels; viewers of Channel 4 afternoon talk shows; conformers, people who want to read the recommended books.

Style of address: a direct address; ironic intertextuality 'Buy it Today' echoes hard sell techniques.

Choose examples to illustrate each point made about audiences in these texts.

■ What terminology and media ideas have been used here? What else might you include?

When you are confident about how to organise your analysis, work through all four questions for each text.

After completing all four answers for all three texts look carefully over your work.

■ Have you discussed details in the text for each question?

■ Have you used media terminology accurately?

Now look at the markscheme for each question in Section A and highlight what level you think you have achieved.

◤ Preparing for the examination

In a sense you have been preparing for the examination throughout this book. You analysed media texts from all the media platforms when you learned about media forms and media concepts and you used planning and analysis tools when investigating the texts in your case study. But don't stop at what you've covered in class. Use the media studies perspective on texts you come across in your daily life. When you read magazines, watch television, visit social websites, play interactive games or any other media activity, investigate and analyse the experience. The more you practise applying your media knowledge and understanding, the better you will impress the examiner when they read your answers.

Whatever the text you should ask yourself the following questions:

■ What does it remind you of? Think within the form and across the media.

■ What are the codes and conventions used in the text? Think within the form and across the media.

■ Is there intertextuality, references explicit or implicit to other texts?

■ What is being represented and how are the representations constructed?

■ How is the audience positioned and addressed?

■ What opportunities are there for interactivity? What does this say about the relationship between the audience and the producing institution(s)?

■ Link

Revise the work you did for Stages 1, 2, 3 and 4 of the study in Topic 4 – The Cross-Media Study.

■ Media in action

The examination paper says 'You are required to:

- ensure that text is legible and that spelling, punctuation and grammar are accurate so that meaning is clear
- select and use a form and style of writing appropriate to purpose and to complex subject matter
- organise information clearly and coherently, using specialist vocabulary where appropriate.'

AQA Examiner's tip

You must read the questions very carefully and choose the one that suits you best. You must answer the question that is asked. Merely re-writing the facts about the texts and topic you have studied won't earn you high marks.

■ Presenting your case study in the examination

You have spent some time making a case study and should be very confident about your knowledge and understanding. However, the skill of writing an essay in an examination is in selecting and organising the right material to answer the question and expressing your ideas within a tight time frame.

In Section B of the examination you will be assessed on how well you can demonstrate knowledge and understanding of your case study and the media products and processes associated with it. The products are of course the texts within your case study and the processes are the ways in which meanings and responses across the media are created and responded to by producers and audiences.

There are two questions in Section B of the examination paper and you must answer one of them. You have to write one essay in 45 minutes. Within this time you should spend between 5 and 10 minutes selecting a question and planning your answer. The quality of your written communication is assessed in this part of the examination, so structuring your ideas and writing clearly and accurately is very important too.

The questions won't refer to your specific topic but your answer must give examples from your cross-media study. If you have done more than one case study you could draw on both.

Analysing the questions

Let's look at how you should go about answering the questions on the specimen examination paper.

Question A

Explore the ways that audiences consume and respond to media products across different media platforms.

Support your answer with reference to examples from your case study.

1 **Break down the question so as to understand its demands**

Audiences – You should focus on audiences. You're not asked about producers in this question.

Explore the ways – You should write about at least two ways; one won't do. You're asked not just to provide facts but to engage in a discussion that might include raising several points.

Consume and respond to media products – You should show how audiences engage with the texts, how they use the technology and how active they are in the reception of and interaction with texts.

Different media platforms – You must refer to texts from different platforms.

Support your answer with examples – You must show that you have studied texts in detail.

2 **Plan the content for the answer**

You know a lot about your case study but this question only asks about the ways audiences engage with texts. You will have covered this and need to remind yourself what they are. You need to identify the audiences.

You need at least one example of each way and at least one example from each media platform.

3 Plan an argument or approach

What are the differences in the ways audiences respond to your case study across different platforms? Which ways are the most popular? Why is this so?

6 Anything else to add?

Are there any changes in the ways audiences are responding to the media products? Why might this be so? Is it because of changes in technology, any other contextual changes?

Media theories, media ideas and media terminology.

Your response can gain a maximum of 32 marks and, like Section A, the markscheme is divided into four levels. When the examiner marks your essay they will look at the qualities revealed in your work and first of all decide which level best fits your response. Then they will assign a mark within that level.

Put yourself in the role of the examiner and read the following extract from a possible answer to Question A. I have not included actual texts or facts and figures but have indicated where they would be. Assume that the references to the case study products are included in some detail and look at these extracts alongside the markscheme. Decide what level could be achieved if the answer were complete.

This candidate has made a case study within the documentary topic and answered Question A. To condense the answer for the purposes of this textbook, where the student provided specific elaboration on a subject. This is omitted and indicated using square brackets.

Case study

'Documentaries are generally moving image products and have a large presence on the broadcast platform with dedicated channels such as National Geographic and Animal Planet channels on Sky and Virgin. Documentaries feature in the schedules of the five mainstream television channels where expositional, observational and reflexive forms and hybrid varieties are screened. *[answer includes facts about scheduling from the case study]*

'One of the reasons that people watch documentaries is to gain information about the world around them. Audiences also get pleasure from being able to see through "the window on the world" and view places and life that few could experience themselves. *[answer includes an example of a scene from a documentary that informs and gives aesthetic pleasure]* So audiences watch some documentaries such as *[answer names examples]* to learn, to satisfy curiosity or for general interest. In the contemporary media landscape individuals can do more than just watch a television programme or listen to a radio documentary. They can take the opportunities offered *[answer gives examples of red-button interactive or links at the end of a product]* to visit a website, to send up for an information pack or follow up their interest by reading an article in a magazine. *[answer gives an example of synergy of moving image, print and internet]*

'Audiences can participate in documentaries in a number of ways and television documentaries often feature ordinary people in everyday situations. *[answer gives example]* We can identify with these people and learn something about ourselves or the situation *[answer gives some detail from one of the case study texts]* or often take the role of voyeurs. Some documentary techniques, by shaping the narrative through editing to give a predominant reading of a person, place or event, lead audiences into taking a particular view of something or someone that could be a mediated view of what actually happened *[answer provides a detailed example of the techniques and discusses how audience might respond]*

'Popular hybrid documentaries *[answer names a format and outlines the content]* have a presence across the media. Often the people who feature in these "shows" appear in spin-off broadcast programmes and provide content for magazines that cater for a similar audience. *[answer gives an example with some detail of the links in content]*

'Extra footage and interviews are accessible on the internet, hyperlinked through news browsers or on specific websites. Audiences can upload their opinions to these sites and they can appear on text or telephone to express their views on the spin-off shows. There are opportunities to download related material, updates and highlights on mobile phones.

'New digital technology means that audiences can make and present documentaries themselves *[the answer briefly outlines the technology]*. Whether it be on video sharing sites or by sending material documenting an event to a traditional media, user generated content has changed the top-down reception of documentary products. *[answer gives an example]*

'Whatever the origin of the documentary on whatever platform it occurs or whoever produced it, the product has been mediated by the producer and can never be more than an interpretation of reality.'

We'll go through the same procedure for the second question.

Question B

Write a talk to present to media producers making a case for using a range of different media platforms to reach consumers.

Support your answer with reference to examples from your case study.

1 Breaking down the question

Producers – You should focus your answer on producers of media products. You are asked to address them directly in the form of a talk.

Making a case – You should give reasons to convince producers of the advantages of different media platforms.

Different media platforms – You must refer to each platform and explain the advantages of using more than one.

Reach consumers – You must refer to how well each platform communicates with audiences.

Support your answer with examples – You must show that you have studied texts in detail

2 Plan the content for your answer

You know a lot about your case study but this question only asks you to explain the advantages of broadcast, print and e-media platforms for producers. You need to identify who the producers are. The question allows for the producer to be a large institution that already

AQA Examiner's tip

There is no 'right' answer to either question. The views you put forward and the examples you give from your own case study are individual to you. These case study examples merely provide a guide to one possible approach to each question.

has a presence across the media or for a number of producers who may be using only one or two platforms.

You could discuss the commercial opportunities or promotional opportunities of each platform considering sponsorship, intertextuality and synergy.

You need at least three examples of products that have a presence across the media and be able to give details of the advantages of each platform for reaching consumers. You will need to identify who the consumers are.

3 **Plan an argument or approach**

You must present your essay in the form of a talk. You need to make your case clearly and strongly. Think about how you will address your audience and how you will organise your talk. Use the second person 'you', or if you wish to talk in the role of a media producer you could address your audience as 'we'. Explain in your introduction what you are going to talk about, and then make each point clearly giving examples.

4 **Anything else to add**

Are there any changes in the ways producers reach consumers? Why might this be so? Is it because of changes in technology, any other contextual changes?

Media theories, media ideas and media terminology.

Put yourself in the role of the examiner and read the following extract from a possible answer to Question B. I have not included actual texts or facts and figures but have indicated where they would be. Assume that the references to the case study products are included in some detail and look at these extracts alongside the markscheme. Decide what level could be achieved if the answer were complete.

This candidate has made a case study within the topic of Sport and answered Question B.

In this essay the references to a particular sport and specific media products have been omitted. However, a number of ideas about sport across the media have been included. Again, square brackets indicate where in the original answer more specific examples were given.

Case study

'Welcome everyone to my presentation where I shall provide the rationale on why you should use a number of platforms to present your media products. Let's look at who your audiences are, what they are interested in and how they access the media for sports products. *[answer states what the case study is about – what the products are]*

'Established media audiences for sport, those who enjoy watching major sport competitions will always consume broadcast sport on television and radio. This will always be the most important way of reaching this audience and the rights to live broadcasting are a competitive and costly business. Deep pockets are needed to buy the broadcasting rights and traditional terrestrial channels like BBC and ITV have been outbid by Sky and Setanta. *[example]* Nevertheless, the programmes of highlights shown on the terrestrial channels are appreciated by family audiences and those who only view free-TV. *[example]* However, sponsorship and advertising revenue helps commercial television channels fund the presentation of live sport. *[example]* Advertisers will always be attracted to broadcast channels that provide them with audiences.

'Audiences want up-to-the-minute and background information. They want to hear this from the people involved such as sports personalities. Sports personalities have an important role to play. *[example]* Information can be provided on the broadcast platform through interactive facilities and breaking news about scores on television *[example]* but don't forget radio. Radio is a medium well suited to live sport for its cheapness and immediacy. Audiences can consume live commentaries and chat while on the move or engaged in another activity. Radio conveys a feeling of intimacy with listeners. BBC Radio 5 Live and Talk Sport cover live sports giving commentaries and opinions as it happens *[example]* and local radio stations cover local sporting activities and events, fostering a sense of community in audiences. Radio phone-ins allow audiences to participate in the discourse of sport. Radio coverage can be accessed through the internet as can live coverage, videos and features. *[example]*

'Sports news and information, including breaking news is ideal for the internet or mobile technology. Younger audiences, particularly, use their phones for sport updates and video on portable technology is growing. *[example]* While there is a slow take up of other video media forms on mobile phones, sporting moments work well on the smaller screen. *[example from case study]* Receiving sport in this personalised way and being able to pass on and share it with others is popular with audiences seeking to keep in touch with events and with each other.

'Sports fans consume DVDs of matches and competitions of historic importance and video material about sports stars. Similar products can provide training and coaching skills for some sports. *[example from case study]* Interactive computer games and coaching videos on the internet broaden the scope for attracting consumers to sports products. *[example from case study]* Dedicated websites for sports, sports fans, fanzines and a sharing of views reach a growing number of consumers. *[example]* The e-platform is an important means of communicating with active audiences.

'The oldest media platform, communicating by the printed word, is not to be forgotten. All national newspapers, red tops, mid-market and qualities feature sport daily and stories about sports personalities and sports business are covered in other parts of the newspaper. *[examples relating to case study]* In the magazine market, sports titles have a strong presence and can appeal to a range of audiences. *[examples relating to case study]*As media producers, whether you have the rights to live sports events and/or access to archive material you should spread your material as widely as possible to maximise communication with consumers.

Investigating media

Plan and write your own answers to Question A and Question B.

Preparing for the examination

You have been analysing media products and processes, meanings and responses throughout your course and have made a detailed study of a particular topic across the media. Keep up to date with what is happening in the area of your case study, particularly noting any changes in the technology of production and consumption. The more engaged you are with your chosen topic and the more ideas you have about the texts within it, the more you will impress the examiner.

Whatever the topic you should be able to answer the following questions:

▪ How much does the content of the texts change across different technologies?

▪ How important is the print media in your topic?

▪ How important is the role of the internet in the production and reception of your topic?

▪ How far does the topic you have studied rely on broadcast or other moving image platforms?

▪ What are the likely future developments in your topic? Think about producers and audiences.

💡 *End of topic summary:*

- The examination consists of two sections, Section A and Section B.

- In Section A there are four compulsory questions on an unseen text. Each question is marked out of 12.

- The questions ask you to focus on media forms, codes and conventions; media representations; media institutions; media audiences, values and ideologies.

- Spend 15 minutes thinking about the text and planning how to answer each question before starting to write any answers.

- In Section B you write about your cross-media study. This response is marked out of 32.

- You have to show what you know about media products and processes by writing a sustained response using your case study to support your views.

AQA Examiner's tip

Don't try to write about everything you know and every text you have covered. If you do this, your answer will be generalised and superficial as you won't have time to develop the ideas that are at the heart of each question. Select detailed examples that you know well, and express your ideas clearly, taking the perspective asked for in the question.

7 Research and planning

For Unit 2 of the course, you will be expected to produce two practical productions from a brief set by the board. You will also present a folder of pre-production work, and an evaluation. In the interests of maintaining creativity and originality in your interpretations of these briefs (more about this in Topic 9) three exemplar groups of cross-platform briefs have been set here. These will be used to demonstrate a number of aspects of research and planning, production and evaluation – all important stages of your work.

💡 🔍 Exemplar briefs

Brief A

Broadcast: create a one-minute trailer advertising a new reality TV show where college-age students train to teach their younger peers in a school.

Print: write the lead article on the launch of the show for the front page of an existing weekly newspaper for a) children, b) teachers.

E-media: design one page of a website for the show featuring a three-minute podcast update of the week's key events.

Brief B

Broadcast: create the opening for an unusual new TV detective series, including pre-credit sequence, title sequence and one minute of the actual start.

Print: design three teaser magazine advertisements to appear in a TV guide in the run-up to the series launch.

E-media: design the first two pages of a website designed to add value to the audience experience of the series by making good use of the interactive features offered by the medium.

Brief C

Broadcast: create two 30-second TV advertisements OR a sequence of five radio adverts designed to promote an environmental message.

Print: create a 'photo-story' two-page advertisement for a teen magazine targeted at boys or girls to promote an environmental message.

E-media: design three pages of a website for use by families to help them work towards a 'greener' lifestyle.

How do I choose the best brief for me?

Your decision about which brief you are going to follow should be based on a careful weighing up of the following three factors:

- your level of interest in the brief itself
- any strengths you already have in particular areas of media production, or the desire to learn a new skill in a media technology that appeals to you
- availability of technologies to you either at your centre or elsewhere.

This is why the choice is so individual. Your tutor should be able to offer you some guidance, but you'll need to make the final decision yourself.

Investigating media

Look at the grid below, completed by an AS student:

Brief A	Appeal?	Skills?	Technology?
Broadcast	I like the idea. I watch a lot of reality TV and feel comfortable with the genre	I made a video text for GCSE Media so have some experience with filming, but not editing as this was done by someone else in my group	I don't have my own DV camera, but am studying in a school, so can film using a school camera on the premises. I would edit on the iMac in school
Print	I'm not really familiar with this type of text but could ask around for help	My written English is good, so I could take advantage of this for a journalistic piece	I don't know what I would produce this on, as all I have is Word. I'll need to find out more about what's expected
E-media	I often use the websites of my favourite TV shows so have lots of ideas about what works and what doesn't	I've never done any web design before and it doesn't appeal to me that much. I like the idea of the podcast though	I don't have access to any web design programs at home, but I think we have a student version of Dreamweaver on the network at college

1. Which two parts of the brief would you advise this student to choose?

2. Draw and fill in a similar grid for yourself for Briefs B and C. Which two products would you choose to make, and why?

Research and planning

What sort of research should I be doing?

Quantitative research uses techniques such as polls and questionnaires to conduct market research. It is used quite a lot in the media industry to establish whether there is a market for a particular product were it to be made. This kind of research usually uses samples of people big enough to be statistically significant, as well as balancing factors such as age, gender, economic status and demographics to ensure a useful outcome. Such research is beyond the means of most AS Media students, and is not recommended here.

Qualitative research looks more into HOW the text should actually be presented to the audience and is much more appropriate for AS students. In the real industry this might include gauging audience responses to a test screening, discussions at production planning meetings and evaluation of the commercial and critical success of other products.

Link

For more information on research, see Topic 2, Researching Audiences.

Link

See Topics 1, 2 and 3 to revise the knowledge you will need.

AQA Examiner's tip

Effective research is crucial to the success of your final product. Simply glancing over a similar text, or even just assuming that since you are familiar with the type of product you will therefore be able to emulate it isn't good enough. This is one of the most common mistakes new students make when beginning practical media research.

Investigating media

Stage 1: Common case study

Read this case study of *Spiral*, which has been done for you. Using the questions asked during the study, write next to each point how you would address it if you were to make this broadcast media product.

For your purposes, it could take the following forms:

- Research into a topic you need to know about such as an environmental issue for Brief C, or some aspects of education for Brief A.
- Precise notes on the conventions and language of media forms, target audience, representations common across your media genre and platform, and institutional values. If you're unsure about any of these things, you can always revisit the relevant sections of Unit 1.
- Interviews with relevant persons in the industry.
- Discussion with your tutor or any member of a target audience about your ideas for your text.
- Finding out about the range of similar texts already available to media audiences and examining your own personal response to these.
- Analysing specific existing texts that have some similarity to what you intend to produce, and learning from them.

It is really worth while seeking out a product similar to your own and writing a case study of this text. This can throw up all sorts of considerations you wouldn't otherwise think through until the evaluation stage. What you can then do is to consider the implications of what you've found out from this text for your own product. At this stage it's worth applying the questions you came up with briefly to at least one other text to see how another media producer has handled some of the conceptual issues you've identified. Keep notes on all of this research – this is all valuable and worth marks for pre-production.

Case study

Pre-production research for the Broadcast Product from Brief B

Analysis of opening from Spiral, *a French detective series made by Canal Plus and screened on BBC4 during autumn 2006.*

Crime and fear of crime occupy an important space in the public imagination, and are therefore fertile ground for media producers trying to engage a mass audience. Crime affects political agendas and fear of crime can lead to social change. There is a proliferation of texts that deal with crime across all media forms and many genres are in existence.

Spiral seems to have a well-defined target audience for its UK showing. The decision to screen the programme on BBC4, a channel which by its own definition attempts to offer 'an intelligent alternative to mainstream TV' already suggests an audience who are middle class and educated. It was broadcast post-watershed, and run during the autumn season as are many high-profile new series. Such an audience may take pleasure in consuming programming with intellectual complexity, and are unlikely to be put off by subtitles. The target audience in France could of course be expected to be much broader, perhaps profiled similarly to the audience for a popular text in the UK such as *Cracker* or *Prime Suspect*. As a conventional detective genre text, it offers the audience **information**, as there is the satisfaction for the audience of following the progress of the investigation not usually conducted wholly in the public eye until trial. **Social interaction** may also be offered through the increasing familiarity of the audience with the main characters and **entertainment** is certainly present in the gruesome nature of the crimes.

- Who are my target audience, and how does this link with the scheduling of the programme?
- Can I find out the remit of my intended broadcast media institution, and will I be able to qualify how my product fits with their commissioning agenda?
- Can I use an audience model such as McQuail's Uses and Gratifications theory to explain the appeal of my product?

Link

Uses and Gratifications is explained in Topic 2, Audience and Genre.

A series of crane shots throughout the opening of *Spiral* establish the genre conventions and conventional invisible editing is used subsequently to allow the audience to focus on the dialogue between the Prosecutor and the Inspector, which is crucial in advancing the narrative. The crane shots are fluid and unflinching as they pass over the body.

- What will I show in my establishing shots?
- Will I need to feature dialogue, and if so do I need to write a script?

Location filming has taken place at night, signifying the unknown, and the audience may feel additional anxiety due to the disorienting effect of the strange camera angles.

- I don't have access to lighting kit, and my DV camera will not take good footage in low light conditions. I'll need to factor this in.
- What locations shall I choose to convey the right atmosphere?
- How ambitious should I be given my current level of camera skills, and can I still storyboard some interesting shots in spite of my lack of professional kit?

The positioning of the audience above the corpse is voyeuristic, and this is particularly significant since the woman is the clichéd vulnerable victim, who dies, we are told, 'because she was beautiful' (punishment of women for their sexual attractiveness is pervasive in this type of media text historically and many others).

- How conventional do I want to be in my representations?

The high-angled crane shots above the forensic scene that follows again privileges the viewer and allows them to feel part of the investigation. This is emphasised by the dialogue between characters – we are 'filled in' on all the relevant background information.

- How will I make sure my audience are drawn in?
- What devices, visual or aural, will I use to convey my narrative?

The male protagonist is given status by his physically high presence over the investigation scene and the low angle shot with which he is filmed; the establishing shot of Paris following the title sequence is grey and unglamorous, and the quick zoom creates intensity for the audience and rapidly draws them in.

- What types of shot will I use to construct my representations?

The female inspector who is introduced secondarily leads us to assume there will be a degree of sexual chemistry between the two main characters – a 'Mulder and Scully' dynamic, which is popular with contemporary audiences.

- Have I considered how to convince the audience my characters will be interesting in the long term, or even just to the end of the 'hour'?

■ Who will I cast in the main roles who will fit the parts convincingly?

The title sequence features a dark background reflecting the dark themes and serious tone of the programme, and the golden letters are reminiscent of a code or a puzzle that needs to be solved. This is accompanied by a soundtrack that uses strings (traditionally emotive and associated with drama and tension). A wooden percussion instrument connotes the ticking of a clock, which may again suggest drama and fits in well with the French title *Engrenages* (links between clockwork wheels). The importance of language as a sign system may be observed in the connotations of *Spiral*, which in English may connote a downward motion, a 'dance' or intricacy of plot. The French title implies more the efficient functioning of an investigative team.

■ What am I going to call my text and what will this suggest to the audience?

■ What can I do with my title sequence to make sure it contributes something to my text and is interesting for the audience?

That the genre conventions are so readily and quickly recognisable is interesting. Given that this text is produced by another European culture, we nonetheless rapidly recognise the format – a body is discovered, a forensic team arrive and provide information, a patriarchal figure suggests a motive for the crime. This may suggest cultural imperialism, or at least the sharing of generic codes across cultures by an industry keen to capitalise on successes observed elsewhere. Genre is a product of the dynamics between audience, industry and text and conventions are established over a period of time and numerous texts.

■ Will my text contribute something new to the genre, and what existing conventions will it use?

Genres can, of course, have a cultural function in the organising of ideas. The content of the crime drama can be cathartic for the audience, since it allows them to experience vicariously their fear of violent crime while watching the crimes being solved and society as a whole served by the detectives. The narrative in this episode opening appears conventionally to emphasise the brutality of those who commit crimes, while glorifying those who protect society and enforce our moral codes enshrined in law.

■ I've thought here about the appeals of the genre to the audience. How can I ensure these are firmly embedded in the text I produce?

The text references mainstream moral values and assumes these on the part of the audience. It exploits the audience's real fear of crime and glamorises it for entertainment purposes. We may have a morbid fear of crime, but ideologically it is very reassuring for us to experience the realities of crime demystified, stripped of their threat in the process of mediation and packaged so securely – and palatably – for our consumption.

■ I can use these points to introduce and frame my ideas in my evaluation.

Investigating media

Stage 2: Individual case study

Using the following as a checklist, write a similar analysis of a website, print media text or broadcast media text as research for either Brief A or Brief C.

Write the case study analysis first. It could be in note form if you prefer.

Consider:

■ the audience for your product

■ the institutional factors affecting production and consumption

■ use of the codes and conventions appropriate to the chosen platform and genre

■ the construction of representations and the meanings these have for the audience.

Read your case study through. What questions for your own intended product does it raise? Write them in around the margins or as a separate list.

Why undertake research?

Quite simply, because that's how things are done in the industry. No media product gets made without prior research into similar products on the market, or finding a niche to exploit outside mainstream products already available. Writers of broadcast fiction, documentarians, digital marketing experts, advertising agencies and journalists all undertake research to lend their work verisimilitude or ensure it has factual weight and authority. Without undertaking research, production companies cannot get funding or commissions, newspapers lose credibility with their audience, advertisers miss their target audience entirely, broadcasters cannot sell advertising slots successfully, innovative web services get lost in the cyber-wilderness, and so on.

Pre-production work

Why do I need to include pre-production work?

No serious media professional would ever consider not completing the pre-production tasks peculiar to their discipline and field. The aim of the practical production is to put your theory about media platforms into practice. You will be set a choice of three briefs to choose from by the board, and you will create two of the three products and collect ideas for a third across media platforms. The brief will be precise, but will in each case offer you the opportunity to think creatively. This is the job of real media professionals. Media study and media production go hand in hand – and the better you understand the connections between the two and use each to inform the other, the better your grasp of the whole subject will become. Your pre-production work is evidence that you aspire to the values of a media professional working in the industry, and is worth marks for your pre-production folder.

What sort of pre-production work should I include for submission?

This list is not exhaustive, and is necessarily generalised to encompass a range of briefs. Check with your tutor, who may also contact a coursework advisor. The brief you are given from the specification will give you precise examples suitable for your final choice:

- storyboards
- annotated analyses of relevant texts
- a log of footage shot or recorded, indicating what was discarded and why
- small annotated copies of photographs either selected or discarded, annotated clearly
- where they will not be too bulky (e.g. a single print advert) annotated copies of texts
- checklists and preparation notes for production
- *findings* from factual research in your own words (e.g. longer copy from a journalistic piece that had to be cut)
- scripts for a shoot, podcast or radio piece
- evidence of planning such as locations lists and schedule
- summaries of research into suitable technologies (e.g. the comparative benefits of using three different types of web design software, with your conclusions as to which best suits your purpose)

AQA Examiner's tip

Good research at the pre-production stage will mean that you have fully thought out how your productions will be linked and how they fit their target audience.

- notes kept documenting your learning experiences in using a media technology new to you
- a CD of real interviews recorded on MP3 as research for a journalistic piece in a magazine.

The following are *not* suitable for inclusion:

- any bulky printouts or photocopies
- anything that is not clearly annotated identifying its contribution to the production process
- quantitative research such as questionnaires and their results in graph or chart form.

The most important thing is that your pre-production work is presented with absolute clarity for the moderator as someone who doesn't know you, and hasn't directly witnessed your working processes. Write a contents page, paginate and label everything.

End of topic summary:

- I know what factors to take into consideration in choosing the overall brief, and which two tasks to select within it.
- I am confident about undertaking suitable and appropriate research.
- I know what sort of work is suitable to undertake pre-production and what should be included in my pre-production folder.

8   Using technologies

In this topic you will:

- gain familiarity with the equipment required for broadcast, print and web-based media production

- learn the flow of processes required in each form of production

- become aware of some of the problems you may face and know how to either avoid or deal with them.

Investigating media

Production planning

As you read through each section on the technologies relevant to your product, produce a page of questions for yourself to help you plan your production process, e.g.:

- Do we have a manual for our college editing software, and if not what sort of support can I expect?

- How many mega-pixels does my camera at home have?

- How will I back up my print media work?

- What institutional values do I think my website should convey, and what does it exist to do?

During this topic, you will be learning about the equipment, processes and problems you might encounter in preparing for practical work in each platform. You should now be ready to start planning your workload for the products. Read the advice on each technology carefully.

Preparing to create a broadcast product

The equipment

Equipment has come down massively in price in the last two decades, making audio and video production of a reasonable quality more affordable than ever before. This section will refer primarily to more modern and affordable equipment, since that is what most of you will have access to. If you're lucky enough to have access to a radio or TV studio, you'll need to consult with a specialist in your equipment and be provided with appropriate training. Here are details of some of the equipment you may be expected to use:

- A digital video (DV) camera, preferably using mini-DV tapes for flexibility and quality. It is possible to use older SVHS or Hi-8 cameras, but if you want to edit digitally using footage from one of these, you'll need some means of converting the footage from analogue to digital.

- A tripod, useful for stability during pans and establishing shots in particular.

- The appropriate connecting leads (usually a fire-wire or USB cable) to transfer your footage from camera to edit suite.

- A PC or Macintosh computer (you will need to make sure the technical specifications are up to video editing, particularly if you intend to use older equipment or a laptop computer).

- Video and/or sound editing software such as Windows Movie-maker or i-Movie, Sound Studio or other programs such as Final Cut Express/Pro, an Avid system or Adobe Premiere. There are numerous editing software titles available and they vary in their suitability in terms of price, robustness and ease of use. You may not have any choice as to which you use, but if you do, read the reviews and preferably ask people with some editing experience what they use.

- The means to transfer your final product from computer to a standard format DVD that will play in a home DVD player. This will usually be a piece of DVD writing software capable of converting files to the correct format.

- A USB microphone connected to a computer and fed directly into sound/video editing software, or used in conjunction with a digital sound recording device.

- A decent set of headphones that can be used for sound recording for radio (and video if your equipment and crew situation is luxurious enough) and while editing.

- Microphone and pole ('boom') connected to DV camera or sound mixer via XLR input.

The processes

Scripting

First you'll need to undertake some essential pre-production work. For radio, this might include the completion of a script or programme outline, including all kinds of production details.

A radio script for a piece of broadcast fiction will require some quite formal preparation. You'll need to write all the dialogue, indicate where you will source and record your sound effects and music, make decisions about where to record (On location? In a basic digital studio with USB microphones?) and casting. All of this will need, for production clarity, to be set out using a standard industry script format such as the one featured here as preparation for Brief C, which is based on the BBC radio play recommendations.

A programme outline is a script that identifies running order, contributors and the nature of their contribution, music etc., but will not script the actual dialogue to be spoken, for obvious reasons! It should show the positioning of phone-ins, interviews with experts etc.

The same advice on scripting given here can be used in relation to a podcast to be included on a website. A podcast may of course not involve as many contributors or be as complex – but be aware that podcasting is a relatively new phenomenon, and as such is changing all the time. Some podcasts do actually comprise repeats of actual radio programmes or excerpts from them.

💡 **Fig. 8.1** *Example of a radio script format*

```
                        ADVERTISEMENT 1
                        THE INTERIOR OF A SUPERMARKET

     F/X:                    TINNY MUZAK, ANNOUNCER, SCANNERS
                             BEEPING, CHATTER


     CHECKOUT OPERATOR: (CORNISH ACCENT) Alright there, my lover?


     WOMAN CUSTOMER #1: Oh yes, fine thanks. Lovely outside today, isn't it…


                             FADE TO BACKGROUND


     WOMAN CUSTOMER #2: (CLOSE)  Look at all that PC stuff in her trolley. Funny-
                          looking light bulbs. Fair Trade bananas – what do you do
                          with them then? Swap each one for an under-privileged
                          orange? Recycled toilet paper – well, you never know where
                          it's been. Those organic cauliflowers look a bit small. More
                          cauli-florets really – ha ha, cauliflorets! Oh yes, very good,
                          you're on form today, Sandra.


     WOMAN CUSTOMER #1: Excuse me, I couldn't help noticing. Your ignorance is
                          showing. Out loud.


     WOMAN CUSTOMER #2: Oh. Um. Thanks.


     F/X:                    JINGLE FADE IN


     ANNOUNCER (V.O.) :  Don't let your environmental ignorance embarrass you in
                          public. Visit www.windsofchange.co.uk. Think outside.
```

For video production, there are several different industry standards for setting out scripts. These differ, for example, for film and television production. Finding and learning to use the appropriate format should be part of your pre-production. Neither format should include the sort of technical detail featured on a storyboard as the two documents are quite separate. Software that provides a template is often used by professional writers for film and TV, but in most cases basic observation of the form and layout in a word processing programme should be adequate. A 'shooting script' for a documentary may be little more than a shot list and collection of production notes about the location, and desirable behaviours and interviewees to film.

Storyboarding

Detailed storyboarding is one of the most valuable activities you can undertake prior to any kind of filming activity. In the industry, storyboards are used in many different ways by production teams according to personal preferences, so this is a model and suggested method that is appropriate for the scale of an AS Media Studies project. It's the first page of a storyboard for the broadcast element of Brief B.

Used correctly, a storyboard should be your best friend. You don't have to be an artist to think visually – stick men are perfectly adequate and have been used by many famous names in directing. These days, computer programmes that act as a storyboarding tool for directors with limited artistic skills are available, although currently these are quite expensive.

Your storyboard should be used...

1 Pre-production: plan shot sequence, length, type, angle, movement and duration. Plan any diegetic sounds you intend to record, and any non-diegetic that will also be added post-production. Also indicate any editing effects such as dissolves or fades, and titling you may wish to use.
2 Production: take your storyboard with you on location and use it!
3 Post-production: use it as a guide during editing to help you assemble your initial rough cut, and then review. At this point you should perhaps put it away, and begin to edit by eye.

The shoot

It's crucial that you familiarise yourself with the technologies you'll be using for production prior to commencing actual filming or recording. Know where the controls are on the camera, and practise framing nice steady shots, moving the camera in practice pans and controlling zooms. Hold a production team meeting to ensure everyone knows what they're doing, and include any actors for broadcast fiction texts. Even if the project is all your own, you're still bound to be collaborating in some way with others and they'll need to be in on your plans for a smooth production to result.

Technical tips

1 To avoid re-filming (testing for all involved, given that there is no budget!), get it right first time you go out. If you're not sure whether a take is good enough, do it again while on location.
2 Make sure you always let the camera roll sufficiently before and after action – and it's always better to shoot more than you need. Take your time.
3 It's best not to review rushes on location as this can lead to the accidental recording over of existing work, which is heartbreaking.

AQA Examiner's tip

■ Not everything you imagined on the storyboard may work as well as you thought on-screen. On location, you may spot extra shots that look good – rely on gut instinct. Following a storyboard slavishly post-production could limit your creativity, so know when the time is right to put it to one side.

■ Even documentary makers relying heavily on actuality for their filming may sketch out 'thumbnails' (a very basic collection of small frames with rough shot types in) to help them remember the range and types of shot they want to get.

Fig. 8.2 *Example of a storyboard*

🔦 Health and safety

1 Always do a recce to make sure you have access, can film or sound record safely with headphones on, and help you to plan your shots.

2 Try not to film or record as a lone operator, and especially avoid tracking backwards without a guide at your elbow.

3 Always let someone know where you're filming and what time you plan to return. Take a mobile phone with you.

4 Make contacts with any interview subjects in advance, ensure they understand they won't be paid for any documentary contribution and get them to sign a permissions letter.

5 Be particularly careful filming or recording in busy places. It's amazing how distracting the processes are, and you must remain aware of your surroundings at all times.

6 Risk-assess everything you do. Don't be tempted with modern and light camcorders to film from unsafe places just to get that perfect shot.

Technical tips

▪ Be sensitive as to how your camera performs in a range of light conditions and don't ask the impossible of it.

▪ Don't expect high quality sound recording of dialogue from a basic internal camcorder microphone – if you want good sound either record it through another source, or make sure your mic is up as close and personal as it can get without you being arrested!

Planning for post-production

If you're lucky, you may get some training on how to use your editing package. At the very least, as part of your research you should experiment with a little practice footage. Internet reviews of software can be very enlightening in helping you ascertain what you can and can't do with your software. Use a manual or get hold of a book. Post-production is easily learnt as you go along with basic editing packages designed for the home user. Make good use of the help topics, and make notes if you need to, to help you remember how to do things. Don't count on post-production to make up for deficiencies in the quality of footage or sound. There is a limit to what can be changed.

Make sure you save your work regularly and back it up if you have the facility to do so. Processing digital footage makes big demands on the average computer and crashes are not uncommon. Be stoical if this happens to you, and be prepared to re-edit small sections of work.

Aside from investigating the potential of your editing package at the research stage, resist the temptation to employ the whole palette of special effects at your disposal. Professional media products often use the most basic cuts and transitions such as fades and dissolves. When was the last time you saw photo frames spinning in out of nowhere in a trailer, or a 'mirror' or 'aged film' effect in a soap? Rely on well-planned techniques such as matched cuts and sound bridges from shot to shot to lend sophistication to your cut.

Problems – avoiding and fixing

Obviously, you are always going to be limited by the technology at your disposal, but this is not what the examiner is concerned about. They want to see that you've made the best use of what you have available to achieve the highest possible level of finish. Audiences can be remarkably forgiving of cheap camcorder footage so long as you try to avoid the following common pitfalls:

- Poor sound recording when it's really vital that the audience hear what's going on (especially dialogue filmed through a camcorder at a distance).
- Glaring continuity errors.
- Overuse of special editing effects in digital suites, or SFX in radio production.
- Zooms that are too fast, or zoom in and then out. Use these types of shot with great care.
- Shaky camerawork – for instance a hand-held camera used for steady shots really requiring a tripod.
- Excessive filming in poor lighting, leading to a grainy finish as the camera struggles to compensate.
- Onlookers in the background taking a visible interest in the proceedings.
- Inappropriate dress codes/lack of convincing props.
- Lack of attention to mise-en-scène, or 'fluffy bunny in the gangster hide-out' syndrome.
- Using the camera to follow the action, when really a range of shots should have been used.
- Shots that are badly framed where the horizon is tilted.
- Takes that are too short (not letting the camera roll before and after the desired shot) leading to a shoddy and 'clipped' feel to editing.
- Overly lively titles that are offensive to the eye, unsuitable or otherwise detract from the filmed visuals. Titling should be subtle and simply do its job.

Preparing to create a print product

The equipment

As you might expect, the production of print media has not escaped the technological revolution. The sheer range of desk-top publishing software available (some of it for free from the internet), widespread ownership of digital cameras and the continued lowering of the costs of high quality printing mean that in the digital age, print media still clearly has a firm place in the media consumer and industry's hearts. Print media is consumed differently; audiences clearly still enjoy the freedom from their computers and portability of the form. Newspapers are still read on trains, magazines out on a sunny day or during factory breaks, and advertisers still spend millions competing for these eyes. Basic equipment you will need to use includes the following:

- A Windows PC or Macintosh computer.
- Desktop publishing software – some, such as Microsoft Publisher for PC or Pages for Macintosh – are expensive to buy but widely known among home users. Beware of the limitations of some of these programs, and particularly of using templates – more information about this can be found in Topic 9, Creating a Print Media Product. Be prepared to research free software such as the packages offered by Serif, which may offer equal flexibility and sometimes quite professional design features.

- A means of making your files portable if necessary to a high quality printing facility, such as a decent sized USB or other mass storage device.

- Access to a high quality full colour printer.

- A scanner to assist with image manipulation if necessary.

- A photo-editing package such as Photoshop Elements.

- A digital stills camera with at least 3 mega-pixel capability and a flash. Any lower and any large images you wish to use will develop a pixelated look, which is most disappointing when you've spent a lot of time thinking about lighting, shot composition and so on. If you know from your brief or research that you need to present photographs in a large format such as A3 to represent billboard or double-page spread adverts, then try to use as good a camera as you can – for this size, really 6 or 8 mega-pixels should be the minimum.

- The proprietary USB connector lead supplied with it *or* a card reader if your camera uses SD or Compaq Flash Cards.

- A tripod for taking good steady shots.

The processes

Generating copy

Writing good copy for a newspaper or magazine/advertisement campaign is a highly skilled area that is often neglected by students producing print media texts. There is a good reason why this happens – like filmmaking and radio production, print media production is generally a collaborative enterprise in the real industry. You are likely to be working alone to produce a piece of print media, or only in a small group. This means that visual concerns about acquiring new skills relating to DTP can take over and come to dominate, resulting in a piece that may look great superficially, but doesn't work well as journalism.

You have a great deal to think about – you'll have to be your own editor and proof-reader for one. Unlike some journalists, you'll also be often writing more than one piece for your magazine or newspaper, and possibly even including some advertisements – again, advertising sales and copy production are always dealt with by different departments, usually working within a graphics department on smaller regional newspapers, or produced by advertising agencies for the nationals. For advertising briefs, it's not uncommon to see students produce fantastic concepts with beautiful graphics and photographs accompanied by copy that is badly written, ill thought out and sometimes even misspelt. Pay attention to detail in whatever you write – it is anything but secondary.

Technical tips

- It can be difficult to write directly into a template you have established for yourself on a DTP program. Generate your copy first on a word processor to allow yourself time to draft it.

- Always get someone else to proofread and offer their opinion on copy at this stage.

Working with graphics and digital photography

Taking good photographs of any kind, like good journalism, is obviously a separate discipline in its own right. You'll need to remember to consider carefully the relationship between what you choose to include as images and the copy itself. You must remember to put into practice everything you've learnt about visual codes and the production of meaning for audiences in planning your photographs effectively to achieve maximum impact. Here are a few pointers:

■ Compose your photographs carefully – consider the position of your subject in the frame, background as well as foreground, colour, light levels and contrast.

■ You can use cropping facilities on photo-editing software, but if you really zoom in on one area you'll lose image quality.

■ Remember that photo-editing packages can correct some slight deficiencies of hue, but cannot make a good photograph out of a bad one.

■ White balance and flash use are the most problematic areas of image production in digital photography – if you don't want bleached out dull photos, make sure you know how your camera performs before you go on that all-important shoot.

If you're using a graphics package of any kind, remember to think carefully about the kind of image you want to project for your publication – and match the graphics to this. Colour is particularly important when targeting certain audiences. Remember that certain publications may also need illustrations such as diagrams and maps, although use of these should be sparing, and certainly secondary in most cases to original photography. See further advice in Topic 9 on 'found' images.

Design considerations

There are variations between DTP programmes, but you should certainly choose one which offers you the following features:

■ A good range and variety of fonts, and preferably the ability to import fonts from external sources.

■ The facility to create your own template rather than choosing one of the ones offered.

■ A good range of text box styles and the ability to import other media such as digital photographs.

■ Some basic graphics or the ability to import these from another program, allowing you to create interesting mast-heads etc.

You should also as part of your research decide on the design basics. Make sure you follow the conventions appropriate to the media form you've chosen – a magazine cover, for example, will need to observe bleeds, cover-lines, menu strips etc. in order to have verisimilitude.

If you have been asked to create a feature article for an existing publication as part of your brief, the most obvious part of the research is to get hold of a copy of the publication. Read it carefully from cover to cover and perform an analysis as suggested in Topic 7, Research and Planning. This will also be useful in establishing the house style. Check whether your publication is listed on www.news-tream.ltd.uk – this site has useful information about size of publication and number of columns. Then make sure you *use* this information in designing your own template. The examples here show some of the thought processes involved in preparing to write for an existing publication for Brief A.

Problems – avoiding and fixing

A checklist for print production:

■ Spend some time choosing your fonts to ensure a professional finish, and consider using a separate graphics or photo-manipulation program to help you with the layering of images and in designing a professional masthead. The best journalism in the world will look amateurish with a standard 'art' setting from a word-processing program.

- You may not be lucky enough to have a large screen to work on. Try to maintain a sense of the actual size your product will be and bear this in mind for font sizing.

- Get to know your software before you make decisions about the 'look' of your product, which practically you may not be able to accomplish. Layering and other aspects of DTP can be quite complex tasks – you'll need to have a careful order of work planned to avoid problems and confusion in this area. You can only do this if you know the program.

- Be wary of 'busy' layout. Over-egging is for cakes.

- Find out about the format your DTP program saves files in. Are there going to be any compatibility issues when you attempt to print? You may find that if you've saved your work on a USB device, the same programme is required to open the file for printing – or, horror of all horrors, the computer opens your file with what it deems to be another 'suitable' application, only to lose all of your careful formatting…

- Design a layout that closely resembles existing publications, being careful to replicate column width, proportion of text to image, and other details and niceties of design. If you're producing for an existing publication, you'll need to scan in the masthead. Use your knowledge of target audience.

- Save your work regularly, and back up regularly on a USB device.

- *Don't* use the stills facility on a video camera or a mobile phone for photography unless you're absolutely certain of the quality of the resulting image.

Preparing to create a web-based product

The equipment

If you are already a student of web design (either formally or as an enthusiast) and competent with programming languages, you may choose to use the tools you are already familiar with for media production. However, if you are a complete novice to web design, there are now a range of suitable programs to enable you to produce very effective websites. These vary considerably in ease of use, functionality and so on – as with DTP, there are some that can be downloaded for free or at very little cost, and others that cost hundreds of pounds. Because of functionality issues, checking that the software available to you can do what you want it to is doubly important here.

For basic web design, you will need:

- a PC or Macintosh computer
- web design software such as Frontpage, Dreamweaver, Namo Web Editor etc.
- a web browser to check how your work would appear if it were to go 'live'.

To add content to of various types, you may also need:

- USB microphone, digital stills camera and standard video production kit
- associated software tools such as Windows Media Player or Quicktime, and the facility to convert sound and video files into these formats ready for uploading
- a program such as Macromedia Flash to add animations and other moving content.

Fig. 8.3 *Front pages from* First News *and the* TES, *what similarities and differences do you notice and how can you account for them?*

The processes

Web design uses some of the same principles and skills, and therefore will present you with some of the same challenges as both print and broadcast media production. These will not be repeated here, and you should refer to the relevant Using Technologies sections for these and take the advice presented therein for some relevant issues (creating video content, using photographs and some aspects of DTP). Superficially at least, some web design programs may resemble a DTP package at first glance. However, there are important differences to consider when undertaking web design:

1 Web pages are not necessarily read from top to bottom, front to back. Web audiences are much more likely to want to choose areas of a site they most wish to access, and will have this expectation. Your design needs to take account of this and provide opportunities to make the 'navigating' experience a smooth, logical and pleasurable one. We've all been to badly organised or just plain boring websites.

2 Video and audio content may need to be kept brief and compressed appropriately to allow for differing download speeds and quality – the same goes for flash animations. Remember to consider your target audience here – someone with a high income living in a city may have a faster computer and better broadband access than someone in a different socio-economic class in a rural area. If necessary, could you offer options or alternatives to video content, such as a downloadable PDF file containing the same information?

3 Websites can contain a huge variety of information and are used for different purposes. Examples may include those that are purely for digital marketing, while others exist to feed a fan-base for another area of the media. Think carefully through the purpose and audience for your site, and particularly hard about the values of the institution, imaginary or otherwise, for whom the site is being designed.

4 Some of your content should be dynamic, and capable of being instantaneously updated. Some people are regular visitors to favourite sites, and will be disappointed to see exactly the same content each time. You wouldn't like to read the same thing in a magazine every month, so bear this in mind. Some information may be constant, but some elements certainly should be refreshed regularly, even if it's only 'click here to see the latest reviews'.

5 Websites sometimes begin small and then grow – try to envisage what room for growth there could be for your site. This will help you to clarify exactly what the needs of your target audience are as well as the requirements of the institution. Will your site be in existence for the foreseeable future, or is it a more ephemeral one, for example to market the cinema release of a new film?

Additional benefits of web design

It's also essential that you consider the possibilities offered by websites not available through other media. Don't ignore the democratisation of audience interactivity the web has brought, and some of its newer phenomena. You could make use of:

■ a viral, moving image marketing tool to be disseminated via mobile phone attachments

■ blogs

■ podcasts and vodcasts in MP3 and MP4

■ message boards and forums and chat-rooms to develop a community of interested site users

- downloadable video content and screensavers
- online sales of merchandise
- printable posters, e-cards
- the facility for users to be alerted via email when content changes, and to encourage them to revisit the site
- a section that allows the posting of user photographs
- a toggle that allows the quick emailing of a link to another user.

Problems – avoiding and fixing

- Most of the problems you will encounter during web design are technological problems. The internet is full of design limitations, quirks and incompatibility issues that may mean you have to be flexible or adaptable rather than waste lots of time trying to do something that is technically too difficult for you, or too expensive. Your experiences can all be recorded in your pre-production materials.

- You will not usually be asked to develop a vast website in its entirety, so it may be that you have to suggest a link to something interesting you had hoped to include rather than actually putting it in. Perhaps adding some video content turns out to be too problematic, and you can substitute a still image in its place, or use a sequence of stills rather than a video clip.

- Make the best use you can of the internet to help you solve problems. Your tutor may not know the answer – web design is a specialist discipline incorporating lots of ways of doing things. Be prepared to use your initiative, and befriend web design enthusiasts.

End of topic summary:

- I understand how to choose the equipment appropriate to the brief I have chosen.
- I know how to plan my order of work, including time to familiarise myself with the equipment.
- I know to be aware of the limitations of the technologies I will be using, and to match my pre-production planning to allow for any challenges.

AQA Examiner's tip

You may not want to actually publish your site to the web – think carefully before you do. Anyone could look at it, so it'll need to be clearly labelled as an AS Media web design project if you do decide to go live – particularly as you could get into legal or copyright issues. A student at one school was recently pursued by an international media company for unauthorised use of their logo on his personal homepage! Luckily they were mollified by an apology and the site was taken down with no further action, but it just goes to show...

9 Creating products

In this topic you will:

- develop an understanding of how to interpret both parts of your chosen brief with originality and creativity

- learn to monitor your projects throughout the production period, including issues arising from group work

- become confident that your ideas can be realised with professionalism and accepting of some of the limitations you may experience.

By this time, we'll assume that you have:

1 chosen both the brief you wish to address and the two platforms you need to work in
2 undertaken all necessary research into existing products
3 identified the appropriate pre-production tasks that need to be undertaken
4 sourced the technologies needed for your product and begun to learn how to use them
5 had some preliminary ideas for turning the products in both platforms from concept to reality.

If you're unclear about any of the above, don't worry. Just re-read Topics 7 and 8, and spend a little time filling in any gaps.

💡 Originality and creativity

Using genre conventions and media forms imaginatively in both platforms

Genre conventions and existing media forms are widely agreed and understood by both audiences and institutions. This means that genre boundaries are usually observed by media producers, but also continually stretched to offer audiences something new. This is important for you to bear in mind when creating your products. You need to ensure that your audience have familiarity with your text; that they can relate quickly and easily to it, but also that they are simultaneously offered something new.

In terms of the briefs outlined at the beginning of Topic 7, this means that you will already have researched and developed a good understanding of how previous media producers have tackled these kinds of tasks before. It's up to you now to both learn from what has gone before, but also try to offer a sufficiently new take on these to keep your audience interested.

What do 'originality' and 'creativity' mean for my products?

'Originality' means trying to ensure that you don't directly copy existing media texts.

'Creativity' means making imaginative use of existing genre conventions and expectations audiences might already have of the text in terms of your original ideas.

It's also important to be creative not just with your original ideas, but also with your use of media language. This is achievable no matter how basic your equipment. Much of the 'creativity' happens in the mind of the person who makes decisions about the 'look' and feel of the product – the storyboard artist, the director, the web designer or the sound engineer.

When filming broadcast media, static camera shots during long takes should be avoided. Film cut-away shots, try using two camcorders (if available) to give two perspectives on the scene, experiment with point-

135

of-view shots, slow zooms, high and low angles. When editing, can you use dissolves to slow the pace down and lend your sequence a wistful air, or accelerate the motion of a sequence to give it energy? Can you make any use of still shots?

Technical tip

Special effects solutions:

- Sam needed a plane crash to establish a narrative situation. He built a model plane, dangled it on string and set fire to it, all filmed with convincing hand-held camera. Please note he did have supervision.

- Sonny, requiring some 0.5 second long flashes of 'gore' to unsettle his audience, visited and filmed in a local butcher's shop. The results were truly astonishing!

- David, needing convincing footage of a house fire, arranged to film at a safe distance during an exercise at a local fire station. In gaining his permission to use his work as an example, he commented to me, 'People don't realise how easy stuff like that is. That phone call took 30 seconds to make.' Easy enough for a student with initiative, that is!

In creating print media, you of course need to observe some journalistic conventions such as being sure of the who, what, when, how and why of a story. But you still need to consider the balance between a professional, polished and eye-catching look and finish to your typography and photographs, and presenting the audience with an unusual slant or attention-grabbing story that will surprise or entertain them when they're least expecting it. Websites in particular offer lots of room for innovation, being such a dynamic, relatively cheap and interactive platform.

Let's look at an example from the broadcast media section of a brief, and see some ideas in action.

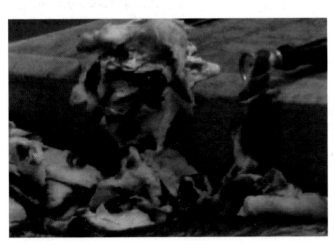

Fig. 9.1 *Stills from Sonny and David's special effects footage – you can see how effective their solutions were!*

Thinking creatively about a broadcast brief – Brief A

Create a one-minute trailer advertising a new reality TV show where college-age students train to teach their younger peers at another school.

You'll hopefully have seen and researched trailers, and have fleshed out a format for your show to help you clarify in your own mind what the show is about (see Topic 7, Research and Planning). You will have probably come up with the following ideas for things you could show/do…

- Encourage your audience to identify with or reject particular participants in the show – preferably including brief shots of them talking to camera, perhaps video-diary style, to quickly create a rapport between participants and your audience.

- You will need to show the contestants in action, doing what they do in the show.

- You will probably want to foreground the range of emotional experiences they go through – this is one of the major appeals of reality TV.

- Given the subject matter, it's likely the audience will want to see some of the tougher or more extreme situations contestants find themselves facing.

Given that you only have one minute, how do you inject 'creativity' into your trailer?

- Could you include a voiceover to narrate the trailer in the style of an action film?

- Should you use titling and sections of black and white video to give it a moody and serious feel?

- Could you pick on a particular mannerism of a participant or typical reaction, and show this repeatedly in a number of quick edits?

- Why not emphasise the chaos of one participant's classroom with the cool calm of another, cross-matching particular moments in their day, and matching music as appropriate?

- Will you edit to the rhythm of a particularly surprising and lyrically appropriate soundtrack, and do away with diegetic sound altogether?

Thinking about media

Look at the two other practice briefs for broadcast media products. Make notes on the conventions and audience expectations of the media form, just as in the case study. Then decide on three suggestions for original or creative approaches to each.

'Found' media

'Found' media is media you haven't created yourself. It might sound obvious that you shouldn't use media created by someone else and pass it off as your own any more than you would plagiarise an essay. However, there are many grey areas in media production. You need to work out how to negotiate your way through these.

FAQs

Why does it matter whether I use footage or images from somewhere else? Real media producers use library images and footage.

It's true that media producers have access to vast and expensive libraries. However, you seldom see them actually used. Producers and audiences always favour the original and fresh over something that is stale, may not exactly fit the context, and could have been seen before.

Are archive footage and photographs used in context and clearly labelled as such OK?

You should only ever use these if the context of your piece absolutely demands it, and you can balance it with appropriate footage or photographs of your own. The majority should be your own.

What about copy for secondary articles, news features or adverts?

All your work should be original, i.e. written by you, without **any** exceptions. To do otherwise constitutes plagiarism.

Is it OK to include something like a clip of an explosion in a broadcast piece?

If this sounds like you, your project may need a reality check in terms of what's achievable realistically on next to no budget! Inserted clips can really jar. A sound effect of an explosion, a cut to black, then a slow fade in with 'fog' effect applied subtly at the start is always preferable to found footage.

Can I use music or TV in the background providing it contributes something to my product?

Avoid using any existing broadcast media in your work, unless it is demanded by events in the sequence you are filming or recording and is narratively or semiotically significant. The same applies to images from the internet, magazines or books, and newspapers. Think extremely hard about using clip-art in any form, since it will be widely used, unoriginal and easily recognised by the audience. Even prominent positioning of brand names can be problematic. Don't forget that if you were to really broadcast or publish anything making use of material from another medium, you would have to seek the permission of its producer and pay a fee. Otherwise you contravene copyright law.

What about music and SFX?

The same principle applies. You can certainly never show your work outside an educational context if it breaks copyright law. There are alternatives to using well-known music. Why not compose your own copyright-free music on an easy-to-use program such as Garageband and record your own effects? With a little imagination this is not as hard as it sounds. You must be clear about where your music and sound come from in your evaluation, since the choices you make count towards your mark. Think how much more the sound of cows mooing or a car starting are worth if you've made the effort to go out and record them yourself.

What about backgrounds, or changing a found image significantly?

An image that has been significantly altered electronically and used in an imaginative way will be considered acceptable – but check this with your supervising tutor.

I need a photograph of something it's impossible for me to get. Can I use one I found on the internet?

Ask yourself why? Can you really not mock up the picture, or find an alternative means of illustrating your point? Check whether your project is on track. You may be straying from the brief, or interpreting it with too much ambition.

Can I use templates on DTP packages and web design software?

Since you should already have designed and sketched out ideas for print or digitally-based texts, it's quite unlikely that you'd want to. You'll effectively penalise yourself if you use a template without altering it at all. Since you won't have designed it yourself, it won't exactly suit your purpose, and you won't be able to evaluate why you've prepared your layout in the way you have. You can always look at templates to give you ideas and practise with them when learning to use the software, but it's preferable by far to create your own.

Thinking about media

In pairs, discuss the possible uses of the following examples of images and sounds.

Then, sort them into two columns – those you feel might be acceptable to use, and those that would definitely not be.

There are no answers provided, partly because you should draw your own conclusions, and also because the acceptability may in some cases depend on the context:

1. A radio playing in the background of a domestic sequence.
2. The masthead from a weekly farming newspaper.
3. A map showing the location of an event.
4. A still of a woman screaming taken from a horror film.
5. A diagram of the heart from a science textbook used as part of a title sequence.
6. A BBC News broadcast viewed by and reacted to by characters.
7. A 'constructed' image of a child living in poverty found on a child protection website.
8. A two-minute sound effect loop downloaded from the internet of background sound in a cafe.
9. The sound of the *EastEnders* theme tune with the reflected light playing on their face as you film someone sleeping on a sofa.
10. A photograph of a rare animal or bird.
11. A video clip of a friend playing football with spectator sound recorded from a premiership game.
12. A personal photograph belonging to a parent showing what teenagers wore in the 1970s or 1980s.
13. A recipe scanned in from a book.
14. A sound effect of a jet engine roaring overhead from an editing programme.
15. A picture of a former British prime minister.
16. The theme tune from *Star Trek*, the first TV series.

■ Organisation

The pros and cons of teamwork

As you already know, broadcast texts are always a collaborative enterprise. For the purposes of your piece of coursework, whether or not you work in a small production team sharing one project may be dictated by external factors, such as tutor preference and availability of equipment, or left to your personal choice.

There are some benefits to working in a team:

- more creative input and sharing of ideas with other interested parties
- less pressure where responsibility is shared for the outcome
- a greater spread of technical skills
- possibly a lighter workload during production as different team members divide up responsibilities.

There are also some disadvantages:

- creative disagreements
- someone not pulling their weight either due to laziness or illness, contributing to extra stress all round
- it can be difficult to unite everyone's vision and contribution
- potential difficulties in defining your contribution to the work where work was done as a team.

Where there are a large number of separate tasks that need to be undertaken, a group may work happily together with no problems. It may be that in the second choice of platform, group members decide to work individually (e.g. when producing a print media text) and this is certainly acceptable or even preferable. If you decide to work as a team, you must make sure of the following:

- That everyone knows what is happening when. For example, for a broadcast media text, write yourselves a schedule. Plan in advance times, dates, people involved. Leave yourselves plenty of time for the edit, and if you need to book facilities, equipment and crew then honour the bookings. You must meet the deadlines you or your producer set. Make alternative plans in case of bad weather, trying to take into account time of day for continuity of light in the shoot or sound if recording in a busy place. Have everyone's contact number and a mobile phone. If you're ill or suddenly can't get transport to the shoot, let the rest of the crew know as early as possible.
- That frequent meetings are held to check on progress and review each other's work, and that you keep a record that clearly identifies who contributed what to the final product.
- That you are flexible and anyone is adequately briefed to take over someone else's role at short notice in the eventuality of someone leaving the team without warning.
- That everyone shoulders fairly their set of responsibilities, and that you all agree to this before you begin the project. To assist with planning, it's worth drawing up a team contract like the one shown here as part of your pre-production work.

The lone operator

Working alone still requires tremendous efforts of organisation. You'll probably still need to draw up a schedule and set yourself interim deadlines to stop the time slipping away from you, one of the biggest enemies even of the brightest and most talented media student.

Either way, never underestimate how long a task will take, particularly when using unfamiliar technologies. Allow time for things to go wrong. Something probably will, for somebody, each year – what if it's you?

P R A C T I C A L   W O R K

Contract

NAMES: J. HILL, K. MAHER, J. COX, Z. DAVIDSON

BRIEF: BROADCAST - OPENING OF DETECTIVE SERIES

AS LEVEL MEDIA STUDIES   EXAM ENTRY 2008

Agreed tasks
and contributions:

K. MAHER	Storyboarding, script & directing
Z. DAVIDSON	Camerawork, equipment booking & locations
J. HILL	Sound recording and post-production
J. COX	Editing, transport,

Additional help: ACTORS/ACTRESSES
N. SHARMA (Girl on swing in flashback)
E. KING (Girl in club) J. COX (Detective)

Schedule

1, STORYBOARD - To be completed for team meeting LUNCH
Subject to review by team ⟶ 10/3/08

2, FILMING - Sequence ① Meet on location (cliffs) ⟶ 10.A.M.
14/3/08
Sequence ② Faculty Office ⟶ 4 P.M.
16/3/08
Sequence ③ 'Club' (Drama Studio) ⟶ LUNCHTIME
17/3/08

3, EDITING - Jo and John booked into edit suite
P 4&5 18/3, P 5 22/3, AFTER COLLEGE 22, 23RD
Whole team review: 24/3/08

DATES PLACES TIMES BOOKINGS TASKS DEADLINES DATES PLACES TIMES BOOKINGS TASKS DEADLINES DATES PLACES TIMES TASKS DATE

💡 **Fig. 9.2** *An example of a contract*

Realisation

Producing the best possible work

Hopefully, if you've followed all the advice for Unit 2, researched effectively, spent the appropriate amount of time on pre-production activities, and allowed plenty of time to produce the work itself, you should now be looking at two products that are very good indeed.

However, whatever the equipment available to you, the chances are that there will come a point when you have to accept that your media product may not be up to a professional standard. This does *not* mean you can't get top marks.

Remember the assessment focus for the actual practical pieces of work:

AO3 Demonstrate the ability to plan and construct media products using appropriate technical and creative skills.

Your practical products are worth 60 of the 80 marks available for the unit. Do the best you can with available resources, and address any technical deficiencies you really couldn't do anything about in your evaluation, where a further 20 marks are available.

The importance of revisiting the brief

One of the most valuable things you can do before starting, at least once during and again when you are close to finishing your production process, is to sit down again with the brief in front of you and check all your plans and work in progress. Look closely at your outline plans for print and digital media. Try an image analysis of any photographs you've taken, and re-read your copy whether in your template or not. Check storyboards and scripts. Log your work either by viewing on the editing suite for broadcast work or through listening to recordings in the case of audio. Ask yourself these four questions:

Am I doing what I was asked to do?
Check carefully the wording of the brief. Have you done everything it asked you to, and where you've made creative decisions, do they match the spirit of the brief, or lead you too far away from it?

Who are my target audience, and could I explain to someone now how I've matched my product to their needs?
Your target audience must be clearly and appropriately addressed – look carefully at guidance offered on how the text is expected to be consumed, and put yourself in the mind of that consumer.

What size/duration is my product supposed to be?
This is vital – a brief will always be given in the media industry, and is often closely tied to production and printing costs, and advertising. A producer will insist you stick to their requirements – in this case, your tutor/ the examiner is your producer.

End of topic summary:

- I understand the importance of originality and creativity in producing two high quality texts.

- I know how to keep track of the production progress whether working alone or in a team.

- I'm aware that a high level of professionalism, flexibility and hard work are required to produce an effective practical production.

10 The evaluation

Your evaluation should be 1,500 words long. It is vital that you observe this word limit – you may find that you want to write more, so this could prove to be an exercise in conveying your ideas with precision and with clarity.

You should clearly demonstrate:

■ your knowledge of the conceptual framework in relation to the media products you have produced, including discussion of exactly how your product meets the needs of the target audience

■ that you are aware of the strengths and weaknesses of your work

■ that you have considered how you would address the third brief.

Stage 1: Analysing your own work

Before you begin your evaluation, it would be a good idea to analyse your own piece of work in note form under headings relating to your learning from Unit 1. You can organise these headings in whichever way makes most sense to you, but ensure you cover all the concepts you have learnt. You must make sure you use appropriate media terminology, not only for the practical processes you have undertaken and the technologies you have used, but also in terms of media analysis.

Perform a checklist on your notes:

Have you indicated clearly who the intended target audience are for each product, and discussed how they have been addressed?

Have you considered what the values are of the institution producing the text?

Have you discussed your representations in sufficient detail, and considered the meanings these will have for different sections of your audience?

Have you discussed the codes and conventions of the genre or media form apparent in your product and how you have made creative and original use of these?

Remember, the evaluation is where the media knowledge you gained from Unit 1 and how it has impacted on the choices you have made as a media producer should be most explicitly obvious to the examiner. You also need to make sure that you reinforce how your intentions in realising the brief have been met, and why your product is absolutely fit for purpose for the target audience.

Try exchanging your product with someone else's as part of your preparation for the above. Using your headings for your notes, question them about your text. Do they read it in the way you intended in every respect? Perhaps they have something useful to say you hadn't thought about?

Stage 2: Writing the evaluation

Focusing on the strengths and weaknesses in your work

Throughout the evaluation, you should demonstrate that you are fully aware of the impact of technological or skill-based limitations you have faced, and how these may have impacted on the look and feel of your final product. It would be a mistake to conceive these as a separate section – rather, you should aim to maintain a tight focus with precise critical observations as to what works well and what doesn't throughout.

Don't forget, this is your opportunity to comment on and justify some of the production choices you made, and also to gain marks in examining critically the flaws in the final pieces. Be honest about the weaknesses of your products. There is no shame in drawing attention to the deficiencies of your products, and you will be rewarded for your ability to do so where something hasn't quite worked as you'd hoped. Likewise, try to celebrate what has worked really well. Don't be modest about flagging up an emotive or powerful camera shot, an image where the light is stunning, composition flawless and the graphics thoroughly stylish, or the high level of varied opportunities for audience interactivity offered by your website.

Crucially, you should never make vague comments such as 'I thought my opening sequence was really effective'. Always frame your ideas conceptually to lend weight and authority to your argument. Substitute the following: 'The animation sequence I included in my titles was time consuming and technically demanding to make, but worthwhile. It clearly shows that this series has a humorous undertone, and references the Pink Panther intertextually.'

Weaknesses in your work may be due to the handling of technologies – but sometimes they might be conceptual flaws, too. There is no harm in acknowledging where something hasn't been thought through well enough until after production. Identify what you've learned from your mistakes. Never say 'Parts of my website didn't really look very professional.' Consider how it could be amended: 'The second page of my website was at times rather clumsy to navigate around, and really only needed a single video clip, some static explanatory text and the scrolling "news" to carry what was intended to be a simple message far more powerfully.'

Investigating media activity

Try writing a sentence or two discussing each of the following weaknesses:

- Lack of reference to an important piece of information or debate in a journalistic piece.
- Imbalance between opportunities for user generated contributions to website and the content generated by the institution.
- An invented sequence for a series that is too similar to existing texts in the genre.
- A radio piece that has insufficient variety in aural codes for the listener.
- A print advertising campaign that is not clearly anchored enough to prevent an aberrant reading.

Addressing the third brief

You should briefly say what such a product would consist of if you were to make it, for example, what images or copy you would carry over to the third platform. If, for example, you have made a moving image and an e-media product, you should consider how you would deal with the print product. In order to make this meaningful given the few words you have available, try to address with precision some of the following points:

■ the potential of the third platform to address its target audience

■ what is distinctive about the codes and conventions of the third product that makes it an equally useful medium

■ what use you would make of the above, giving a brief outline of perhaps three of the features you would include.

Investigating media

Choose one of the media from each of the practice briefs that you have not used for any previous activity. Write a short paragraph for each one for an evaluation, practising how to address the points made above.

Case study

Exemplar evaluation: Brief C (1,499 words)

The brief I chose required me to produce two media products designed to promote environmental responsibility on behalf of the target audience. I imagined my institution ('Winds of Change') to be an organisation similar to the Centre for Alternative Technology, whose website I analysed and was impressed by as part of my research. The briefs I addressed were the website and the radio advertisements. In addition to promoting awareness of environmental issues, I would hope to sell some products associated with energy-saving behaviours. This would promote their use and make a small profit to contribute towards the continued research of my organisation, which would have charitable status. I hoped to engage my audience through their needs for surveillance (finding out about environmental issues and solutions), personal identity (a sense of contributing to a better future for all) and diversion (the entertainment values I hope are present in my texts, and the ability to contrast my products with the doom and gloom messages about climate change).

The digital media brief asked specifically that I target 'families hoping to work towards a greener lifestyle'. With web access being so widespread now this seemed a good way of engaging families with the issues. Websites can be accessed at any time, suiting parents. I decided that to meet the needs of the target audience, I would have to consider the needs of both genders and possibly their children too. Simultaneously, I would need to try not to alienate non-traditional families such as single parents by pushing the 'nuclear family' too much in terms of my representations in images etc. I've also considered the needs of minority groups and used an Asian family with mum dressed in a salwar kameez for the beach-clean feature.

Rather than developing part of the website specifically for children, I decided to target their parents alone, focusing on those of younger children, probably in their mid 20s to early 40s who perhaps are just becoming interested in environmental issues. The site is intended to cater for casual interest and a no-nonsense approach to the debates, but also for serious eco-enthusiasts (both male and female) with a part of the site dedicated to building complex alternative energy projects. This combined the feel of the 'Green Baby' merchandise site I looked at, with the complexity of the technical information available on sites and forums for alternative technologies such as 'Permaculture'. I wanted them to be able to bookmark my site as a resource – somewhere on the web they could return to again and again. I felt that part of the website could deal with encouraging kids to 'go green' and also provide links for safe surfing to websites geared for their age groups with fun activities and so on.

I did feel that I was probably addressing primarily quite a middle-class audience (or at least an audience who aspire to middle class and liberal values concerning the environment) but was aware that young families from all backgrounds often don't have a high disposable income. I hoped that the radio ad campaign might encourage more families from lower socio-economic groups to also view the site. I also varied the complexity of articles on various issues. Because the website should be frequently updated to maintain consumer interest, I envisaged a 'monthly' look to the site, and in this I was partly inspired by my research into the print publication *Organic Life*. While certain features would remain constant, it would ensure a seasonal and relevant feel. My site was designed for August, with the holiday season in mind (see appendix).

All of these were regular features the consumer would expect to see, and links were displayed clearly with the best feature (the beach clean with kids) being the focus, providing as it did a very sunny beach photograph of a happy mother and son. I also included a scrolling news banner so that while skimming the précis of this feature, the audience could clearly see if there was anything else of interest. Other links including those to permanent resources appeared to the right of the screen, observing eye movement as a guide.

I was particularly pleased with the strength of my branding for my fictional institution. I felt that the predominance of bright greens and yellows in the design signified effectively environmental concerns, and the straightforward and bold layout of the site made it distinctive but unobtrusive, allowing the content to stand out. I was particularly pleased with the wind turbine and tree logo I produced on Logo-maker, which was striking, but simple enough to repeat in different sizes at numerous points throughout the site. I thought 'Think Outside' as a slogan worked well, connoting both outdoors lifestyle and appreciation for the environment, but also alternative lifestyle choices environmentally. I chose the beach image for the main feature as Salia and Nassur, who modelled, looked so natural and the colours were so vibrant on a hot day. It was worth experimenting with the digital camera on a manual setting, and the focus on the mother and son with softer focus on the background looks quite professional. The further images accompanying the feature on the second page looked stylish as a 'storyboard' sequence of five contrasting images from the day, and I made the most of these by positioning them prominently within the design.

My sequence of radio adverts was designed to promote features of the website to a different section of the target audience. I hoped through researching demographics of listeners to commercial radio to reach those who are at home all day, perhaps doing childcare, and those in unskilled or semi-skilled occupations who may also be regular listeners while at work. Each advertisement raised awareness of five separate regular features on the site. I was pleased with the scripting of each of these. Intended for daytime schedule on a local station such as Pirate or Atlantic FM, I imagined that each could be recorded in a range of regional accents. Perhaps due to cost implications I would roll these out after assessing how much impact they were having in attracting new visitors to the site. This could be evaluated quite easily through the 'where did you hear about the site?' toggle.

I spent a great deal of time, after listening closely to numerous radio adverts I had recorded, writing the humorous scripts that I decided immediately would work best as a dialogue between two people. These were slightly eccentric, and conveyed what I hoped was a 'Pythonesque' style of humour. I hoped these would genuinely make the audience laugh, and I also hoped that listeners who have the radio on all day (in the workplace, for example) might still raise a smile even on hearing the advert for the fourth time. As well as using actors with local accents the audience can trust, I incorporated some local dialect. However, the delivery by my non-professional actors was lack-lustre and not as pacey as I'd hoped. Because of time constraints due to the technical unsuitability of an earlier recording I had to re-record the fourth advert, which should have been mums in a supermarket, using two 17-year-old girls. One of them sounded too young when recorded, spoiling the verisimilitude of the advert. I'm also not sure that all of the jokes would translate to all regions. The one about 'getting round to it "dreckly"' in the second advert set in a park, which would be understood in Cornwall, might not be understood elsewhere or be as funny. The third advert, which was recorded on location in a working garage using a laptop and USB microphone suffered from excess background sound that proved impossible to balance post-production as well as I would have liked. I was pleased with the jingle I produced on Garageband, as it sounded upbeat and optimistic, and the simple but authoritative voiceover (for which I used Received Pronunciation) that ended the advert and gave out the website over the jingle unified the adverts well with good sound balance. This also reinforced the branding of the website, with repetition of the enigmatic slogan 'www.windsofchange.co.uk. Think outside'.

The third brief would have required me to produce a photo story advert aimed at teenagers. I thought a good focus for this might have been a light and portable wind-up universal charger, which could be used to power MP3 players and mobile phones. The teen market has been brought up with greater environmental awareness than many of their parents, but also many feel alienated from issues like global warming or helpless to make a difference. I conceived the photo story as one of a series targeting girls in magazines such as *Sugar* and *Cosmo Girl*. I felt that addressing their need to conform and the importance of peer endorsement and self-image might be good selling points, and that the photo story could focus on a 'what-if' scenario where someone's mobile phone runs out at a crucial social moment. Perhaps a web-link could take them directly to the merchandising section of the website.

Appendix:

August features

Green kids:
A feature on how to do a safe beach clean while on holiday and rewarding kids for the rubbish they collect

Reducing your carbon footprint:
Holidaying at an unusual or surprising UK destination – what the Lincolnshire coast has to offer

'Bio-fuel':
Eating seasonally and locally

Gadget of the month:
Wind-up low-cost universal charger for holidays

Home improvements:
Installing roof-top grey water collection to save on your water bill

Examiner's commentary:

This candidate has offered a clear explanation of how they have met the needs of their target audience, and linked this well across the two parts of the brief addressed. There is also a clear awareness of and insight into how their product is likely to be consumed. They have dealt with issues of representations in both texts, offering again sound reasons for their choices. There are also some effective references to other inspirational texts found during research. The language of Media Studies is used with confidence throughout. Clear reference is made to the media language employed and the stylistic aims of this in both cases.

This candidate has provided a frank and realistic assessment of the strengths and weaknesses of their products. They have recognised that the website is technically the more successful of the two products, offering explanations for the deficiencies in the radio adverts without dwelling on these.

Finally, there is a clearly argued consideration of how the third brief would be approached and how it fits with the other two products.

The evaluation is overall well written and communicates its message well. It is clearly structured and organised, offering firstly an analysis of their approach to the brief for both products and the institutional values they hoped to convey. Secondly and thirdly, there is a section on each product that includes considerations of media form, conventions, representations, institution and audience issues. Integrated throughout these sections there is clear sense of perspective with regard to the strengths and weaknesses of each product. The third brief is addressed by way of conclusion, quite an effective strategy in this case.

This evaluation therefore meets the criteria for Level 4 (16–20 marks).

End of topic summary:

- I know how to use my learning from Unit 1 to inform my writing of my evaluation.

- I can evaluate the strengths and weaknesses of my products with confidence.

- I know how to address the third part of the brief not actually produced.

Glossary

A

anchorage: a fixing device – the text directs the reader through the signifiers of the image towards a meaning chosen in advance by the producer of the text.

animation: pictures or words that move on the screen.

audience share: the measure of audiences viewing channels and programmes.

B

banner ad: internet adverts which contain a link to either a different section of the website or a different website altogether.

banner headline: page wide headline

brand image: how an institution, a media product or even a person is promoted to create a particular perception or belief amongst the public.

byline: name of the writer.

C

caption: headline under a photo.

case study: a factual example or a set of related examples about media platforms, media institutions or media products. Used to make or illustrate a point.

CGI: computer generated imagery. 3D computer graphics used for special effects.

cliff-hanger: a dramatic device at the end of an episode in a series which leaves the audience eager to discover what happens next.

codes and conventions: A code is a network of signs, written, visual, artistic or behavioural, which signify meanings that are culturally accepted and shared. A convention is a conduct or practice or method that is commonly accepted and has a tradition. Media texts are constructed using a number of codes and conventions which have agreed meanings.

concepts: ideas that can be applied to a media text in order to understand it.

connotation: meanings arrived at through the cultural experiences a reader brings to a text. (also see **denotation**).

contemporary media landscape: the changing contexts within which media texts can be found.

convergence: the coming together of the media technologies.

copyright: the legal ownership of the text. The owner gets a fee for giving permission for a media product or part of a product to be reproduced or shown.

D

deck: the number of lines in a headline.

denotation: refers to the simplest and most obvious level of meaning of sign be it a word, image, object or sound (also see **connotation**).

discourse: a set of statements or body of language on a particular topic or theme unified by common understanding.

E

editing: the process by which the shots and sounds (and sequences of shots and sounds) are assembled into the finished narrative.

editorial: an expression of opinion by the newspaper's editors, reflecting the views of the publisher or owner.

establishing shot: what is shown to let the viewer know where and when the action is set.

exclusive: story published by only one newspaper, a scoop.

expectations and pleasures: audiences understand genre through their familiarity with the **codes and conventions** used in the text. They expect and take pleasure in repetition and recognition of the generic elements of content, style and form.

G

genre: a term of classification which groups together media texts of a particular type.

globalisation: Encyclopaedia Britannica defines globalisation as 'the process by which the experience of everyday life…is becoming standardised around the world.'

google: a leading search engine.

H

headline: words in large type found at the top of the story summarising it, the head.

hybrid genres: texts which are formed with elements from more than one genre, perhaps producing sub-genres.

hyperlinks/links: website links which, when clicked, take you to another area of the same website or to another website entirely.

I

iconic: a sign which in some way resembles its object- looks like it or sounds like it.

iconography: particular signs we associate with particular genres.

ident: an identifying image or sound.

ideology: the opinions, beliefs and ways of thinking characteristic of a particular person, group or nation.

institutions: the organisations or companies that produce and/or distribute media.

interpellation: term used by Louis Althusser to describe how the media hail us as an individual who has a shared understanding of the ideology within the text.

intertextuality: within a text, visual or audio references are made to other texts. It is expected that audiences will recognise such references.

L

layout: arrangement of content, pictures and words, on a print or web page.

lead: the first paragraph or two of a news story – sometimes in bold or larger typeface.

logo: the identifying design used by a brand to provide recognition.

M

masthead: the top of the front page which gives the title and publication date of the newspaper printed in every issue.

media forms: the distinguishing characteristics of types of media products.

media franchise: the capacity to extend the life of characters, settings or trademarks by producing further products.

media platforms: the technology through which we receive media products.

media products: TV and radio programmes, films, advertisements, websites, newspapers and magazines etc, produced for audiences.

media texts: anything that has been constructed to appear in the media.

mediation: the process by which an institution or individual or a technology comes between events that happen in the world and the audience who receive this re-presentation.

mise-en-scène: An expression from film studies meaning the composition of the shot.

N

narrative: the processes by which stories, fictional and non-fictional, are constructed by producers and understood by audiences.

navigation: how the user accesses different parts of the site.

network: a television broadcasting system made up of linked television stations.

news agenda: the planned content of the news programme, the running order and the time allocation.

news values: the relative importance of certain stories over others.

niche audiences: the separation of the media audience into segments, each of which have different tastes and concerns.

P

polysemic: more than one meaning, open to interpretation.

post-modern: the idea that in our society old certainties no longer apply, that with the globalisation of the media and the interactive virtual reality of the internet, the cultural meanings and forms of the media are subject to constant change.

product placement: the inclusion of a product in sound or vision in return for cash or services.

protagonist: the main character in a play, story or film or any person at the centre of a story or event.

public service broadcasting (PSB): a broadcasting system whose first duty is to a public within a democracy, serving to inform, educate and entertain rather than to make commercial profit.

puff: a promotion of a product or service.

R

readings: the understandings taken from and brought to the text by the audience.

repertoire of elements: the number of **codes and conventions**: technical, symbolic, narrative and setting, from which a selection can be made.

representation: media texts are artificial versions of reality.

S

schedules: the timetables of programmes on television or radio.

scheduling: the positioning of programmes within the schedules in an attempt to keep audiences tuned in.

semiology or semiotics: the study of the meanings of signs.

shot: the image captured by the camera during the photographic process. It covers framing, camera position and movement, lighting and other technical choices made by the cinematographer.

stereotype

stereotype: a standardised, usually oversimplified, mental picture or attitude towards a person or group, place or event.

strapline: a short statement that sums up a story in a newspaper or magazine in a few words and may appear with the main headline for that story.

synergy: the process through which a series of media products derived from the same text is promoted in and through each other.

T

target audience: the specific group of people towards whom a media text is directed.

terminology: specialised vocabulary used in any particular sphere of life. As students of the media you will need to use media terminology.

transitions: the ways in which shots and sounds and sequences of shots and sounds can be joined together to convey specific meanings.

U

UGC, user generated content: contributions to media texts from audiences.

V

viral marketing: the spreading of a message, like a virus. It applies to any strategy that encourages individuals to pass on a marketing message to others.

vox pop: the voice of the people – short interviews gathering the opinions of members of the public, usually in the street.

W

web 2.0: a term coined in 2004 to describe the second generation of web based communities such as social networking sites, wikis and folksonomies. These changes are in the ways the platform of the World Wide Web or Internet is used and not an update in technical specifications.

wiki: a software that enables documents to be written collaboratively using a web browser.